Warrior Kids

'Warrior Kids is COOL!'

Warrior Kid

'Every child and every adult in New Zealand should go through Warrior Kids.'

School principal

'Warrior Kids was good because it was something that complemented the kids' education and helped them deal with stuff at school and at home.'

Parent

'I like the balance of physical, emotional, spiritual and fun aspects of each session. I like the way the facilitators relate to the children with respect; firm yet focused, caring and supportive. Warrior Kids should be part of every school curriculum. As a parent observing, I have learnt also.'

Parent

'My son's behaviour and confidence has improved noticeably since attending Warrior Kids. He has learnt ways to appropriately deal with anger and he stops to think before reacting. He mixes in better with other children, enjoys responsibility and understands his feelings better.'

Parent

'I was paying heaps for a counsellor, so I tried Warrior Kids instead. Warrior Kids has really helped my son and given him so much more. He's improved at his school work and gone up reading levels since he started.'

Parent

'I was going to pay $400 for an 8-week parenting course, but then I found Warrior Kids. It's teaching me to be a better father.'

Parent

Warrior Kids
Warrior Training for Children

Tim Tipene

*Special thanks to Catherine and Joe Hannken
for their support over the years.*

In the interest of gender equality, the pronouns he/she, him/her and his/her
have been alternated in the sessions of this manual.

Published by Libro International, an imprint of Oratia Media Ltd,
783 West Coast Road, Oratia, Auckland 0604, New Zealand
(www.librointernational.com)

Copyright ©2011 Tim Tipene
Photographs ©2011 Paul McSweeney
Many thanks to Paul for his generous contribution to this publication.

The copyright holders assert their moral rights in the work.

This book is copyright. Except for the purposes of fair reviewing, no part of this publication may be reproduced or transmitted in any form or by any means, whether electronic, digital or mechanical, including photocopying, recording, any digital or computerised format, or any information storage and retrieval system, including by any means via the Internet, without permission in writing from the publisher. Infringers of copyright render themselves liable to prosecution.

This book is presented as a guide to the Warrior Kids programme. Neither the author nor the publisher makes any representation, warranty, or guarantee as to the administration of the material described or illustrated in it. The author and publisher accept no responsibility for any injury or loss sustained as a result of using the material contained herein.

ISBN 978-1-877514-22-7
Ebook ISBN 978-1-877514-41-8

First published 2011 by Libro International

Printed in New Zealand

Contents

Preface	7
What is Warrior Kids?	11
How to use this manual	17

Part 1: Establishing and maintaining a programme

A positive image	19
Making a living	20
Don't do what I did!	20
Funding	21
Providing the In Breath and the Out Breath	21
The Out Breath — open group	21
The In Breath — closed group	22

Instructors' Code of Conduct — 24

1. Guiding principles	24
2. The Instructor–student relationship	25
3. Maintaining professionalism	26
4. Responsibility to the community	26

Systems — 27

A promotional portfolio	27
Guidelines	27
Enrolment form	28
Attendance roll	28
Handouts	28
Progress reports	28
Incident report	28
Completion reports	28
Evaluation forms	31

Managing a group and addressing behaviours — 34

- Consistent Positive Regard — 34
- Watch for traps — 35
- Take control — 35
- Students presenting issues — 36
- The value of NO! — 37
- Focus on the behaviour that you want — 37
- Non-compliance — 37
- Do not put up with nonsense — 37
- Warrior Kids is supposed to be fun — 38
- Finally … — 38

Part 2: Warrior Kids In-school Programme

- Preparing for a session — 39
  - Setting up the space — 39
  - Guidelines for Instructors — 40
  - Sessions — 41
- Session 1 — 42
- Session 2 — 77
- Session 3 — 100
- Session 4 — 124
- Session 5 — 145
- Session 6 — 155
- Session 7 — 170
- Session 8 — 184
- Session 9 — 197
- Session 10 — 207
- Grading — 223
- Beyond the programme — 228

Preface

A warrior raises hope and direction for those who have none.

For some children life is a battlefield and they must learn to be warriors in order to get through. Even children from good homes have battles to face. This is the origin of Warrior Kids.

To some, the word 'warrior' speaks of war, power, violence and abuse. Warriors are portrayed in movies and computer games. They are on the sports field, in the military and in other areas such as the martial arts. Too often warriors are depicted as violent and destructive. In the *Oxford Dictionary*, 'warrior' is stated as meaning a *person famous or skilled in war; fighting man (esp. of primitive peoples)*.

Yet, to many people, the word warrior speaks of courage, bravery, fortitude, resilience, honour, respect and nobility; a servant of his or her community. The warrior is seen as one who defies all odds and stands tall in the face of adversity.

In Maoridom the word for warrior is 'toa', which also means 'brave', and 'champion'. When used the word encompasses all three meanings. Maori have a long tradition of fighting warriors who have been glorified for their cunning and ferocity in battle. But Maori also have a long history of courageous heroes, such as Te Whiti-o-Rongomai, who used peaceful resistance to oppose European incursion and the confiscation of land in the late 1800s. Te Whiti and his relative, Tohu Kakahi, were the leaders of an inland village called Parihaka. They led their people to plough confiscated Maori land occupied by European settlers. Parihaka became a focal point for many Maori who were opposing European injustice. In 1881, 1600 Armed Constabulary and volunteers, under the command of Native Minister John Bryce, invaded Parihaka. Instead of resisting, the people of Parihaka greeted the soldiers with bread and song. Te Whiti was arrested and held without trial until 1883. However, he did not give up and was arrested again in 1886.

I hold the belief that there is a warrior within every person. Away from the fields of sports and battle, the warrior is that part of a person who, after putting up with an abusive relationship, finally decides that enough is enough and leaves. The warrior is that part of a person who, after sacrificing time with their family for work, finally decides that enough is enough and makes a change. A true warrior, for me, is a person who is willing to face himself or herself, who is willing to take responsibility for mistakes, who is willing to change and willing to stand up for what he or she believes in.

Have the courage to stand when it is easier to sit.

Have the courage to speak when it's easier to be silent.

Have the courage to go on when it's easier to go back.

I was raised in a Maori family so I was taught values such as mana (prestige), manaakitanga (caring and respect), whanaungatanga (community), wairua (spirit), kaitiaki (guardianship), aroha (love), and toa.

While my immediate family didn't practise these values, the wider family did, in the form of service to the whanau (family), hapu (subtribe), iwi (greater tribe) and community. My grandfather, William (Tim) Waitai Tipene, and grandmother, Dollyanne Tahu,

Preface

were proud to have two white grandsons. My grandfather was a chiefly man who had a tremendous sense of responsibility to the family and tribe. He led the family and, even after passing over 30 years ago, is still well respected.

On my mother's side, my grandmother was one who cared for many and my grandfather was a free spirit who taught wrestling in a hall in a small town called Helensville, north of Auckland.

As a boy I followed my immediate family's example and inflicted my anger, hurt and frustration on others. It was commanded of me. If I didn't physically punish those who upset my sister I would get a beating when I got home. If I had a falling out with a friend at school I was expected to sort him out. As my dad once said to me, 'You go to school, pick up a hunk of wood and smack that boy across the head with it. If you don't I'll give you a f***** hiding when you get home.'

Just a boy, I was my mother's protector. She had me sleep in her bed when my father worked the nightshift. If there was a noise in the house I was sent out to investigate while my brother and sister slept soundly in nearby rooms. The different treatment was not because I was the favoured child, it was because I was the expendable one.

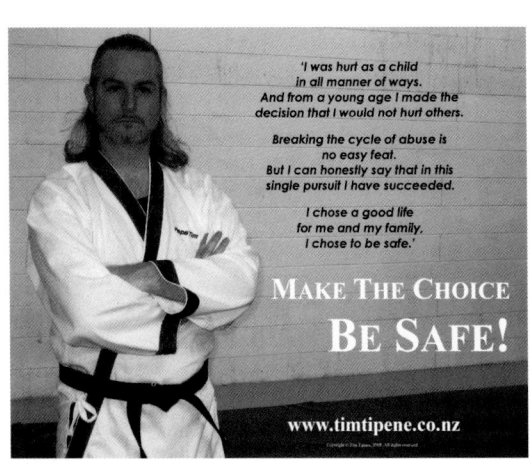

In 2008, the 'Make the Choice, Be Safe' campaign shared the Warrior Kids message.

When my mother came home in the early hours of the morning from a night out on the town and it was raining, she sat in her car at the bottom of the drive with her hand on the horn because she didn't want to get out to open the gate. It was my job, and my job only, to get out of bed and to brave the weather to open the gate for her while everyone else remained beneath their covers. By the time I returned from shutting the gate my mother would have already disappeared into her room.

At the age of 12 I was introduced to martial arts through stories and movies. What impressed me about the exponents of the arts was not their ability to hurt others, but rather their apparent control, discipline and desire to master themselves. This was the complete opposite to the lack of control demonstrated by the majority of adults in my life. Alcohol and drugs fuelled their emotionally charged lives, their endless dramas, sexual perversions and violent outbursts. When my mother found God and took the family to a church of strict doctrine the turbulence escalated, even though my dad and her gave up alcohol and drugs.

By attending classes and learning martial arts I felt empowered and my internal strength was given an outlet in which it could constructively emerge.

In giving my aggression form, I found peace.

But my desire for a better life went beyond the arts and I found other influences. One was Mahatma Gandhi, whom I studied when I was 14. I was impressed with his strength, compassion and wisdom when dealing with conflict and injustice. For me he was the epitome of a martial arts master, a true warrior like Te Whiti-o-Rongomai; one who transcended violence.

In my late teens I became involved in community work. This included training and it was at this point that life forced me to face my past. I had to make a choice: follow in the footsteps of my

Preface

A warrior raises hope and direction for those who have none.

For some children life is a battlefield and they must learn to be warriors in order to get through. Even children from good homes have battles to face. This is the origin of Warrior Kids.

To some, the word 'warrior' speaks of war, power, violence and abuse. Warriors are portrayed in movies and computer games. They are on the sports field, in the military and in other areas such as the martial arts. Too often warriors are depicted as violent and destructive. In the *Oxford Dictionary*, 'warrior' is stated as meaning a *person famous or skilled in war; fighting man (esp. of primitive peoples)*.

Yet, to many people, the word warrior speaks of courage, bravery, fortitude, resilience, honour, respect and nobility; a servant of his or her community. The warrior is seen as one who defies all odds and stands tall in the face of adversity.

In Maoridom the word for warrior is 'toa', which also means 'brave', and 'champion'. When used the word encompasses all three meanings. Maori have a long tradition of fighting warriors who have been glorified for their cunning and ferocity in battle. But Maori also have a long history of courageous heroes, such as Te Whiti-o-Rongomai, who used peaceful resistance to oppose European incursion and the confiscation of land in the late 1800s. Te Whiti and his relative, Tohu Kakahi, were the leaders of an inland village called Parihaka. They led their people to plough confiscated Maori land occupied by European settlers. Parihaka became a focal point for many Maori who were opposing European injustice. In 1881, 1600 Armed Constabulary and volunteers, under the command of Native Minister John Bryce, invaded Parihaka. Instead of resisting, the people of Parihaka greeted the soldiers with bread and song. Te Whiti was arrested and held without trial until 1883. However, he did not give up and was arrested again in 1886.

I hold the belief that there is a warrior within every person. Away from the fields of sports and battle, the warrior is that part of a person who, after putting up with an abusive relationship, finally decides that enough is enough and leaves. The warrior is that part of a person who, after sacrificing time with their family for work, finally decides that enough is enough and makes a change. A true warrior, for me, is a person who is willing to face himself or herself, who is willing to take responsibility for mistakes, who is willing to change and willing to stand up for what he or she believes in.

Have the courage to stand when it is easier to sit.

Have the courage to speak when it's easier to be silent.

Have the courage to go on when it's easier to go back.

I was raised in a Maori family so I was taught values such as mana (prestige), manaakitanga (caring and respect), whanaungatanga (community), wairua (spirit), kaitiaki (guardianship), aroha (love), and toa.

While my immediate family didn't practise these values, the wider family did, in the form of service to the whanau (family), hapu (subtribe), iwi (greater tribe) and community. My grandfather, William (Tim) Waitai Tipene, and grandmother, Dollyanne Tahu,

Preface

were proud to have two white grandsons. My grandfather was a chiefly man who had a tremendous sense of responsibility to the family and tribe. He led the family and, even after passing over 30 years ago, is still well respected.

On my mother's side, my grandmother was one who cared for many and my grandfather was a free spirit who taught wrestling in a hall in a small town called Helensville, north of Auckland.

As a boy I followed my immediate family's example and inflicted my anger, hurt and frustration on others. It was commanded of me. If I didn't physically punish those who upset my sister I would get a beating when I got home. If I had a falling out with a friend at school I was expected to sort him out. As my dad once said to me, 'You go to school, pick up a hunk of wood and smack that boy across the head with it. If you don't I'll give you a f***** hiding when you get home.'

Just a boy, I was my mother's protector. She had me sleep in her bed when my father worked the nightshift. If there was a noise in the house I was sent out to investigate while my brother and sister slept soundly in nearby rooms. The different treatment was not because I was the favoured child, it was because I was the expendable one.

When my mother came home in the early hours of the morning from a night out on the town and it was raining, she sat in her car at the bottom of the drive with her hand on the horn because she didn't want to get out to open the gate. It was my job, and my job only, to get out of bed and to brave the weather to open the gate for her while everyone else remained beneath their covers. By the time I returned from shutting the gate my mother would have already disappeared into her room.

In 2008, the 'Make the Choice, Be Safe' campaign shared the Warrior Kids message.

At the age of 12 I was introduced to martial arts through stories and movies. What impressed me about the exponents of the arts was not their ability to hurt others, but rather their apparent control, discipline and desire to master themselves. This was the complete opposite to the lack of control demonstrated by the majority of adults in my life. Alcohol and drugs fuelled their emotionally charged lives, their endless dramas, sexual perversions and violent outbursts. When my mother found God and took the family to a church of strict doctrine the turbulence escalated, even though my dad and her gave up alcohol and drugs.

By attending classes and learning martial arts I felt empowered and my internal strength was given an outlet in which it could constructively emerge.

In giving my aggression form, I found peace.

But my desire for a better life went beyond the arts and I found other influences. One was Mahatma Gandhi, whom I studied when I was 14. I was impressed with his strength, compassion and wisdom when dealing with conflict and injustice. For me he was the epitome of a martial arts master, a true warrior like Te Whiti-o-Rongomai; one who transcended violence.

In my late teens I became involved in community work. This included training and it was at this point that life forced me to face my past. I had to make a choice: follow in the footsteps of my

Preface

dysfunctional family or address the abuse I had endured and carve a new, more promising life for my future. I began years of counselling, psychotherapy, anger management and other forms of treatment.

During this time I had become chief instructor of one martial art and an instructor of another. My classes were popular and people started to travel long distances to attend. Parents brought their children to me because they felt as an instructor I was safe and responsible.

The lack of accountability and social responsibility in what many martial arts schools taught bothered me. It seemed to me that honour and integrity had become a myth in the martial arts, existing only in movies and stories. I came to realise that the bulk of martial arts schools were caught up in ego and aggression. Perhaps there's something in the nature of martial arts that generates this sort of competitiveness. The instructors and higher grades become more stuck in their ways the further they move up the ranks. While Western practitioners develop fighting abilities and muscle control, often they are not emotionally in sync with their bodies or attuned to their internal experiences, which results in many of them developing long-term health issues, something very uncommon in Eastern martial artists.

What also concerned me was that martial artists around the world were overrepresented as perpetrators of physical assaults, sexual assaults, domestic violence, child abuse and drug-related matters. Many instructors and high-ranking students have been convicted for such crimes. When interviewing me about Warrior Kids, various media have openly conducted investigations into me and my work because they know numerous martial arts clubs have gang affiliations and clubs are often used for recruitment.

In many of the Eastern traditional schools it has been touted that it was common for a prospective student to be asked why he wanted to learn martial arts. If he answered he wanted to know how to fight or that he wanted to protect himself, he would be turned away. The correct answer to give would be that he wanted to grow as a person and to cultivate a life of peace; learning how *not* to fight.

Martial arts have been portrayed as a means to confront the ego, find a way through violent tendencies, to master the self and attain self-control. In today's world, to know a school and its values, one need only look to the high-ranking students.

When I was training in counselling, group work and other therapies, I saw that there were aspects of the martial arts that had the ability to heal and change lives, however, they needed to be reworked into a more holistic approach that could address the shortcomings that were prevalent in the arts.

When working with adults, I realised how shame, powerlessness, fear and guilt blocked lives moving on from abusive cycles. A survivor of an abusive childhood myself, I began to understand the need for a preventative programme. In 1994 I changed my children's martial arts class to Warrior Kids and Warrior Training became the focus. This allowed me to incorporate Maori values that were so ingrained in my life.

The posters for the 'Make the Choice, Be Safe' campaign went out to every intermediate and secondary school in New Zealand.

Since that time I have provided Warrior Kids to schools and communities, teaching thousands of children. I have continued to develop Warrior Kids, trying to make it an ever-more-empowering experience for all who participate in it. Warrior Kids heals and changes lives. And now, thanks to overwhelming demand, the release of this manual expands the history of Warrior Kids further and my hope is even more lives will be touched and enriched.

From humble beginnings, Warrior Kids has grown into the reputable, professional service I have strived for it to be; all in the aim of serving my community.

Tim Tipene

What is Warrior Kids?

Warrior Kids is a high-impact, full-on, non-stop adventure involving games and challenges where children learn to be warriors in the truest sense of the word.

Warrior Kids empowers children. The focus is on bringing out the warrior within; self awareness and personal development, instilling self-control and leading children to become champions in life. Much like athletes, Warrior Kids are conditioned to succeed. They become more confident, focused, flexible and self-determined.

All movement within Warrior Kids is natural and has long-term health benefits. Students gain self-assurance and competence with their body, and a sense of security, connection and independence, as well as self-defense skills.

In Warrior Kids students learn to manage their emotions. They also learn the true value of emotions and how they can harness and cultivate their emotional energy to serve them. Through this they gain a more harmonious existence, not only with themselves, but also with those around them and with the natural world.

Warrior Kids is a non-intrusive yet therapeutic form of training that offers freedom: freedom for children to be themselves, freedom from negative influences and freedom from behaviours that don't serve them.

Children gain interpersonal skills that allow them to constructively relate to others and the world around them. Families are welcomed and encouraged to be a part of a student's training. Children are supported towards becoming a constructive member of their family and their community.

The aim of Warrior Kids is to equip children with the tools and skills to face whatever comes their way, now and in the future.

The overall aims of the Warrior Kids programme

- To pass on life-skills.
- To prevent violence and abuse.
- To improve the health and well-being of students and their families.
- To provide positive role models.
- To strengthen and support students and their families.
- To provide a positive, holistic approach to mental health.
- To teach students to become prominent, consistent, permanent, stable and supportive points of reference in the community.

The guiding values of Warrior Kids

Integrity Respect
Honour Resilience
Peace Dignity
Fortitude

What does Warrior Kids offer?

Self protection

Constructive Response features postures, short forms, releases, holds, blocks and an understanding of strikes and throws.

Warrior Kids introduces students to Constructive Response, which is a form of de-escalation and containment of aggressive behaviour. While inspiration has come from a variety of martial arts, Constructive Response is unique and innovative, with its own ethos and approach.

I developed Constructive Response in reaction to students asking for methods of dealing with altercations in a way that wouldn't get them into trouble. Traditional martial arts are restricted in their methods of responding to altercations and usually resort to striking, throwing or grappling. The reality is that if a student utilises these methods at school, or even on the street, there is a high probability that he will get into trouble for doing so.

Keeping safe or self-protection is an essential skill for life. The students will face adversity at times, and some of that adversity will be in the form of threats, both physical and emotional. Whether from external or internal influences, the threat of harm has always been part of life and the human experience. There are physiological reactions when faced with threats and as humans we have intuition and natural instincts for survival; this is something that we explore early in the programme.

However, in today's world many of us don't have to hunt for food and fight for resources as earlier people did. In present-day society intuition and survival instincts can be numbed and rendered mute owing to the comfort found on the reliance on services that supply essential needs such as food and shelter, and a reliance on others to keep us safe. Then, of course, there is our reliance on electrical power and communication.

Television and computers also add to the numbing of senses and instincts. Such distractions can cause us to lose touch with our surroundings and environment. Intuition and survival instincts get overlooked, dismissed and ignored.

However, these senses have real value in today's world, especially when it comes to keeping safe.

One of two main survival instincts arises when responding to a threat: fight or flight. In Constructive Response the aim is give the students a framework of control of the instinct towards fight or flight; that is, a conditioned constructive way of responding to threat. The emphasis of Constructive Response is on safety and solving problems in peaceful ways.

Protection for everyday living includes knowing how to fall safely, care in using a knife in the kitchen, dodging a hot pot falling from the stove and saying, 'No.' Students need to understand that the best ways of protection are relaxed and flexible and allow them to keep a balance of inner and outer focus. Opposing this are defensive reactions, which are focused outwards and have little regard for consequences; hence I often use the term 'self-protection' and not 'self-defence'.

Understanding actions and their consequences helps students to choose constructive ways of expressing themselves. They can look at a particular action and where it's likely to lead. If the result is not in their own best interests, then they are encouraged to choose another course of action, one with positive outcomes.

What is Warrior Kids?

If a bully pushes a student at school and the student punches the bully back it is likely that the student will get into trouble. If a student raises their fists they are threatening to harm and will, rightly, be in trouble for doing so.

If an aggressor walks up to me on the street and pushes me and I punch that person, I can be charged for assault. That is the way it should be in a civilised society.

Constructive Response and self-protective choices are about choosing the best short-term and long-term consequences for our lives: choices that don't get us into trouble or bring us further harm and adversity. This is being clever: Instructors should always remind the students that they are clever and to be clever when faced with adversity. Students should be encouraged to breathe and to think when faced with a threat.

Constructive Response is about being assertive and protecting one's well-being. It is not about punishing or hurting others, even if they're out to hurt us. I want my students to be able to look after themselves and to protect themselves from harm and to stand up for what they believe in. But I do not want my students hurting others and getting into trouble. This would not be in my students' best interests and is certainly not protecting their lives.

Overall it is the students' manner that keeps them safe. If students are confident and hold their heads high they are a lot less likely to be picked on.

For a non-violent person, the whole world is one family.
He will thus fear none, nor will others fear him.
Mahatma Gandhi

Bodywork

Bodywork deepens the overall holistic experience of Warrior Kids. Working with and enhancing basic motor skills, students learn a variety of tumbling, conditioning and co-ordination while also being given the opportunity to physically exert themselves in challenges and games.

Many children's lives have been improved just through the Bodywork in Warrior Kids.

It is common for prospective Instructors to have issues with the physical aspects of Warrior Kids. However, the Instructor should be careful not to let his own fears and inhibitions get in the way. The activities and challenges of Warrior Kids are for the students.

When conventional counselling is used for children they feel a level of discomfort and it tends to be more comfortable for adults. Warrior Kids is the other way around. Children tend to feel comfortable in Warrior Kids where adults can feel confronted and challenged.

Emotional Awareness

In Warrior Kids we explore healthy, safe methods of dealing with emotions through useful skills that we can fit into daily life.

There are five steps in the development of Warrior Kids emotional awareness. These steps are explored through activities, challenges and discussions throughout the programme and in the ongoing community classes.

By learning to live in harmony with our emotions, our emotions no longer hinder and hold us back, but rather assist us in venturing forwards.

1. The first step of emotional awareness in Warrior Kids is identifying emotions, triggers for emotions and the physical and mental sensations and manifestations of these emotions.

2. The second step is learning to be with emotions and to safely manage them.

3. The third step is understanding the value of emotions and their place in our lives.

4. The fourth step is acceptance of emotions.

5. The fifth step is learning the art of detachment, that is, being able to separate from emotion.

This is ongoing learning that goes beyond a 10-week programme, but it is the mountain that all students are expected to climb throughout their life.

Anger management

While emotions in general are explored in Warrior Kids, special attention is paid to anger. Challenges such as the Run and Yell and the wrap-up have the students getting in touch with and expressing their anger, and such challenges are always followed with techniques for maintaining self-control and for appropriately expressing and managing anger. In this way the students solidify their learning experience so that in time the appropriate strategies for managing anger become automatic.

Self-control

Every aspect of Warrior Kids promotes self-control. From the very beginning students are encouraged to be the masters of themselves, physically, mentally and emotionally. They need to become good drivers behind the wheels of their lives.

This is not about being perfect. The students are entitled to make mistakes and with compassion and understanding this is to be accepted. But each student is encouraged to continue to pursue self-control. I often point out to the students that, 'Regardless of what is happening in your lives, you still have a choice about how you choose to be.'

In Warrior Kids, students do not master the art of fighting. They learn to master themselves.

I've had students stand before me in the grading at the end of a 10-week programme and challenge me, saying, 'What would you know?' My last such encounter was a boy telling me he couldn't help behaving the way he does because 'My Dad's in prison.' I acknowledged his statement, then leaned forwards and told him that my father had been in prison the majority of his life, which is the truth. That boy and every other student in the room straightened up, eyes wide. I then went on to say, 'But I'm not going to be like my dad. I've chosen to be different. I want a good life. I don't want to go to prison.' This proved to be a very valuable experience for that boy, enabling him to understand that he had a choice about the sort of person he was going to be.

In the 18 years I have been running Warrior Kids there has never been a serious accident. With all the challenges and activities no one has been seriously hurt. This is because of the control I maintain over the class, and my goal to ensure every student demonstrates self-control. Students need self-control when performing a forward roll, a handstand, when playing with others, when faced with a classroom task or when feeling enraged.

Social skills

Communication is a key aspect of Warrior Kids. In each session students are given the opportunity to verbally express themselves and their life experiences. Group discussions allow the students to share their ideas and it is the safety of Warrior Kids that empowers students to speak up. In realising that their words are valued by the Instructor and the rest of the class, the students tend to become more vocally expressive in the other areas of their lives. In being heard the students are validated.

As well as learning to convey themselves the students also learn the power of listening and validating others.

Confidence

Every part of Warrior Kids is designed to uplift the students and empower them. Through fostering confidence the Instructor is in a position to change the students' lives. Instead of telling themselves that they can't do something, students start to realise that, in fact, with effort and planning, there is a lot that they can do. When the students leave the class beaming, with a positive outlook of the world and their lives, I know I'm on the right track.

Through building confidence students gain fortitude and resilience. They become brave and prepared to risk failure in order to succeed. They realise they can speak up in the classroom, introduce themselves to others, give new things a go, follow their dreams and aspirations and believe in themselves.

Conflict resolution

Students do not have to hurt or use power-over tactics on others in order to be heard or to be validated. Nor do they have to put up with others trying to do it to them. The very core of Warrior Kids is about addressing issues constructively. Like the other areas previously mentioned, conflict resolution is an essential skill for life, and along with Constructive Response and the self-protection aspect of Warrior Kids, students are taught to deal with issues in peaceful, life enhancing ways.

Fun

Any programme or class that isn't fun for children is void of meaning and depth. Fun keeps Warrior Kids alive and vibrant. If Warrior Kids was boring, I wouldn't do it myself, let alone expect children to want to do it. I want every child to want to be there, and if that is the case then the majority of my work is already done. While the other areas of Warrior Kids are extremely important and valuable it is fun that determines whether the programme is successful. Happy students are willing to learn, to change and to grow.

Warrior Kids moves at a steady pace, changing from action to talking, learning to experiencing, and trying to being.

Fun in this controlled sense allows the students to relax and to feel safe. It encourages them to be themselves and they are celebrated for doing so.

How to use this manual

This manual is laid out in two sections. The first section explores the background and foundation of Warrior Kids, while the second section presents each session of the Warrior Kids in-school programme.

While the background to Warrior Kids is informative, the foundation section explains what structures were used and developed in providing the programme. This covers areas such as systems, funding, the Instructors' Code of Conduct and group management, which will be of some use to those serious about providing a professional service.

As for the second section, the two main ways to use the class material are simply to run the programme as it is outlined from sessions 1 through 10, or to apply the various activities and exercises to existing work.

Part 1
Establishing and maintaining a programme

The foundation determines the success. Therefore the setting up of your programme is an extremely important and vital stage.

A positive image

What would the people in your life think if they found out that you were a participant in an anger-management course? What would your employer think? You have the skills to reason a good explanation to them, but what if you were a child or an adolescent? If the programme has a positive image and reputation, half the work is already done. Students and their families will be lining up to take part.

However, if the programme is labelled as being for 'at-risk kids', how many parents would be wanting their children to take part? Would you like your child or children to be labelled as 'at-risk'? These negative labels and reputations not only threaten those we seek to serve, but also undermine our attempts to realise our focus and to be approachable.

One intermediate school organised a Warrior Kids programme for some of its students. Once a week I would visit the school and run the programme. However, when the school was choosing the students to attend, they chose those with challenging behaviours rather than a mixed group, as was prescribed. The programme was labeled a 'bad kids club' and, because those attending were having such a rewarding experience, a wave of other children started to misbehave so that they could join the Warrior Kids programme too. Furthermore, as those participating had clearly been labelled as bad kids by the school, their challenging behaviour increased.

I promote Warrior Kids as a class for good kids. This enables children and their families the opportunity to step out of any projections. I was once approached by a current-affairs television programme that wanted to run a piece about Warrior Kids. The opportunity for such an exposé was exciting. However, when the producers made it clear that they were wanting to film students throwing tantrums and their parents failing to control the behaviour, I said no. As much as it would have glamourised the image of Warrior Kids and present me as a hero, it would have damaged the reputations of all those involved, and therefore damaged the integrity of Warrior Kids.

Establishing and maintaining a programme

When it comes to mastering the art of living we all have something to learn. Hence a proactive name encompasses all, including staff. When families have the understanding that we are addressing these issues together and that no one is deemed to be above another, they know that we are truly on their side. The maintenance of a positive profile welcomes all.

Making a living

Providers and Instructors of Warrior Kids are expected not to just make a living from running classes and programmes, but to prosper. I charge a fee to schools for providing a programme, and those who attend the community classes are expected to pay a fee. In the early days when I was still emerging from the effects of my childhood abuse my confidence was low and I practically gave my work away. I undervalued myself and Warrior Kids.

As a result I ended up funding the bulk of the classes and programmes through other work. The majority of students attending the community classes were doing so for free. Whenever I heard a sad story I let the person train without payment. The little money that did come in didn't cover running costs. I was running my operation as a charity.

While this may appear a noble thing to do, it was in fact detrimental physically, emotionally and financially. I ran into debt and began to feel resentful. Because I was providing a charitable service, people began to treat me as a charity and expectations grew — families expected me to be at their beck and call, and I started to take on responsibility for the children, responsibility that wasn't mine to bear. Government agencies jumped in as well, sending children my way and often failing to pay the small invoices I sent them. As I was practically giving my work away, funders didn't see the need to fund it.

In the end I crashed and burned, and vowed not to do Warrior Kids again.

Don't do what I did!

Today I am a single parent with two beautiful children. It is up to me to feed and clothe them. There are bills to pay and, most importantly, I have come to realise that I am doing valuable work and should be paid for my expertise.

I had started Warrior Kids before gaining any qualifications or becoming a published author. Yet it was through those two achievements that I started to value my work. On realising that I couldn't do it on my own, I knew I had to charge for my services and thereby elicit the support of the community through the payment of fees. I believed that if the community wanted Warrior Kids they would endeavor to keep it. They did, and because of that Warrior Kids has been able to stand strong on its own, without any charitable funding.

It is the families that keep Warrior Kids running. The fees that they pay feed the programme and in turn the programme feeds them and their children. The families support me to support their children. Hand in hand we move forwards. Through membership, families develop a sense of belonging and ownership around the class. There are no handouts and Warrior Kids is not dependent on funding.

I am aware that I could be charging more than I currently do, however, it is important that I don't outprice my students and their families. I expect any provider and Instructor of Warrior Kids to be paid for their time and energy when supplying the programme or classes. How can you support others if you cannot independently support yourself? If you do not look after yourself physically, mentally, emotionally and financially, you will end up in a position where you can no longer run Warrior Kids.

In the right hands Warrior Kids can be a good business with enormous earning potential. There is income to acquire from class fees, school programmes, grading fees, Warrior Kids clothing and books and running workshops and seminars.

Funding

Schools and services who have taken on the Warrior Kids programme in the past have found it easy to gain funding. Funding agencies have even sought them out.

It is important that when seeking and accepting financial assistance from funding authorities, or sponsorship from businesses, that the provider of the programme retains autonomy over the programme. When supporting a project funding bodies outline conditions, detailing what they expect from the programme provider. These expectations can sometimes involve changes to programme content, set-up, and image. Funders may even pressure the provider to work with only one group of society such as boys or girls, those from lower socio-economic circumstances or of a particular ethnicity. Regardless of the conditions, providers of Warrior Kids should protect the integrity of their programme, even when faced with institutional or political pressures. Don't sell yourself out, it will cost you in the end.

When accepting financial support, providers should fulfill all of their obligations to the funders and uphold the guiding values of integrity, honour, respect and dignity. Not to uphold these values would be to jeopardise one's reputation and the reputation of the programme, and could lead to severe repercussions, legally and emotionally, for the provider.

Providing the In Breath and the Out Breath

Warrior Kids has been provided in two ways. These ways I call the In Breath and the Out Breath as they give two different perspectives in the development of Warrior Kids.

- The Out Breath is the community classes, or open groups.
- The In Breath is the in-school programme, or closed groups.

Both have been the breath and life of Warrior Kids.

The Out Breath – open group

Community classes are where it all began: the martial arts class that became Warrior Kids. The community classes are open to all and are under the full control of myself as the provider. In this form Warrior Kids is a part of the community. The level of participation is decided by the public and Warrior Kids is promoted and nurtured by local organisations and the people it caters for. Government and community agencies are able to refer their clients.

As an open group students have the freedom to enter and leave the training at any time. This means that the training is ongoing and that students are able to obtain further grades, and that some students have the opportunity of becoming assistant Instructors. Long-term students would also be able to become fully-fledged Instructors.

The relationships between the Instructor, the student and the student's family are long-term, which allows more trust to be established and puts the Instructor in a prominent position to give guidance and direction.

Students and their families develop a sense of belonging and ownership with the Warrior Kids community-based classes, even nominating to help out and assist with day-to-day operations. Parents pay fees in order for their child to attend. Two fee payment options are available.

1. A casual fee is a payment to attend one class.

2. A membership fee is a payment for the week and allows a student to attend up to four classes per week.

Depending on circumstances, there are often opportunities for individual students to be funded or sponsored to attend the classes by outside organisations.

More parents attend to observe the community classes than the in-school programme. They find the environment less threatening and less associated with their own personal school experiences. Parents tend to be more trusting of the Instructor when he is not associated with a school, as they don't feel that an authority is involved in their lives. This enables parents to be more forthcoming in seeking help and disclosing issues in the home and lives of the family.

Clear guidelines are required in the community classes as interruptions can come from the observing parents and families. Children who are not taking part in the classes need to be kept to the side and under parental control. There are some moments though where parents can join in the class; these are an enriching event for all.

There are costs involved in running community classes. Classes are usually run in a hall, community centre or from their own venue that bears the cost of rent and power. Advertising is needed to draw prospective students and their families in, along with phone access so that contact can be made. There are printing requirements such as certificates, enrolment contracts, attendance forms, invoices and newsletters. There is a price for having T-shirts, uniforms and other promotional clothing; these items can all help to bring in revenue. These costs are on top of those required to attain the basic tools to run Warrior Kids such as gym mats, Koosh balls and a padded sword.

The In Breath – closed group

Owing to the success of the community-based Warrior Kids classes, schools requested an in-school programme. This began the closed group, the In Breath, where children are nominated by their school to attend; the group of kids that starts are the group of kids that finish. The programme is closed to others.

The in-school programme is run in the hall of the contracting school during school hours. The school takes care of costs and supplies equipment such as gym mats. As an in-school programme,

however, it is often expected to fit in with the school, meaning that when a special event requires the hall, Warrior Kids is postponed.

As it is a closed group there tend to be fewer distractions, which means that more attention can be given to individual needs. New groups of students are enrolled for each new programme and students rarely get to repeat. This ensures that more children get to experience Warrior Kids, and some that would never get a go can do so. As the school takes care of the costs, parents don't have pay.

When providing Warrior Kids it is wise to get assurances from the school that they will endeavor to support the programme and be committed to its success. Such assurances would include the following.

1. A representative of the school management team should be present for each session of the programme. This helps to integrate the programme into the school.

2. Understanding the serious nature and value of the Warrior Kids programme, the school must ensure that each session is free from interruptions. There is nothing worse than having a class of children invade the hall during a session because the hall has been double-booked.

3. The school needs to involve the Instructors in matters of behaviour and disciplinary action concerning students of the programme.

4. The school must have parent/caregiver consent for each student attending the programme.

5. The school must endeavor to make the parents feel welcome to attend each session of the programme.

6. School management must be willing to meet with the Instructors to discuss issues concerning the programme or the students.

7. The school must understand that the programme is not a simple, quick-fix formula. It takes time. The programme is more productive the longer students are exposed to it.

A formal written agreement between a school and the Warrior Kids providers is strongly recommended to ensure that both parties are looked after.

Instructors' Code of Conduct

Instructors must master themselves in order to become a master of Warrior Kids.

The utmost professionalism is expected from Warrior Kids Instructors as they, and their conduct, can make or break a Warrior Kids class or programme. The purpose of the Warrior Kids Instructors' Code of Conduct is to establish and maintain standards for the instruction and delivery of Warrior Kids, which in turn protects the integrity of the programme, the interests of the Instructor, the students, the students' families and the community.

The Warrior Kids Instructors' Code of Conduct comprises such values as integrity, competence, confidentiality and responsibility. Instructors of Warrior Kids should assent to such conduct and accept their responsibility to students, the families of students, fellow Instructors, schools and community bodies.

Instructing Warrior Kids

Instructing Warrior Kids involves the formation of special relationships characterised by openness and trust through the activities carried out in the programme.

Warrior Kids Instructors assist students to increase understanding of themselves and their relationships with others, and/or to develop more satisfying and resourceful ways of living, and/or to bring about a change in their behaviour.

1. Guiding principles

1.1 Respect personal freedom

Instructors should respect the dignity and worth of every student, the integrity of the students' families and the diversity of cultures and religious beliefs. This implies respect for the students' right to make decisions that affect their own lives, to choose whether or not to consent to anything that is done to them or on their behalf, and to maintain their own privacy.

1.2 Cause no harm

Instructors must avoid any diagnostic labels, exercises, techniques, use of assessment data or other practices that are likely to cause harm to students and their families. Instructors must also avoid promoting their own values, beliefs, judgments and discriminations that are likely to cause harm to students and their families. In class settings Instructors have to protect students and families from physical and/or psychological harm resulting from participating in the class or from interaction within the group.

1.3 Behaviour	Instructors need to act in ways that promote the welfare and positive growth of students. As a role model, Instructors must consider their behaviour in terms of language, self-indulgences and social activities. They need to ask themselves if it is proactive and if they would want their students doing it.
1.4 Equality	Instructors should be committed to ensuring that their Warrior Kids class or programme is made available to all individuals and their families. Instructors should increase the opportunity for all members of the community, with special regard for the disadvantaged, to attend their programme.
1.4.1	Instructors must be committed to ensuring that all students and their families are treated equally, without favouritism or bias either in word or action.
1.4.2	Instructors are expected to do all programme activities and exercises they expect participants to do.
1.4.3	Instructors should work to promote social justice through advocacy and empowerment.
1.5 Manner	Instructors need to be safe, honest and trustworthy in all their relationships. Instructors need to uphold a high standard of performance, quality and professionalism in all conduct concerning Warrior Kids.

2. The Instructor–student relationship

2.1 Informed choice	Instructors must ensure that students and their families understand what is meant by Warrior Training and that they freely consent to participate. Participation in any research should also be based on free and informed consent.
2.2 Confidentiality	Communication between Instructor, student and the student's family should be confidential and treated as privileged information unless the student and their family gives consent to any particular information being disclosed. Exceptions to this rule occur when there is clear and imminent danger to the student, the student's family or others. In these circumstances the Instructor should take reasonable personal action or inform responsible authorities.
2.2.1	Any records of the Instructor–student relationship should be considered professional information for use by the Instructor. The records should not be considered the property of the Instructor or any group the Instructor is representing.
2.2.2	When information gained from the Instructor–student relationship is used for purposes such as training or research, the Instructor should protect the student's identity and the identity of the student's family.
2.3 Value all people	Instructors must avoid discrimination against students and the student's family on the basis of their race, colour, sex, sexual orientation, behaviour, social class, age or religious or political beliefs.
2.4 Abuse of position	Instructors should not abuse their position by taking advantage of students or members of the student's family for purposes of personal, professional, political, financial or sexual gain. Instructors

Instructor's Code of Conduct

are responsible for setting and monitoring the boundaries of their relationships and for making such boundaries as clear as possible to the student and to members of the student's family.

2.4.1 Instructors should avoid being alone with a student or a member of the student's family at any time in or out of class.

2.5 Sexual relationships

In the Instructor–student relationship the student and the family need to be free from the possibility of sexual exploitation or sexual harassment. Instructors cannot engage in any form of sexual activity with their students or with members of the student's family.

2.6 Fees

Instructors should, at the outset, clarify with students and the student's family, any cost for attending Warrior Kids and methods of payment.

2.7 Referring

Instructors should refer students and their family on when they cannot meet their needs. It is the Instructor's responsibility, as far as possible, to verify the competence and integrity of the person to whom they refer a student and their family.

3. Maintaining professionalism

3.1 Instructors should monitor and work within the limits of both their own competence and their own personal resources.

3.2 Instructors should hold a current First Aid certificate.

3.3 Instructors should seek to increase their professional development through training with an approved Warrior Kids Instructor whenever possible.

3.4 Instructors should be vigilant in monitoring and maintaining their fitness to practice as a Warrior Kids Instructor with respect to their emotional, mental, physical and spiritual well-being.

4. Responsibility to the community

4.1 Any person who has been convicted of a crime against a child/children is considered unsuitable to be a Warrior Kids Instructor.

4.2 Instructors should treat fellow Instructors with respect, courtesy, fairness and honesty.

4.3 Instructors should take action through appropriate channels against any unethical conduct by any person involved in providing Warrior Kids to the community, especially where it is harmful to individuals or their families.

4.4 Instructors should adhere to and uphold the Warrior Kids Code of Conduct and avoid compromising them in the face of organisational, institutional or agency requirements.

4.5 Instructors should do their utmost in addressing any issue, incident or complaint arising during or after a class.

4.6 Instructors need to be fully committed to the success of their class or programme.

4.7 Instructors understand that any breach of the Warrior Kids Instructor Code of Conduct could bring the Instructor's practice and any group, institution or agency that they represent into disrepute.

Systems

Systems are necessary for maintaining the day-to-day running of the programme. Good systems mean less work, and that if you want information you know where to go to get it. Systems are also designed to protect all those involved: the students, their families, Instructors and the providers of the programme. The systems used in Warrior Kids include the following.

A promotional portfolio

First and foremost, no one is going to use a service unless they know that it exists. The community needs to learn of Warrior Kids, so information has to be put out. This requires a promotional portfolio consisting of business cards, brochures and any other informative or promotional material.

Standard posters, brochures and letters are a low-cost yet effective way of informing the community you exist. When people learn of a service they like to have information that they can take away. Local organisations are usually happy to pass information on and support a good service.

Once Warrior Kids is up and running, word of mouth can bring more attention. Articles in local papers and other publications such as school newsletters and magazines build a programme's profile and instil public confidence. Television and radio networks are often keen to support local projects as well.

Guidelines

The Guidelines outline appropriate behaviour and conduct for Warrior Kids and can be written out and displayed on the wall. This helps the students know what is expected of them. The Guidelines include:

- Warrior Kids are safe kids.
- Warrior Kids are respectful to others.
- Warrior Kids are careful with the earth, with animals and nature.
- Warrior Kids practise self control.
- Warrior Kids remember that they are loved and treasured.
- Warrior Kids choose to be a Warrior Kid every day.

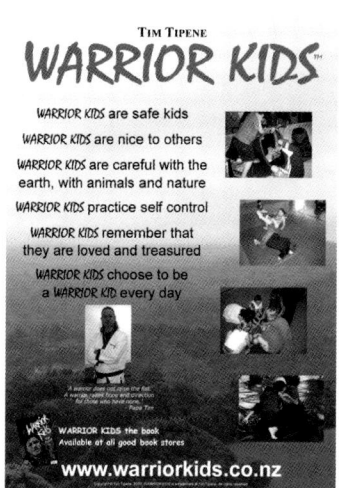

The Warrior Kids poster describes the Guidelines that underpin the programme.

Enrolment form

Regardless of whether the student is attending an in-school programme or the community classes, parents are required to complete a Warrior Kids enrolment form. The enrolment form gathers the required information and consent from parents for their child to attend Warrior Kids. The form also informs parents what is required of them. The Membership Registration Form that I currently use for students enrolling in the community classes is shown on page 29.

Attendance roll

It is important to keep a record of the students' attendance. By ticking off names of students who attend the class the Instructor will be able to have an overall record of numbers attending, keep track of payments and more readily determine grades. In the Warrior Kids community classes students have to attend a minimum number of sessions before being eligible for their next grading.

Handouts

In the past I have prepared and given handouts at the end of sessions for the students to take home. The handouts tended to highlight an aspect that was covered in class and built on the students' Warrior Kids experience, deepening their learning and having the information taken into the home where the rest of the family could be involved.

Progress reports

Progress reports are useful for maintaining a professional practice. They allow Instructors to map each student's manner and conduct throughout the programme and they assist the Instructors in consciously planning their objectives for each student, thereby optimising the student's growth and learning, and addressing behaviours.

For example, Tom may have done really well in the session, giving everything a go. But as he left the venue he verbally put another student down. An objective for the Instructor in this case could be to phone Tom and discuss the issue with him, or to make a point of bringing it up at the start of the next session as a valuable point of learning for the group. A progress report might look like the example shown on page 30.

Incident report

In the event of an incident a record should be kept. Incidents can be anything from a disclosure of abuse, an altercation involving students during a session or a parent verbally insulting another or the Instructor. What happens with the information contained in the incident report is entirely up to the Instructor and the contracting school.

An Instructor of Warrior Kids must never get themselves in the position where they can be accused of failing to keep sufficient records, or be accussed of negligence.

Completion reports

Completion reports can sometimes be requested from schools. A completion report will inform the school of the progress of each individual student and will raise any concerns and recommendations the Instructor may have regarding that student.

WARRIOR KIDS™

Membership Registration Form

Please print clearly as names will be used on certificates.
All information is obtained solely for the purposes of participating in WARRIOR KIDS.

FIRST NAME: ....

LAST NAME: .... DATE OF BIRTH: ....

PARENTS'/CAREGIVERS' NAMES: ....

ADDRESS: ....

PHONE: .... MOBILE: ....

EMAIL: ....

Is there anything that you would like the Instructor to be aware of?

TERMS AND CONDITIONS
1. Failure to agree to these terms and conditions will mean that the prospective student will not be able to take part in WARRIOR KIDS classes.
2. Students who fail to keep their fees up to date forfeit their WARRIOR KIDS membership and are not able to attend classes.
3. Although every reasonable safeguard is taken at all times, WARRIOR KIDS and its representatives cannot be held liable for any injury incurred as a result of attending WARRIOR KIDS.
4. WARRIOR KIDS and its representatives reserve the right to cancel any membership of any student and dismiss them from the school for any behaviour in or outside the school that could be regarded as misconduct.
5. All materials pertaining to WARRIOR KIDS, including class material, training, exercises, lesson plans and supporting literature and forms, are copyright and cannot be used without written permission from the copyright holder, Tim Tipene.
6. WARRIOR KIDS is a trademark of Tim Tipene. All rights reserved.

   Permission to use photos and footage
   Due to the high profile of WARRIOR KIDS, there are times when classes are photographed and filmed. These images may be used by various media for publications and productions, the promotion of WARRIOR KIDS and for the WARRIOR KIDS website. Please complete the following.

   I .... do / do not give permission for Tim Tipene and WARRIOR KIDS to use my image/s or the image/s of my child/ren for the purpose of promoting and preserving WARRIOR KIDS.

I .... acknowledge that I have read, understand and agree to the above terms and conditions.

SIGNED: .... DATE: ....

WARRIOR KIDS™

Progress Report

VENUE: Jane Doe School　　　　　　　**DAY:** Tuesday

DATE	STUDENT	COMMENTS	OBJECTIVE FOR NEXT SESSION
2 March 09	Tom	Tom was focused this session and gave everything a go. However, on his way out of the hall at the end of class he told Samantha that she was fat.	Start of next session, have Tom sit in the centre of the circle. Praise Tom for the effort he put in to the class then address his comment to Samantha and discuss appropriate ways of talking to others.
	Sally	Sally entered class positive, however, she found the leaping challenge difficult and was clearly apprehensive about failing. Sally is a high achiever and puts a lot of pressure on herself.	Make a point of encouraging Sally to relax in the next challenge and let her know that she is okay whether she gets it right or not. Encourage her to be brave. No risk no gain.
	Eric	Eric is reliant on the attention of others. He is constantly seeking the approval of those he looks up to and tries to get them to laugh at him. He also strives for their approval with demonstrations of defiance towards the Instructor.	Encourage Eric to relax and remind him that he doesn't come to Warrior Kids to make others laugh. Have him forget the others in the class and to focus on the activity in front of him, and then praise him for doing well.

Evaluation forms

Feedback is a good way of evaluating one's performance and programme. The gathering of feedback shouldn't occur at the end of every programme, only every now and then. It will allow the Instructor to ascertain the quality and impact of his work. It also allows the students, parents and teachers the opportunity to have their say. The results from evaluations will be a great resource for research and for collating more extensive feedback over various time periods, which can be useful for funding applications. The following are two examples of evaluation forms I have used. The first one (page 32) is for the students to fill in, the second (page 33) is for parents. The parents' form can also be adapted for teachers, allowing them to give feedback concerning the pupils who have attended the programme.

WARRIOR KIDS™

Student Evaluation Form

NAME: ....

Please circle your answers.

A = Always   U = Usually   S = Sometimes   N = Never

I enjoyed going to the programme.	A	U	S	N
I enjoyed the warm ups.	A	U	S	N
I enjoyed the stretching.	A	U	S	N
I enjoyed the different challenges.	A	U	S	N
I enjoyed talking with one person.	A	U	S	N
I enjoyed talking with the group.	A	U	S	N

Now you have the opportunity to write some answers.

The programme has taught me how to:

Things I don't like about the programme:

People I talk to about the programme:

I came to the programme because:

WARRIOR KIDS™

Parent Evaluation Form

CHILD'S NAME: ....

Please circle your answers:

A = Always F = Frequently S = Seldom N = Never

Before attending the programme:

My child was able to talk about his/her feelings openly.	A	F	S	N
My child expressed emotions in a constructive way.	A	F	S	N
My child displayed a positive self-image.	A	F	S	N
My child had a positive approach to school work.	A	F	S	N
My child interacted with others in an appropriate manner.	A	F	S	N

Comments

After attending the programme:

My child is able to talk about his/her feelings openly.	A	F	S	N
My child expresses emotions in a constructive way.	A	F	S	N
My child displays a positive self-image.	A	F	S	N
My child has a positive approach to school work.	A	F	S	N
My child interacts with others in an appropriate manner.	A	F	S	N
My child appeared to enjoy attending the programme.	A	F	S	N
My child shared with me about the programme.	A	F	S	N

Comments

Managing a group and addressing behaviours

There are times where it is best to be unwavering.
There are times where it is best to go with the flow.
There are times where it is best to be direct.
There are times where it is best to evade.
There are times where it pays to follow your intuition.

A good Warrior Kids Instructor practises each of these five responding strategies.

Where martial arts seek to repress behaviours, Warrior Kids is designed to instigate them. Warrior Kids is about benefiting each student and addressing behaviour allows students to shift beyond them. Students are able to be their natural, authentic self.

Martial arts on the whole tend to be authoritarian, enforcing will and power over students in order to control them. Warrior Kids is authoritative in that it supports students in developing self-control and personal responsibility. Students are made to be responsible for their own manner and conduct, instead of that responsibility lying with someone else. Boundaries, guidance and expectations are given, but without being overbearing. Rather than suppressing, this approach is empowering. Students are encouraged to make constructive choices and thereby choose to succeed, as opposed to being forced to succeed.

Note the activities described in the in-school sessions are carefully detailed with regard to outline and setup and cover possible issues that may arise. Instructors can refer to this information if such issues arise.

Consistent Positive Regard

Consistent Positive Regard (CPR) is the attitude a Warrior Kids Instructor maintains towards each student. When the students know that the Instructor's regard for them is consistently positive they will trust him and readily consider his guidance and direction. This puts the Instructor in a powerful position in the students' lives. It is the Instructor maintaining the best intent for each individual. Even when a student pushes at the boundaries of the class and tests the Instructor, the Instructor keeps CPR in mind and seeks the most beneficial way to address and assist the student. In keeping CPR in mind for each student, the Instructor's manner and conduct is influenced and that will be seen in his work.

When organisations have referred children or adolescents to me I typically choose not to have much background information. Nor do I allow parents or caregivers to relay stories of how bad their child can be. I choose to take each new student at face value and build on that, because the power of CPR proves itself time and again. When

Right:
Students are taught to be responsible for their own behaviour.

Far right:
Consistent Positive Regard is the foundation of Warrior Kids and the Instructor's greatest asset.

someone believes in a child, especially an adult, it makes it easier for the child to believe in himself. When an adult believes in a child, magic happens.

Watch for traps

A big trap for Instructors to avoid is falling into the 'mate role' with students, where the Instructor is trying so hard to get along with the students that no one is in charge and directing the programme or group.

Children and adolescents want strong, safe adults in their lives, adults who can uphold appropriate boundaries. I am not a friend to my students, I am not a mate. I am their Instructor. The students can then relax and enjoy the Instructor–student relationship. Just as a parent always remains a parent, an Instructor always remains an Instructor. Regardless of age, students will offer you the respect of having been their Instructor. In Warrior Kids students call me Papa Tim. Papa is a Maori term of address for a teacher. I have adults walk up and greet me as Papa Tim as they had once been my students in the past. They proudly claim me as their Instructor and speak of the positive impact I had on their lives. I find this very rewarding, as you will too.

What is also important is that the Instructor does not take on the parents' responsibility. Clear boundaries need to be in place from the start and upheld, especially when dealing with parents as they may expect the Instructor to parent their child. I have been phoned at all hours of the night, had parents linger after class, even approach me at the supermarket, with the intention of discussing issues that they are having with their child and wanting me to fix it. It is common for parents to want me to talk to their child outside of the class and not want to pay for it. There are sometimes requests for one-to-one sessions between myself and a child.

An Instructor should keep his contact with students and their families confined to the sessions as much as possible. In just giving a little, further expectations develop. It is good for the Instructor to have on hand brochures promoting parenting help and courses and to give these out to parents who are wanting further support.

Take control to enable each student to feel they are safe. As much as you may want to, you cannot do it all. Focus on the students in front of you. While you may have a positive influence on a family, you cannot fix them.

Take control

The students are looking to the Instructor to keep them safe. It is the Instructor who is in charge and any unsafe conduct in the programme could jeopardise trust between the Instructor and the students.

To aid in the management of a programme the Instructor can make reference to the Warrior Kids Guidelines, explained in the Systems section (see page 27). During a session the Instructor can stop the class and get students to read the Guidelines that are on the

Managing a group and addressing behaviours

wall, reiterating any of those guidelines that students may need to be reminded of.

The Instructor should always look for control. The promotion of self-control should start as early as possible in Warrior Kids. The Instructor can even say that he is looking to see who has good self-control. Those who do things correctly should be openly acknowledged in front of the class.

To help control and maintain an overall appropriate level of behaviour in class, the Instructor should fully claim his role of guardian of the space and the group. If the Instructor is well prepared and sets up an ideal environment for the programme, the students will feel as though they are entering a nest where they are valued and appreciated.

To further attain a safe, controlled environment, the Instructor can promote class ownership among the students, prompting them to take responsibility for themselves and for ensuring that they work together to keep the class flowing and on task. The Instructor should also strive to state instructions clearly so that students know exactly what is expected of them and be fully present and attentive to the moment.

The promotion of the Warrior Kids guiding values can also aid in developing constructive behaviour. Integrity, Honour, Peace, Fortitude, Respect, Resilience and Dignity are values we all benefit from if we live them.

Students presenting issues

At times students may demonstrate aggression, sadness, elation or absent-mindedness. Such a demonstration may indicate that something has occurred prior to the student attending the session that may need to be cleared, acknowledged, and in some way maybe addressed before the student can continue. The Instructor might need to take a participant aside to do this. However, the Instructor must also ensure that the rest of the students are safe, and as Warrior Kids requires constant supervision from the Instructor, any activity may need to be paused until the Instructor is ready to monitor and control again.

One way to limit a student's reaction to an early incident from interfering with the class is to simply acknowledge it quietly or aloud, depending on the Instructor's reading of the group and what's appropriate at the time. For example:

> 'Tristan, I see your tears, I see that you're not happy. You will have the opportunity to share later in the class if you want; or if you are wanting to speak to me now, by all means you can come and stand beside me and talk as the others continue. Otherwise dear, I want you to let it go. I know that you may have good reason to feel sad right now, but if you can I would like you to let it go and allow yourself to enjoy your class.'

I will also remind the student to breathe easily, as when we are emotional we tend to breathe short and sometimes even stop breathing.

If it is obvious that the student has experienced something major, then extra support will be required. Depending on the reason for the child's reaction, I may very well take them under my wing for that session, asking them to help me shift mats, giving them a place to sit on the side if need be. I may even place a hand on their shoulder or put an arm around both of their shoulders and hug them to my side.

Managing a group and addressing behaviours

If their parent, caregiver or teacher is present I would possibly also involve them in supporting the child.

Some students may be tired after a late night or hungry from having no breakfast. Children do have late nights from time to time and not having enough breakfast does happen. If a child is continually tired because of late nights or not having breakfast, the Instructor should raise this with the school.

In the community class I would openly discuss it with the child so that their parent can hear on the side and so that everyone else hears as well. I would endeavor to protect the integrity of the family by keeping it light.

The value of NO!

The word NO is extremely valuable and the Instructor should be prepared to use it. A child displaying harmful behaviour towards others should be told 'No', and told that such behaviour is not okay. Children need to know when they have crossed the line and they need to know what is acceptable and what is not acceptable behaviour.

Focus on the behaviour that you want

When addressing behaviour it is good to focus on the behaviour that you want rather than on the conduct you don't want. For example, if you want a student to walk, tell them to walk. By telling a student to 'not run' you are in fact putting the image of running in their mind. It would be like me telling you to 'not think of a purple elephant'. I have inadvertently encouraged you to think of a purple elephant. When I want a child to stop talking, I tell them to listen and focus. When I want a child to stop hurting others, I tell them to be nice and caring towards others.

Non-compliance

Every now and then an Instructor may have a student who is non-compliant. For any number of reasons the student has come to Warrior Kids unwillingly so that student is set on not being there. A non-compliant student may refuse to take part and may even sit down and refuse to budge.

New students to Warrior Kids can be shy and unwilling to join in to begin with, which is perfectly understandable. The Instructor can certainly attempt to encourage new students to give the class a go or allow them to join in when they are ready.

However, if a student is actually on the mats and refusing to take part or is even intent on sabotaging the class, that student should be removed. In such an event I would inform the student that their time at Warrior Kids is finished for today and if they like, they can try again next week. I would then have the school representative present take the student from the room.

In the community class I would have the parent remove the student. This has proved very successful and those who have chosen to return have done so knowing that boundaries are in place and that inappropriate behaviour will not be accepted.

Focus on the behaviour that you want from your students.

Do not put up with nonsense

As the Instructor the class is my responsibility. It is up to me to ensure that every student is having a great experience. When faced with a confrontational student it can be tempting to dig the toes in and work to get the upper hand. Yet it is best to simply let it go.

Managing a group and addressing behaviours

A student must be a willing participant of Warrior Kids otherwise it is best that they move on. The success of the programme for the students cannot be put at risk because of one. By retaining a non-compliant student the Instructor could lose other students who feel that the group is not safe. Support from parents could also be lost.

Warrior Kids is for good children. If a child is non-compliant then they are clearly not ready to be a warrior. I share my disappointment with such students and then tell them that I hope that they get the chance to do Warrior Kids again some time in the future.

Losing students can be disheartening, but there are so many wanting and needing to be Warrior Kids.

Some prospective students will run out the door straight away, especailly children who are in a position of power in the family and feel that their position will be challenged. For example, I had a mother bring her 10-year-old son to a community class. The boy refused to take part. The mother said that she was helpless in controlling her son. When she started her car to leave the boy was sitting on the top of the car. It was only when the car started moving that he jumped off and got inside the vehicle. I would have been keen to work with the boy. However, his mum didn't feel that she had the power to encourage him to give Warrior Kids a go.

Warrior Kids is supposed to be fun

There have been occasions when the whole class has been disruptive and I've had to work hard to keep them on task. During times like this I often point out to the students that I'm bored. Warrior Kids is supposed to be fun, it's supposed to be non-stop. I get bored when it's not. I talk about the activities planned for the session. This usually provokes the students into focusing.

An alternative I sometimes use is to have the class sit on the mats in a circle and as a group we discuss what is happening. I'll even ask the students what I should do when they are being disruptive. I then ask if we're able to continue. If not then it would be best to quit for the day and send the students back to their classes. From this they will understand that Warrior Kids needs to be taken seriously. I've never had a class reach this point and I hope you don't either.

Finally …

Don't be disheartened or put off by these potential problems. Time and experience will make dealing with them second nature. Look to developing your systems and your programme over a period of time. The way to get to the top of a steep hill is by taking one step at a time.

What kept me alive and safe when I was a child in an extremely abusive house were those few adults who believed in me. No one came and rescued me from the horror. My parents were never called up on their abuse. My saving grace was those adults who spent little pockets of time with me. If in the end that is all you can give, your contribution will never be forgotten and it may be the very thing that helps a child through the hard times.

Part 2
Warrior Kids In-school Programme

Preparing for a session

The ideal set-up for Warrior Kids is a clean, welcoming space with a large, safe surface for movement and gym mats for tumbling and other exercises.

Setting up the space

Warrior Kids requires a large open space, such as a hall. The room should be clean and welcoming. Every Warrior Kids session requires gym mats that are 1200 x 1800 mm, usually eight of them. These are laid out in a rectangular formation at one end of the room. The mats are the main focal point for each class. It is on the mats that the students form a circle to start and end the sessions.

It is good to have plenty of natural light coming into the room. If the room is lacking natural light then turn on the lights. This will help to keep the students focused. It is also important to ensure that

Providing a comfortable seating area for parents and other family members and friends will make them feel welcome.

the room is private, closing any doors or windows where a possible disruption could intrude.

Chairs should be set up at the opposite end of the room from the mats. This will give the students some privacy during talking activities. The chairs should be on the side, along a wall so that they are out of the way of the games and other activities.

A table should also be set up near the chairs. Here, information about the programme can be displayed, along with brochures for parenting courses and other self-help groups.

Guidelines for Instructors

1. **Be prepared**
   - Prepare and plan for each session.
   - Be presentable and tidy.
   - Make sure your breath smells fresh. You want the students to listen to you, not to focus on bad breath.

2. **Be on time**
   - Be at the venue 30 minutes before the class starts to set up and prepare.

3. **Greet everyone**
   - Smile and give every student and their family a warm welcome. Let them know that you are pleased to see them.
   - Sign each student in and collect any payments.
   - Ensure students remove footwear and socks and put them to the side in an orderly fashion. The shoes should be out of the way.

4. **Be mindful of your role**
   - Be a positive role model to adults and children alike.
   - Take control. You are in charge.
   - Support your fellow Instructors.

5. **Speak clearly**
   - Know what you are talking about. If you have prepared well, it will show.
   - Be open and direct. However, if unsure, say so.
   - Present logically and give clear instructions. Make sure it all makes sense.
   - Silence is okay. Gather your thoughts.

6. **Be aware of your spoken language**
   - Model 'I' statements. 'I like the way Samantha is sitting quietly.' 'I'm feeling angry that someone hurt Jacob.'
   - Keep it simple. Speak in terms that people can relate to.
   - Be interesting. Use your voice to your advantage.

7. **Be aware of your body language**
   - When addressing the group, be the focus of attention.
   - Be aware of what your body is doing. Watch for nervous actions such as scratching, shuffling, sniffing and so on.
   - Eye contact with your audience is vital.

8. **Avoid having all the answers**
   - Elicit the answers from the group. Have the students take responsibility.
   - Discuss the appropriateness and effectiveness of answers.

9. **Address behaviours**
   - Praise and acknowledge constructive behaviour.
   - Look for and give positive feedback to each student.
   - Name disruptive behaviour, for example, 'I notice you keep interrupting the group. Why is that?' Make each student accountable to the group.
   - Acknowledge anything else of importance that you may notice, for example, 'You are not looking very happy.'

10. **Keep an eye on the time**
    - Start and finish on time.

11. **Conclusion**
    - If there are handouts, give them out.
    - Acknowledge each student as he or she leaves.
    - Address any issues there may be, with students or with their families.
    - Pack up and tidy the room.
    - Check in with a colleague, letting them know how the class went. It could simply be a high and low point of how the class went.
    - Consider anything you could have done differently or that needs to be addressed in the next class.

Sessions

The in-school Warrior Kids programme as outlined here runs over a 10-week period with a 90-minute session each week for 16 students. The allocated time and set-up of each activity is based on these figures. This differs to classes given in a community-based course because a community-based Warrior Kids programme will run indefinitely; the different activities can therefore be spread out over a much longer timeframe. As the students have ongoing exposure to Warrior Kids, activities are broken up and delivered over a number of sessions.

Instructors should take time to practise the various exercises before presenting them to the class.

Session 1

EQUIPMENT

- 8 x gym mats, size 1200 x 1800 mm
- 1 x Koosh ball (it's always good to have some spare Koosh balls on hand)
- 1 x padded wooden sword
- chairs for parents and caregivers

Introduction

In session 1 students are given an introduction to the core principles and skills of Warrior Kids. The foundation is laid for the 10-week programme and the format and boundaries of a Warrior Kids session and each exercise are clearly demonstrated, so the students know what to expect and what is expected of them.

The first session is non-threatening, with ample opportunity for each student to express him- or herself. Group orientation and team building is a big theme.

The outcomes for session 1 are that the students will:

- have a basic understanding of Warrior Kids,
- relate to other students,
- be able to demonstrate stretches and a side and a forward roll,
- be able to vocalise a high point or a low point, and
- gain a basic understanding of evasion.

Lession overview

1. Opening words.
2. Round of introductions: a round of names and a colour that stands out for each student today.
3. Warm-up game: Chain Tag.
4. Conditioning: Stretching 1st form; Brain exercises.
5. Tumbling: side roll and forward roll.
6. Roll Tiggy, 1st version.
7. Breathing exercise.
8. Sharing Circle: a low and high point.
9. 'Instructor Says': postures.
10. Evasion.
11. Closing words.

The beginning

Recommended time allocation: 3 minutes

The Instructor directs students to remove their shoes, socks, watches and jewellery and to sit on the mats in a circle.

The Instructor welcomes everyone to Warrior Kids. The Instructor may like to ask the students what sort of things they think they might do at Warrior Kids. This is a good way to elicit early participation and it demonstrates to the students the openness of the programme.

Note The removal of footwear is a ritual that signifies the specialness of the class and assists the students in relaxing and in letting go and shifting their attention to the training ahead. It also prepares the student's mind and attitude for physical activity and is essential for overall safety. If shoes are worn, students are at risk of having their feet trampled. The concern with the wearing of socks in class is that students may slip during games and challenges. In cold rooms I have allowed students to put socks on for the sitting down activities such as the Sharing Circle or the Emotion Squares.

Watches and jewellery can also be harmful and can get damaged, but exceptions can be made. There may be significant cultural or spiritual items that students wear. These are fine. For items worn around the neck I ask the students to tuck the item underneath their clothing so that it is out of the way.

Grading

In the community-based Warrior Kids classes, students are eligible for their first grade after their first 10 sessions. However, the student is not graded until it is certain that he or she will pass. Students would be told privately if they weren't up to standard, and given time to amend their manner and conduct. The first grade in the community-based classes is Red Belt. There is no White Belt, and Orange Belt is awarded at a later date.

Once the Instructor has welcomed the class members it is important that the Instructor explains to the students that they will be attending Warrior Kids for 10 sessions and that at the end of that time there will be a grading. The Warrior Kids school programme concludes with three possible grading outcomes for each student: orange, red or white belt. This is explained fully in the section about grading on page 223.

The Instructor needs to tell the students that near the end of the programme their parents and their school will get to comment on their manner and conduct, and that such information will be taken into consideration when the Instructor determines the grades.

The Instructor should point out that it's not about being perfect; the students are not being rated on the grades that they may get at school. But they do have to be striving to do their best and to be choosing constructive outcomes in the different areas of their lives. We're all entitled to make mistakes, but if behaviours keep recurring, then they're not mistakes.

1. Opening words

Recommended time allocation: 1 minute

A relaxed yet formal start to each session. Staying in a circle, the Instructor and the students stand. A circle has no beginning and no end. There is no hierarchy or superiority among the participants, nor is there any exclusion. In the circle we see the other students and we ourselves are seen. We are equal, regardless of any belt grade we may hold. No matter age or experience, we each share the same thoughts and feelings, we each have successes and trials.

Once the members of the circle are settled, the Instructor asks for a volunteer from the group to say some opening words to begin the class. The opening words could simply be something like, 'I'm happy that we are all here today. Let's have a good time and keep safe.' This should be explained clearly so that the students know exactly what is expected of them.

The opening words can be in any language, especially where English is a second language. This acknowledges cultural differences and helps participants to feel that they are represented and valued in the group.

If no one volunteers to say the opening words, the Instructor can use the opportunity to demonstrate an appropriate opening. This should only happen at the first class though; from then on responsibility for starting the class should be in the hands of the students. It is also good to share the task around, allowing various members of the group to commence each class.

I find this activity to be a great way to start and finish a class. It empowers the participants, allows them to be heard, and focuses the group's attention. It also gives the participants a sense of ownership of Warrior Kids.

2. Round of introductions

Recommended time allocation: 3 minutes

Introductions follow the opening words and vary from class to class. Once the Instructor has explained the Introduction for the day, she should say her introduction first as an example. For session 1 each member of the circle, from left to right or vice versa, takes a turn to say their name and a colour that stands out for them at that given moment.

Introductions strengthen the group and assist each participant in feeling included and welcome. Students get to stake their claim to a place in the group. Introductions also enable everyone to learn each other's names and to build connections, as someone in the class may have a similar like or experience.

As the Instructor, I make a point of acknowledging each participant; I thank each student directly once they have shared or I paraphrase/repeat aloud what they have said. The latter gives the students the opportunity to correct me if I've heard wrong. Repeating names also assists me in learning them. I say to the students, 'I don't like pronouncing names wrong, so please make sure I say your name right.' I further point out that it is going to take me a little while to remember everybody's name so I might ask them to say their name a few times throughout the class.

3. Warm-up game: Chain Tag

Recommended time allocation: 10 minutes

Games are a fun and exciting way to warm up. As well as offering fitness, co-ordination and improved motor skills, warm-up games allow students to burn off excess energy, to let go of any negative and stressful thoughts and tension they may have picked up during the day, and to relax and focus on the present. This leaves them more open to the challenges and activities that will follow. If the participants are fully focused on the task at hand, then there will be less chance of injury and challenging behaviour arising during the class.

Not only is the warm-up game preparing the participant's mind and body but, also, when they play a game they let down their guard, allowing connections and relationships to develop that will lead to the formation of a cohesive group, where every student can gain a sense of ownership and belonging.

Games also allow the Instructor to identify and address any behaviours or issues that may arise, for example:

- feelings of anger or resentment between students (especially in a school-based programme or when working with siblings),
- the ostracising of a student; whether through their own doing or the group,
- the reaction of a participant who feels that the game has been unfair to them,
- a lack of confidence in one's ability,
- the fear of failure,
- the inability to be able to connect with others positively,
- demonstrating aggression, sadness, elation or a lack of interest, and
- identifying any restrictions in terms of processing or understanding instructions; or restrictions in terms of body movement and motor skills.

With each warm-up game the Instructor will need to explain the rules clearly. It is best to keep the explanation straightforward and simple so that it is not confusing for the students and so they know exactly what is expected of them.

The Instructor should also point out that she can change the rules at any time. This is a workable strategy if the game isn't going so well. For example, if the room is proving to be too big for a particular game, the Instructor can use chairs or a line on the floor to make the game space smaller. The Instructor also has the option of using herself as a line indicator, saying that any one that goes past her will be 'in'.

It should also be pointed out to the students that if at any time a student makes a cheeky, smart or put-down remark or gesture to any person during the game, then that student will be automatically tagged. The Instructor reminds the class that Warrior Kids treat others respectfully.

Safety

Before playing the game it is important to limit the risk of injury. To do this, instruct the students to take note of their surroundings. Point out any obstacles, any chairs or other objects in the room. The students need to stay away from these. If there is a stage or platform make it a rule that it is also out of bounds. Direct the students' attention to the mats, telling them not to forget that the mats are there as they might trip over them. The mats can also be slippery on some surfaces and the students need to be aware of this.

Another thing to acknowledge is that the students are different shapes and sizes; they need to watch out for one another. The students need to focus on what they are doing. There is no reason for anyone to get hurt.

If at any time during the game a student gets knocked over or is behaving in a reckless manner, the Instructor should pause the game and remind that person to be mindful of what they are doing and to settle. Games are no fun when someone gets hurt.

If a student is hurt and feels unable to continue, then the Instructor will have to ascertain the seriousness of the injury. In the many years that I have been running Warrior Kids I've never had a serious injury in any class, and there is no reason for there to be one.

The students' safety and well-being is paramount in Warrior Kids. If a serious injury does occur then the Instructor must respond accordingly. The Instructor should remain calm and in control. Utilise any support that is on hand and seek further support if required. Apply first aid or get medical assistance. The Instructor should contact the injured student's parents, and the Instructor should also contact their supervisor. The other students should be contained and looked after while the injured is being addressed.

Sometimes a student will exaggerate an injury or even make one up to seek attention from the Instructor or their fellow group members, or even to test the Instructor. My first response is to isolate the student by telling the other students to move away and to carry on playing the warm-up game. Fellow students can crowd around a hurt student and try to emotionally rescue them. It is nice to care, and to support others, and it is nice to be needed; however this will not help the situation.

I then check the student, talking to them and ascertaining the seriousness of the injury. Next I move the student off to the side and get them to sit down. I tell them to stay there and that when they fell better to rejoin the game. I avoid giving them too much attention. My aim here is to give students the opportunity to find constructive methods of attaining attention, not to rely on emotional manipulation tactics to have their emotional needs met.

The Instructor needs to remember that she is there for all the students, not just for one. Avoid being a rescuer and avoid any ego boosts from being wanted or needed. An Instructor must train to be above requiring reassurance from students.

In the early days of Warrior Kids I had an incident where a student got hurt during a game. I took the student to the side and sat and spoke with him while an assistant kept the game going. Soon another student was hurt so I took him to the side as well. Shortly a third child was hurt so I ended up sitting on the side comforting three students. However, it didn't end there. In a short space of time I had the majority of the class on the side, all trying to outdo one another for my attention. No one was seriously hurt. I realised my mistake.

In the next class I changed my response and told students that were hurt to sit on the side and to rejoin the game when they were ready, then I left them alone. Instead, I focused on giving the active students my full attention and affirmed and boosted their constructive conduct. Before long no one was getting hurt.

It is not uncommon for children to get carried away in any of the games and challenges in Warrior Kids, especially if their life is unsettled in any way or if they lack personal boundaries. I stop everything in order to get such a student to settle, relax and keep safe.

I openly acknowledge what it is I am seeing in her behaviour. This helps her to be aware of it herself, as she may not be. And this may also create the opportunity for her to open up about an experience that she had or she may even burst into tears. Warrior Kids is the perfect place for this and as an Instructor I am in a position to offer support.

A student's decision to get carried away or to act out in Warrior Kids is a wise choice. It is her way of letting the Instructor know that things are not okay and that she requires support. It is not a time for her to be punished. Certainly her non-constructive behaviour needs to be addressed. But it should also be understood that the student could have good reason to be acting out. Some of the reasons my students have presented to me include a student getting a hiding from Dad that morning when she hadn't done anything to warrant one, the witnessing of a sibling getting a beating, fighting between adults (parents or otherwise), and even a mum throwing a student's breakfast on the floor because she was going through a hard time.

However, a student that gets carried away can hurt another student during a game or challenge. If this happens I make sure that there is no serious injury then I move the hurt student to the side. I then get the student who caused the mishap to sit alongside the hurt student and support them. The student who got carried away cannot rejoin Warrior Kids until the injured student rejoins. This is not so much about punishment but more about understanding the consequences of actions and that when we behave in a non-constructive manner (even unconsciously in a child's case), we must address and take responsibility for the outcomes. This will enable the student to work towards being more conscious of her behaviour and assist her in gaining more self-control.

Chain Tag

Note For Chain Tag it is good for the Instructor to be in as the chaser first. This will assist the Instructor in establishing relationships with the students. It also allows the Instructor to get a bit of a warm up.

Chain Tag is a fun game for team-building, making it a wise choice for the first class.

When the Instructor calls 'Go' the students run to one end of the room, stopping before the wall without touching it, and wait for the next set of instructions.

As with all of the games in Warrior Kids the aim is not winning, it is about the students building connections, learning about themselves and having a great time. Students should be encouraged to relax and enjoy themselves.

1. One person will be the *Chaser*.
2. The *Chaser* must pursue the students to tag one.
3. When the *Chaser* tags a student, the *Chaser* and that student link hands to form a short chain. Working together, the pair pursues the remaining students to tag one.

    Each student that is tagged must link on to the end of the chain that they were tagged from, making the chain longer. Only students on the end of the chain can tag with their free hand.
4. The game keeps going till the last person is caught.
5. If at any stage the chain breaks, any tags during that time are not counted. The students' hands are linked to form a chain and only when the hands are linked is the chain complete. Only then can tags be counted.
6. If cornered, students can dive under the connecting hands of the people forming the chain to escape being tagged. The people making up the chain can lower their arms to prevent this, but not let go of one another.

Students cannot attempt to break through the connected hands or to leap over them. If someone is trying to escape over the top a natural reaction for students of the chain would be to raise their hands. This could result in a child being tripped and their face hitting the floor, which would be disastrous for any class, but especially so for the first class.

At times there may be an issue with students not wanting to hold another student's hand. This could arise between girls and boys, or children who have an issue with one another. The game cannot continue until they hold hands. Any child who gets upset over this can take a seat on the side and rejoin when they are ready to hold hands with the student they were trying to avoid. This is the same for those students who have a strong issue with being tagged.

Depending on time, another round of the game can be played with one of the students starting as the chaser. If time won't allow this, the Instructor moves on to the next activity. Sometimes there is time left at the end of the first class. If this is the case then another round of Chain Tag can be played.

Chain Tag is played for a set amount of time then simply stopped. There doesn't need to be a particular outcome for the game to stop.

4. Conditioning

Following the warm-up, it is time to condition the body. The health benefits associated with conditioning are enormous. The conditioning used in Warrior Kids rejuvenates the body, speeds up recovery time, enhances motor skills and body awareness, strengthens co-ordination and limits the risk of injury during class.

Conditioning focuses and settles the student's attention and prepares them for training; in preparing for training the students are ultimately preparing themselves for life and the issues and challenges that they will face. Conditioning involves flexibility exercises; in practising flexibility with our body we are also training ourselves to become more flexible with our mind and behaviour. Flexibility exercises can also highlight blocks, physical, mental and emotional, that may be inhibiting the student from fully engaging in life and relationships.

When teaching conditioning we are passing on the value and importance of self-care, and students get to practise simple breathing methods that are a component of the emotional awareness aspect of Warrior Kids. The conditioning exercises should be performed by the Instructor alongside the students. It is vital that the Instructor leads by example.

The conditioning exercises and other activities of Warrior Kids will aid the Instructor in retaining a good level of fitness, health and sense of well-being, as well as reducing stress. In practising these activities in and out of Warrior Kids the Instructor will gain these benefits and become more experienced, confident and skilled in teaching conditioning.

Conditioning exercises have been compiled into 'forms' and these are performed by all students in every class following the warm-up. The conditioning forms allow the students to memorise the exercises and in time they can practise these at home, and even lead them in the class. In the first 10 classes I use four basic conditioning forms.

It is good to remind students that they don't compare or compete with others in the class. They perform each conditioning exercise to the best of their ability while avoiding injury. The more the students practise these exercises the more they'll be able to achieve.

More experienced or higher-graded students can be prompted to push themselves, but not to the point of injury. Progress can be slow with conditioning; it can take months and even years, and there's nothing wrong with that.

The Instructor brings students together to form a circle while standing up. As with most of the exercises and activities described in this book, the explanation outlined is for the Instructor. When explaining the exercises and activities to the students, the Instructor should keep it simple and straightforward.

> If a student gets injured then they cannot train. Make a point of reminding them of this when the opportunity arises. Instructors should also avoid pushing themselves too far.

Stretching 1st form

Recommended time allocation: 8 minutes

There are a number of different versions of this exercise, commonly known in yoga as the Salute to the Sun. The students should be encouraged to relax and soften into each stretch.

> **Note** Watch the noise level of the group. Some students may try to attract attention by breathing loudly or even snorting. If need be, tell the students that no extra noise is required during the stretches. Everyone should be able to hear the Instructor.
>
> If interference does occur due to either noise or non-compliance of some form, tell the students that the present position will have to be repeated because it wasn't done properly by everybody. The Instructor can even openly acknowledge the student and their interference, thereby enlisting the frustration and cohesion of the group to bring the student into line. Students get annoyed when they have to keep repeating stretches, especially when they know that games and other challenges are ahead.

Position 1

Stand with feet together, legs straight and fully stretched. Stretch neck without tensing the muscles so that the head is slightly tilted forwards, as if someone is pulling on a string that is attached to the crown of the head. Lower abdomen is pulled in and up. Sternum is also lifted and chest is broadened. Weight is mostly on the heels. Tell the students to breathe in slowly through the nose, then out slowly through the mouth. Should feel the stretch right through the body and feel the spine lengthen.

Position 2

Raise arms out to the sides and up towards the ceiling. Palms face forwards. Lengthen body. Instructor tells the students to 'breathe in', taking a long, steady breath. Then the Instructor tells the students to 'breathe out', making a long, steady exhale. The commands for breathing can be said in any language. I use the following Maori instructions: 'Ha ki roto' (breathe in), then 'ha ki waho' (breathe out). The Instructor controls the pace of the breathing. As with Position 1, Position 2 should be felt right through the body as the spine lengthens.

Position 3

Weight is placed equally on both feet. Keep legs fully stretched. Breathe in and, while exhaling, bend forwards from the waist, hands reaching towards the floor. The aim is to place the hands on the floor in line with both feet; this could be palms or fingers. However, for many students (and maybe for the Instructor) this is something to work towards. Getting as close as possible without causing injury is what is required at this stage. Relaxing and softening the body will aid this. The torso is taken closer to the legs so that the chin moves closer to both knees. Weight should be slightly forward so that the legs are perpendicular to the floor. The stretch should be felt along the back of the legs, the waist and through the spine.

Instructor tells the students to breathe in slowly through the nose and out slowly through the mouth. The pace of the breathing is the same for each position.

Position 4

If palms or fingers are not already on the floor, they are placed on the floor through the following movement. Right leg is raised and taken back, stretching out to the rear, while bending the left knee. Right knee is lowered to extend the stretch, but does not touch the floor. Head faces forwards and up. Left knee does not extend over the left toes. Breathing commands are given: 'Ha ki roto, ha ki waho.'

Position 5

Left foot is placed back so that it is in line with the right foot. Both feet are shoulder-width apart. Hands are also shoulder-width apart, the left hand in line with left foot, the right hand in line with the right foot.

Raise waist and shift pelvis and torso back towards legs, keeping arms and legs straight. Try to lower heels so that feet are flat on the floor. Tuck head underneath and look towards tummy button. The stretch should be felt through the arms, shoulders, back and especially through the legs. Breathing commands are given: 'breathe in, breathe out.'

Position 6

Raise the head, eyeing the floor directly in front. Keeping the hands and feet where they are, shift weight forwards, lowering the face to floor and then up, followed by the chest and abdomen. Lower hips to the floor and arch back, pushing the chest forwards and turning face upwards to look skyward. Should feel the body lengthening and feel the stretch along the spine. Breathing commands are given, 'Ha ki roto, Ha ki waho.'

Position 7

Knees are on the floor. Raise torso, bow head and arch back, pushing it up towards the roof. The stretch should be felt through the back. Breathing commands are given: 'breathe in, breathe out.'

Position 8

Shift torso further to the rear, sitting back. Lower face, resting forehead on the floor. Hands are shoulder width apart. Stretch arms and shoulders. Breathing commands are given: 'Ha ki roto, Ha ki waho.'

Position 9

Position 9 is the opposite of position 4.

Shift torso forwards and lift the right leg. Bending the right knee, bring the right foot forwards and position it between the hands, ensuring that the knee does not extend over the toes. Stretch left leg out to the rear. Left knee is lowered to extend the stretch, but does not touch the floor. Breathing commands are given.

Position 10

Position 10 is the same as position 3.

Before moving into position 10, breathe in. When breathing out, bring the left foot alongside the right so that both feet are together. Place weight evenly on both feet. Keeping palms or fingers on the floor extend both legs until they are fully stretched. Again, if students are unable to place their palms or fingers on the floor then they stretch as far as they can. Torso is taken closer to the legs so that the chin moves closer to both knees. Weight should be slightly forward so that the legs are perpendicular to the floor. Breathing commands are given.

Position 11

Bend legs, raise torso and stand upright, lifting arms out to the sides then straight up towards the ceiling. Palms face forwards. Lengthen body. Breathing commands are given.

Position 11 is the same as position 2.

Position 12

Lower arms to the sides, the right palm facing the right leg, the left facing the left. Feet are together and legs are straight and fully stretched. Head and spine are in a straight line. Stretch neck without tensing the muscles. Lower abdomen is pulled in and up. Sternum is also lifted and chest is broadened. Weight is mostly on the heels. Breathing commands are given.

Position 12 is the same as position 1.

Run through the stretches two times. On the second round, exhale as you move into each position. For example, with position 4, I slowly breathe in, then as I slowly breathe out I lift the right leg and take it back, I raise my head so that I face forwards and sink into the stretch, lowering my right knee towards the floor and allowing myself to fully feel the extension.

Then I slowly breathe in and as I slowly breathe out I move into position 5 and so on.

Alternatively, you could inhale as you move into each position. This is a faster way of performing the 1st form. Students should aim to keep up with the Instructor.

Brain exercises

Recommended time allocation: 3 minutes

The following brain exercises stimulate co-ordination, awaken the students' mentally and improve mind processes. The exercises also stimulate awareness, helping the students to be more present, thus limiting the chance of injury even further. These exercises alone can have students improving in all areas of their lives, from reading and maths to becoming more agile and skilled in sports. The more often the students practise these exercises the more they'll benefit from them; hence these exercises feature in each of the first 10 classes.

The brain exercises may prove to be a challenge for some students. I don't expect students to get these exercises straight away, it can take time, maybe even 10 sessions for some; and that's okay. I often tell the students that it took me a while to get a particular exercise, such as exercise 3, but I kept going and over time I got it. If they persist, then they'll get it too.

Remaining in a circle, Instructor leads students through the brain exercises.

Exercise 1
Cross-overs. Raise left knee and touch it with the right hand. Then swap over and raise the right knee, connecting it with the left hand. Alternate sides for 20 seconds.

Exercise 2
Reaching behind, right hand connects with the raised left heel. Then swapping over, the left hand connects with the raised right heel. Alternate sides for 20 seconds.

Exercise 3
Slowly turn left arm around to complete a circle forwards on the left side of your body, with the arm passing your left ear. Continue to turn your left arm forwards and at the same time start turning your right arm backwards in a circle on the right side of your body. Arms should now be making circles in opposite directions. Do so for 20 seconds.

One way of starting this exercise is to have the students hold both arms straight out in front of them. Then take the right hand up and the left hand down and try to complete a circle with both arms and come back to the starting point. Then try it again.

Another way is to have the arms raised above the head. One arm falls forwards and the other falls backwards.

If students don't get the exercises today then there is always the next class. It shouldn't be rushed. As with the first conditioning form, the brain exercises are something that the students can practise at home with their families.

Water break

Normally in a class I would let the students go for a drink of water following the conditioning exercises. It is good for students to keep hydrated throughout the class. By hydrating the brain the students are able to take in more information. A drink of water also helps to break up the intensity of a class and allows the students to process the learning.

However, the students should only be able to go for a drink of water if the Instructor can contain them. Containment of students outside of the Warrior Kids room can be an issue in school-based programmes. In the early days I used to let students leave the room to go and get a drink of water, but after some time I put a stop to it as the students interrupted classes on their way to the taps, had water fights at the taps and in some cases took too long to return, meaning a loss of time for the next activity. Today, in school-based programmes, I encourage students to bring a bottle of water to class to keep in the room for the duration of the class so they can access it at allocated points through the session.

Containment is a lot easier when water and cups are on hand in a room adjacent to the Warrior Kids room. This is the case in the Warrior Kids Centre and the students are able to go for a drink of water at points during the class. Students need to understand though that they can only go for a drink of water when the Instructor says so. In no circumstances should a student be able to walk off the mats or training area without the Instructor's approval.

You will notice that I have specified a drink of water rather than simply saying a drink. Warrior Kids is a class that encourages and advocates healthy and happy living. Soft drinks, energy drinks and fruit juices contain a lot of sugar and preservatives. Water cannot be beaten in terms of healthy refreshment and hydration.

5. Tumbling

Recommended time allocation: 10 minutes

At any time during an explanation if a student or students are moving about or talking and not paying attention, regardless of the activity, the Instructor should stop what she is doing and wait. When the Instructor has every student's attention she should point out that she cannot talk when others are talking or not paying attention. I would go on to say, 'I need everyone to listen so that everyone knows what they are doing and so that there are no accidents and no one gets hurt.' I may then ask the student or students who created the disruption if they are okay to pay attention now or I might ask, 'Can I continue?'

Tumbling is an essential part of Warrior Kids. It extends the benefits of everything that has come before in the class and ripples out to all the other areas of the students' lives. Tumbling enhances and improves motor skills and co-ordination, enabling students to become more supple and agile. It helps overall fitness and well-being. Further benefits of tumbling include improved circulation and the ability to have the body moving and working as one, as opposed to feeling disconnected. Students gain confidence, greater internal and external awareness, self-assurance, self-control and focus, while at the same time being challenged and having fun.

I use a number of different rolling methods in Warrior Kids and the aim is for students to be able to roll eight directions in various ways. In the first class of Warrior Kids we focus on two simple ways to roll sideways and two simple ways to roll forwards.

Looking around the group the Instructor chooses two students who have role-modelled appropriate and constructive behaviour and acknowledges their behaviour aloud to the class. For example, 'I really like the way you've come in here today. You have paid attention right from the start and you've listened really well. I'm going to make you a leader for our next activity.' If the class is of mixed gender then I would usually choose a girl and a boy.

The Instructor leads both students to the front of the gym mats and has them sit down, with ample space between one another. The Instructor then tells the remaining students that at the command 'Go' they are to line up behind one of the two leaders to make two teams in lines, sitting down. The Instructor should ensure that no one moves until she says go.

Once all the students are lined up and the lines are as even as possible, the Instructor introduces the next activity and goes on to explain and demonstrate the first tumble.

Side roll from the Crouching Frog posture

Starting nice and simple, the side roll is easy to achieve; it is a natural movement even for those who find rolling difficult.

When I first teach the side roll I give the students two options. I say, 'I am going to give you two ways of doing a side roll, you can give both ways a go if you like or just choose one.'

When the Instructor has finished explaining and demonstrating the two options for the side roll she instructs the students to stand. At the command 'Go' the students perform two rolls in a line on the mats then go to the back of their team line. Students moving to the back of their team line should walk around the gym mats. The gym mats must be clear for the next student to perform her rolls.

The Instructor should also inform the leaders of both lines that when they are next at the front of their team line they should pause, as the Instructor can then change the roll.

It is good to point out at the beginning that tumbling is more about doing rather than thinking. If students find this activity challenging, encourage them to give it go and get it over and done with quickly. The Instructor may even need to get alongside some students and walk them through it.

The Instructor should positively acknowledge all attempts and successes no matter how minimal. Also, the Instructor should encourage students to flow throughout the roll and to roll softly, avoiding thuds and bangs. Instructor might say, 'Let's look after our bodies. You can't keep rolling if you get hurt.'

The Crouching Frog posture.

First side roll

Start from the Crouching Frog posture. Place left hand down on the mats, followed by left knee. Left shin is then lowered to the mat along with left forearm and elbow. Bending further, press chest against top of left thigh. Turning left, place left side of body on the mats and roll over on to back. Continue the roll over and on to the right side of body, up on to knees and then feet, returning to the Crouching Frog posture.

Regardless of the type of roll, students will typically end it on their knees. Although just giving it a go at this stage is the achievement, encourage the students to use the momentum of the roll to end on their feet.

The Instructor should also demonstrate this first roll from the right so that students have further choice. Some students may favour a particular side while they are learning the roll.

Second side roll

A faster and more concise way of rolling sideways. Starting from the Crouching Frog posture, place both hands down on the mats to the left. Take left shoulder down to the left and turn over, rolling across the shoulders or upper back. End roll back in the Crouching Frog posture. Instructor should also demonstrate the second roll from the right.

The teams go through twice. When the students are finished the Instructor sets them up to go one last time, saying something to the effect of, 'I wonder which line is the fastest?' Any inhibitions should be lost at this point as the students race to be the winning team. I'm actually not interested in having a winning team. I just want the students to relinquish their hesitations and doubts and simply roll. After this, move on to the forward roll.

Assisting students with the side roll

Some students will have never performed a side roll and may benefit from some hands-on assistance from the Instructor. When physically touching students the Instructor should always be aware of appropriateness and safety: that is, appropriate and safe areas of the body to touch, and appropriate and safe ways of touching. By doing so the Instructor will be role-modelling suitable conduct for a supporting adult and at the same time protecting himself and the students.

The last thing any Instructor would want is to be accused of touching a child inappropriately.

The student crouches in position, ready to attempt the roll.

When assisting students with the side roll, the Instructor should verbally declare her every action and the reason for it in the following fashion: 'I'm going to place my hands on either side of your back, and gently direct you to roll sideways.' The verbal declaration should be loud enough for others to hear. The positioning of both hands should be deliberately clear for all to see and witness, including the other students, supporting staff and parents and family members observing from the side.

Instructors should ensure that they always behave in this manner when touching students.

Once the student is turning over sideways the Instructor removes her hands and steps back.

Forward roll from the Crouching Frog posture

Again, I give the students two ways of performing the forward roll.
They can give both ways a go if they want, or just choose one.

1st forward roll: over the centre

Starting from the Crouching Frog posture, place both hands down in front on the gym mats, shoulder width apart. Bowing forwards, press chest against knees, tuck head underneath body, curling into a ball. Roll over, placing the top of the back on to the mats and running the length of the spine, returning to the Crouching Frog posture. It is important that the head is tucked right underneath, protecting the neck throughout the roll. Apart from maybe the rear base of the skull, the head shouldn't touch the floor at all.

2nd forward roll: over the shoulder

The forward roll over the shoulder is a gentle alternative to the roll over the centre and may suit less-able students who struggle with the first forward roll. Regardless, both rolls are valued in Warrior Kids. Higher-graded Warrior Kids are expected to be able to perform both.

Starting from the Crouching Frog posture, place right hand in front down on the mats, in line with the right foot. Tuck left arm and head under and through the right armpit, curling into a ball and taking the left shoulder down to the mat. Turn over and roll diagonally across the back, returning to the Crouching Frog posture.

The Instructor should also demonstrate the second roll by swapping sides and placing the left hand down, tucking the right arm and head under and through the left armpit, and rolling over the right shoulder.

As with the side rolls, the two teams should go through twice. Afterwards, the Instructor can have them race through, allowing the students to loosen up and enjoy the rolling.

Assisting students with the forward roll

Some students may benefit from some hands-on assistance from the Instructor. As with the sideways roll, when physically touching students the Instructor should always be aware of appropriateness and safety: appropriate and safe areas of the body to touch, and appropriate and safe ways of touching.

The student crouches in position ready to attempt the roll.

The Instructor verbally declares, 'I'm going to place one hand on the back of your head, and gently direct you to tuck your head underneath your body, between your legs. I'm going to place my other hand on the back of your leg to help you over.'

The hand should be on the back of the thigh of the closest leg, halfway between the buttocks and knee.

Once the student is turning over forwards, the Instructor removes her hands and moves back.

6. Roll Tiggy, 1st version

Recommended time allocation: 12 minutes

Time to test the side and forward rolls; Roll Tiggy is a fun and challenging game to do this. Roll Tiggy is another way to get the students practising and perfecting their rolls, while at the same time further developing their self control. There are two versions of Roll Tiggy in the first 10 classes of Warrior Kids; the following is the first version.

The Instructor organises the gym mats into a square, with an empty space in the middle. The students can stay in the lines they were in for the tumbling activity, seated and waiting as the Instructor moves the mats into place. The Instructor may even like to have a couple of the students assist with the setting up of the mats.

When the gym mats are set up the Instructor tells the students that at the word 'Go' they are to sit around the outside of the mats. Once the students are seated in this fashion the Instructor ensures that there is a buffer space between the students and the gym mats. This is a safety precaution as students will be rolling over the mats and could knock into or kick anyone sitting too close. To create a buffer space the Instructor tells the students to move back. She then walks around the mats ensuring that there is a clear path.

The Instructor goes on to explain the rules for Roll Tiggy.

1. Four students are on the gym mats at one time, one student in each corner of the square in the Crouching Frog posture. The students turn to their right and face the student in the corner of the mats directly in line with their own.

2. When the Instructor calls 'Go' the students roll sideways or forwards on the gym mats, chasing the student ahead of them.

3. The aim is for the student to catch up to the student ahead — by rolling, not running — and tag her with her hand. Any contact with the feet and legs must be avoided. This is another safety precaution. Students must control their feet as much as possible as someone could get a foot in the face. Only tags with the hands are counted.

4. When a student is tagged she is then out of the game and must quickly move off the gym mats and out of the way of the other students rolling.

5. When a student tags the student ahead of her, she then turns her attention to chasing the next student in front of her.

6. The last one remaining on the gym mats without being tagged is the winner.

Students must remain in the crouched position unless they are rolling. They cannot stand and they cannot move by sliding, crawling or shuffling. They must roll. Rolls must be clean. Bodies need to be tucked up. There is no rolling with the body straight.

Rounds of Roll Tiggy shouldn't last any longer than 60 seconds. Otherwise the students will get too dizzy and co-ordination and balance will become impaired.

Every student gets a turn. If a student does not want to have a turn but is physically able, gently remind her that, 'You come to Warrior Kids to do Warrior Kids, not to watch others do Warrior Kids.' Encourage the student as much as possible. If she is still resistant to having a go ask her to think about who she would like to play Roll Tiggy with out of the students in the group. This will give her some power in choice.

Of course this should be done tactfully and the student should not be made to feel embarrassed or ashamed. It can even be done discreetly, with the Instructor sitting alongside the student as Roll Tiggy is in play. However, the Instructor's attention should also be on the game. If the student is still resistant I tell her, 'I'm going to let you off today, but next time I want you to give it a go, okay?'

The Instructor should refrain from taking part in Roll Tiggy as her attention needs to be on the class as a whole; and as I tell the students who request that I have a turn, 'Warrior Kids is for the students.'

If the last round of Roll Tiggy requires someone to have another turn to fill the four corners, then the Instructor can ask students to put up their hand if they would like to go again. From there the Instructor can choose a suitable student or students. In the interest of reinforcing appropriate behaviour, I would choose someone who has been a model student, or there could be someone who didn't get much of a turn the first time and deserves another go.

The Instructor needs to ensure that a high level of respect is held throughout the game. This is a good opportunity to pick up on language and comments from students. Every student in Warrior Kids should feel safe enough to play Roll Tiggy, regardless of their ability or level of skill. The game is not about winning, it is about having a go, practising tumbling, building confidence and most of all, it is about having fun. Address any put-downs or belittling remarks. Encourage students who are out to win to relax and enjoy themselves.

Don't forget to acknowledge the effort of each student.

7. Breathing exercise

Recommended time allocation: 3 minutes

Time to refocus the students' attention. Breathing exercises are another good way to develop self-control and self-awareness. As with the conditioning aspects of the class, breathing exercises promote the value and importance of self-care and lead the way to constructive management of the emotions. A number of different breathing exercises are used in Warrior Kids.

Moving on from Roll Tiggy, the Instructor has the students form a circle standing around the gym mats. The Instructor leads the students, demonstrating and talking them through the first breathing exercise.

When taking the students through this exercise I mention that, 'I'm looking to see who has good self-control and who can focus on the task.' I also point out that students need to keep the same pace as me throughout the exercise: not too fast, not too slow. Sometimes this may mean that as a class we have to run through the exercise a number of times until everyone gets it right. By being open about this the students take further ownership of the group and pressure one another to do the activity properly. When we have to wait on others it gets boring. Warrior Kids is not supposed to be boring, and I even point out to the students when I am getting bored. However, allowances should always be made for younger students and for students who have special learning needs.

Hands are placed together with the forearms perpendicular to the floor (1). Slowly breathing in through the nose, raise the hands together towards the roof; keeping eyes forward. When the arms are fully extended upwards (2), hold the breath; bring both arms slowly out to the sides and down, with palms facing out. Keep holding the breath and take the hands right down, with the fingers pointing towards the floor (3, 4). Draw the hands in and up and when they are at chest height, turn them over so that the fingers are now pointing upwards (5). Slowly breathe out and extend arms, pushing hands gently forwards (6). Run through this exercise five or six times.

Acknowledge those students who are demonstrating good self-control and focus.

Alternatives

The Instructor could have the students close their eyes during the last two turns. With this the Instructor should encourage the students to pay attention to what's going on inside their bodies and minds as they do the exercise. The Instructor will need to talk the students through this version as the students will not have a visual guide.

Another alternative to the breathing exercise is having the students bring their hands right down when they are holding their breath so that their hands come together. Cross one hand over the other with the palms facing out. Raising the hands, the palms face upwards and turn over to face the chest and then downwards to face the floor with the hands pivoting to re-cross. As the arms are slowly extended and the hands gently pushed downwards, slowly exhale.

8. Sharing Circle

Recommended time allocation: 20 minutes

An opportunity for the students to share

The Instructor and the students sit on the gym mats in a circle. Each student should be facing the centre of the circle and be clearly visible to the Instructor so that no one is in any way disassociated from the group, whether by their own positioning or by the positioning of another student.

The Instructor presents the Koosh ball and explains the Sharing Circle process. Each student has a turn to share a low point and a high point. A low point is something that happened that the student did not like. It could have happened a long time ago, it could have happened today, or a low point could be something that is coming up in the future. A low point for the future is something that the student is not looking forward to. Maybe someone in their family is leaving to go somewhere and the student is going to miss that person.

The high point is the opposite of the low point; it is something good that happened, it could have happened a long time ago, it could have happened today, or a high point could be something that is coming up in the future. A high point for the future could be something that the student is looking forward to such as an approaching birthday.

Everybody is expected to share. It doesn't matter how big or little a thing is that a student has to share, what's important is that they do share. During the Instructor's explanation of the exericise, students can start to think about what they might like to say.

The person who is sharing holds the Koosh ball. Only the person with the Koosh ball can talk. When that person is finished sharing, students who are ready to share put up their hand and the person with the Koosh ball throws it gently to one of them. A student must have both a high and a low point ready in order to share; not one or the other.

The Koosh ball is an effective textile focal point that stimulates the brain and aids the student in finding the words to share their high and low points.

A prompter for getting students to put their hand up in the start of the exercise is, 'Who is ready to start?' or, 'Put up your hand if you are ready.' A prompter for later in the exercise is, 'Raise your hand if you haven't had a turn.'

The Instructor should acknowledge each student when they have finished sharing with a 'thank you' or 'kia ora' (Maori), 'malo' (Samoan) or something similar. At times the Instructor can also query what is being said. This can show that the Instructor is indeed attentive

Session 1

to what's being shared and values what each student has to offer. This can also aid in clarifying important information, highlighting valuable life lessons and assisting in establishing the relationship between the student and the Instructor.

However, it is also important that the Sharing Circle flows and that the Instructor is aware that too many questions on her part or questions that are probing may cause students to withhold and perhaps become resistant to contributing. However, don't be afraid to ask questions as this is a valuable opportunity to do so. Only the Instructor should be asking questions; if students have a question for the person sharing then they can ask their question at the end of the session.

What is also important is that the Instructor (or Instructors) has a turn to share a high and low point as well. This is leading by example and opens the Instructor up to developing greater levels of trust and relationships with the students. If you have experiences that offer insight and value to the learning of the group, then share them.

The Instructor should be restrained when it comes to sharing personally in the group. Remember, the class is for the students. If an Instructor is wanting support for her own life experiences then she should utilise external support networks beyond the class. The Instructor should always share last out of respect to the students.

Issues that may arise during Warrior Kids sharing activities

Disclosures

Students may choose to disclose incidents of abuse or violence when sharing in Warrior Kids. In such instances the Instructor should get as much information as possible; for example, exactly what happened, when and where it happened and who was involved.

If the content of the student's sharing is too explicit for the other students to hear then the Instructor should shut it down and tell the sharing student that they can share with the Instructor after the class.

In some instances though, with the guidance of the Instructor, it can be appropriate for a student to disclose within the group. There are always secrets around abuse and violence and such a disclosure may relate to another student. It may also instigate support for the sharing student from another student, a teacher or a family member if they are present; people who are more involved and consistent in the sharing student's life. For a disclosing student it might even be safer to speak out in a group with more witnesses.

Any follow-up should take place after the class, unless of course a student is clearly injured or distraught and requires urgent attention. The first step for an Instructor should be to involve a third party. If the programme or class is being run in conjunction with a school or agency, the Instructor should speak to the head of that particular organisation. It is also wise for the Instructor to fill out an incident report or to write a letter detailing the disclosure. This will make the disclosure official, which will move the process along. Once completed a copy of the Instructor's written account should be passed on to any third party, that is the school or agency who are the contracting body. A copy should be retained for the Instructor's records.

If the Instructor is commissioned or contracted to provide a programme or classes for a school or organisation, then responsibility for addressing disclosures will be with the commissioning or contracting body unless otherwise stipulated in any contract or agreement. When a disclosure has occurred in a school programme, I have always passed it on to school management.

If a disclosure occurs in a community class that is completely under the management of the Instructor, then a third party can be found in either the form of a professional supervisor, a colleague, an agency or even a friend. The act of sharing with a third party and in writing a report of the disclosure will assist the Instructor in clarifying, reflecting and ascertaining the disclosure in its completeness and it will assist in the planning of appropriate follow-ups.

If the Instructor chooses to discuss the disclosure with the sharing student's family, she needs to be careful that she does not make things worse for the student in terms of the possibility of severe repercussions. Being tactful is the key. I have spoken to a number of families over the years, and in many cases I have found this more useful than involving an agency.

To protect a student from any retribution I will steer away from talking about their disclosure. Instead I have asked parents and caregivers how things are at home and say that I have concerns. What is important here is that the Instructor, in the first instance, strives to establish good relationships with the parents and families of students over time; a relationship where they can speak frankly to the parents. If the parents and families know that the Instructor is on their side and that the Instructor wants the best for their child, then there is an opportunity for trust to develop.

In such cases the parents or caregivers tend to let down their guard and confirm the disclosure. On a number of occasions it has been the parents themselves who have disclosed, not the student. I've seen tears and cries for help, and from there we have moved together to learn about strategies for safer parenting, reducing stress and for gaining support.

It is wise for Instructors to have knowledge and connections to other services in the community that can assist parents and families; having brochures on hand that promote such services is a good idea.

Some disclosures are about trouble in the home or embarrassing events within the family. I have heard numerous accounts of arguments between parents or things that parents have done to one another, and about other family members. With such disclosures there is no physical threat to the student or anybody else in the family; things may have not been the best for the parents or the family at that given moment or there was an incident the family would rather forget and move on from.

Regardless, depending on the content of the account it is still good for the student to share such things in the privacy of the group as it gives them the opportunity to process and integrate it into their level of understanding. Then they're typically able to move on from that event.

The Instructor should be conscious of protecting the autonomy of the family though and should ensure that the content is shared in an appropriate manner. If the content could be damaging to a parent's or the family's reputation, then it would be more appropriate for the student to share the account at the end of class with just the Instructor. It would be abusive and detrimental to the family to have their dirty laundry displayed for all to see.

Separated parents present a number of issues and there can be accusations from one another that students pick up and share as a disclosure. This can also occur with wider members of a student's family, especially when there are differing opinions on parenting, or where there has been a history of dysfunction in the family. With all disclosures, Instructors should tread tentatively and strive to ascertain the truth. While a few disclosures have had to be taken further, most of the disclosures I have dealt with lead to nothing.

Issues of safety regarding a student's care and protection, or the safety of another, override any issue of confidentiality between student and Instructor. I have always been clear about this to any student who has disclosed.

The use of inappropriate language or the sharing of explicit content

If students use the Warrior Kids sharing activities to test boundaries and use explicit or inappropriate language, the Instructor should shut it down quickly. I do this by raising my hand in a stop gesture, frowning, and calmly saying to the student, 'Let's stop there.'

If any of the students are laughing at the language I look at them and point out that I am not laughing. My attention returns to the student who made the remark and I ask them to think about their language. I question if they think what they said was appropriate and what would happen to them if they used that language in the classroom or at home. I state that it is not appropriate to use such language: 'I don't speak like that, so my students shouldn't be speaking like that either.'

Some experiences may also be inappropriate for the other students to hear, such as an account of abuse, cruelty, the witnessing of a death or even something explicit that a student may have witnessed in a movie. It may even be something that a student heard someone else say. The Instructor should gently bring such a story to a close and tell the student that they can share it with the Instructor at the end of class. It is a good indication of trust if the student is willing to bring up a particular experience in the group, and it is important that the student does get to talk about it. However, it may be damaging for some of the other students to hear. In the meantime, the student in question may like to choose something else to say instead, with the understanding that she'll get to tell her original experience to the Instructor after the class.

Rarely have I had to shut down such sharing. Students do share experiences of abuse, cruelty, the witnessing of tragedies or of explicit digital material, yet the language that they choose and the impact on the class is typically minimal. As an experienced Instructor I actively direct the telling of the experience and guide the student who is sharing and even reinterpret the information appropriately for the group.

Exaggerating the truth or simply not telling the truth

Some students get into competing with stories, wanting to outdo one another. Some students want to appear as if they have exciting lives or that they have the coolest and best belongings. At other times it may be that students want to make out that they've got it bad at home. There are many reasons why students exaggerate or make up stories when they are sharing in the circle.

As an Instructor one will become good at differentiating between the truth and the lies. Yet, usually when students are exaggerating or not telling the truth, I allow it without question. I thank them for their sharing and move on to the next person.

This is because I have found that children who exaggerate or tell stories in Warrior Kids soon let it go and relax after the first few weeks. Their stories become simpler as they come to realise that they are accepted for who they are as opposed to what they own or what they have or have not experienced.

In some instances the exaggeration or lie may affect another student in the group. Depending on the content, I inform any student who is being spoken about that they are not in trouble and that they do not need to respond. Even if it wasn't a lie this would still be the case. I might share my disappointment with the student in question but they're not in trouble. I then simply question and work at getting the whole story straight from the sharing student.

Sharing of loss and suffering

At times students may share the experience of a loss or suffering such as the death of a family member or pet, an accident or of a family break-up. This is exactly what the sharing activities are for and the Instructor needn't be afraid of such content arising in the group. Simply allow the student to speak and to express their emotion.

The Instructor will notice that the other students will naturally fall quiet and empathically give the voicing student the space to share. If the student sharing the experience starts to cry or is visibly getting upset, the Instructor has some options to support the student.

Have a fellow student or sibling (if there is one in the group), sit close beside the sharing student. If the parent or caregiver of the child sharing is in the room they could come into the circle to support their child.

However, with a fellow student, sibling or parent, it is important to avoid rescuing. The supporting person shouldn't try to smother or stop the child from feeling the emotion. The idea here is that the child gets to feel the emotion in a safely contained environment and that the healthy expression of emotion is validated by the group. The supporting person need only sit close to the student, place a hand on that student's shoulder or rub their back.

If it is a school programme then the teacher attending the class could support the student.

If the child is very distraught then they could go and be with their parent in attendance.

Another option is that the sharing student move and sit by the Instructor, who can then support the student with a hand on the shoulder.

Once the student has shared I would acknowledge the experience by saying, 'That is very sad to hear, it is sad that you experienced that.' The Instructor should then take a slow deep breath in through the nose and slowly breathe out the mouth, then continue with the Sharing Circle.

Feelings in their natural state are typically quick to arise and quick to shift, and the times that they tend to stay around are when we as adults are holding on to them. Children demonstrate the ability to move through emotions constantly: one moment they're crying, the next they're running around laughing and playing. This is natural and healthy.

There are times when adults and even therapists look for more when talking with children. They think that since the child has had

Session 1

a sad or troubling experience they need to keep talking about it in order to get over it. If given the space, children will do this of their own accord and in their own way. It doesn't work to force them.

Hence the Instructor should avoid talking too much at this point. Avoid trying to get the student to feel or express more. The Instructor should also avoid trying to cheer the student up or expect the student to get over it no matter how long ago it was.

The Instructor will notice that the group of students will naturally give the sharing student a respectful pause once she has finished speaking. Then the group, including the sharing student, will simply move on.

Later in the class, or even in the sharing activity, the Instructor would be best to check in with the student who shared the experience of loss and suffering, and ensure that they're in a good place. The Instructor can ask the student what they're planning to do after class and make sure that they have a plan, asking if it possibly involves some form of play and fun. It can also be good to ask who will be around to support the student, who can the student talk to? This will mean that the student will have a strategy should they feel upset later.

Themes

Students may direct the focus of the sharing activity, creating a theme. When one student speaks about a death in their family, others can follow suit and share about a loss that they have experienced; therefore death becomes a theme.

Themes can also occur when students talk about other experiences such as achievements and the misconduct of others; these are all valuable points of discussion and exploration.

Group discussions feature in other sessions of Warrior Kids so the Instructor should avoid trying to create a theme of their own in the sharing activities. The sharing activities need to be open. It is perfectly appropriate for the students to simultaneously create a theme, because the sharing activities belong to the students.

Instructors can certainly gently direct the theme and may even need to. For example, death is nothing to shy away from; instead it is a valuable opportunity to highlight the cycle of life and how life involves times of loss and sadness. The Instructor could also ask the student sharing the loss, 'So, what is something that you did, or could do, to support and be nice to yourself?' or, 'What do you do to look after yourself when you feel sad?'; 'Who can you talk to at home?'; 'Where can you get a hug?'

This leads into the emotional awareness aspect of Warrior Kids and supports the students through their experience.

Students may have a lot to say

Students enjoy the Sharing Circle. It gives them the opportunity to share and to be heard. Some have a lot to say. However, it is best to try to keep the sharing to a minimum as time is a factor.

For example, in the Sharing Circle, the Instructor would be wise to point out that everyone shares **ONE** low point and **ONE** high point. It is common, however, for students to try and stretch the boundaries and go for two. In such instances the Instructor should ask the student to pick one of the two points to share.

Nothing to say

From time to time a student may try to avoid sharing or even have an attempt at rebelling and refuse to share.

New and younger students may be uncomfortable talking in the group; this is understandable. I give a lot of encouragement to these students and may try to get them to share a simple high point and talk them through the process. However, I may remove the pressure completely and let them off sharing during their first time at Warrior Kids.

Instead, I will let them share when they are ready. This does work and usually in a short space of time these students can't wait for the sharing activities.

This also applies to existing students who are going through a difficult or challenging time in their life and who may find it hard to open up to a group of people as opposed to a one-on-one situation. While one student might grab the opportunity and benefit in sharing about a difficult situation that they are facing, another might burst into tears and run off the floor when it is their turn to speak. The latter would clearly not benefit in sharing with the group and nor would they benefit from being pressured into sharing.

> **In fact, in Warrior Kids a student should never be forced into doing anything, but should be gently encouraged. Students can be challenged, but never pressured or forced. Such tactics would simply cause a student to withdraw and shut down emotionally. It could also mean that they refuse to come to class in the future.**

Of course there are other students who might refuse to share for different reasons to those above. Students will sometimes look for a chance to rebel and push at the boundaries, to challenge the Instructor. There is often a need on the student's part to see how safe it is for them and to check out how the Instructor will respond.

They may even share inappropriately or in a cheeky manner, such as, 'My high point is that I don't have a low point,' or something similar. They will often try to entice other students to go along with them. I shut this down promptly. If other students are laughing I give them my attention and calmly, yet sternly point out that, 'I'm not laughing.'

I may challenge the student presenting the behaviour, exploring why they are choosing to behave in such a manner; or I may simply say that everyone shares in Warrior Kids and that I will come back to them later, giving them more time to think of an appropriate experience to share.

Giving them more time to think about what they would like to say works on other occasions too, such as when they aren't ready to share or are fairly new to Warrior Kids.

Interruptions

Every aspect of a Warrior Kids class should flow, including the quieter activities such as moments of sharing. The Instructor needs to minimise interruptions.

Parents or caregivers watching the class may have younger ones who may be noisy. They may even start to run around, even on to the mats while the class is in progress. It is important to keep the boundaries for the class and to put a stop to such behaviour before it escalates. I may ask the parents to keep the noise down please or even speak to the younger children. If they're on the mats then I will tell them that they have to move off and that there is no running around while a class is in progress. If they're being noisy then I will simply place a finger to my lips and ask them to be quiet.

Parents and caregivers can also be disruptive in conversation, they may have mobile phones ringing, and their management of younger ones might be noisy. They need to be reminded to keep the noise level down. It can help to have signs visible that ask people to 'Please remain quiet while class is in session.'

Disruptions can also come from the students themselves. Close friendships form in Warrior Kids, as they should. However, at times these friendships can become disruptive. Friends like to sit beside one another; not a problem in itself, but when the friends start talking or playing around during activities when they are supposed to be focused, that is a problem.

I tell my students that I like it when they have friends at Warrior Kids. But if the friendship interrupts the class then the friends will need to be separated, meaning that they cannot sit together until they can be more responsible with their friendship during class. This is a good lesson and I often relate it to their school experience, asking if this is what happens for them at school. Do they get into trouble with the teacher for interrupting the class? I point out that 'true friends don't get you into trouble. They keep you out of trouble and help you to make good choices. A friend is someone who makes your life better.'

Another way I deal with student disruptions is I stop the sharing activity, focus on the disrupting student, calmly say their name and then say, 'When it is your turn to talk, I only want to hear you, I don't want to hear anybody else. Right now it is Jamie's turn to talk, so right now I only want to hear Jamie, I don't want to hear anyone else. Okay?' I do not proceed until the disrupting student demonstrates that they have understood what I have said with a 'Yes'. I do not accept yeah, yep or a nod. It must be a definitive 'Yes'. I ask the student to 'Please respect the person talking.'

Students shuffling or playing about with the mats can also be disruptive during the sharing activities. In some cases the children doing so may be younger, new or have special needs; or they may even be an active listener, one who hears and processes better when they are physically active. I respond to this type of interruption by either having the student come sit next to me and/or getting a Koosh ball for them to hold on to. Of course this is a different Koosh ball than the one that is being used for the sharing activity.

Before giving the student the Koosh ball I tell them, 'I have an important job for you. I would like you to look after this Koosh ball for me. However, you cannot pass it to anybody else, nor can you throw it around. You can roll it in your hands and jiggle it. Can you look after this Koosh ball for me?'

Make the most of the opportunity

The Instructor should be an enquirer and explore the experiences that the students talk about. She can reflect and repeat back to the students what she is hearing. This will show that she is listening, that she is interested and that she values what each student has to say, in turn building the student's confidence and interpersonal skills. Reflecting also helps the student to clarify exactly what it is that she is wanting to say and clarifies the experience, allowing the student to integrate it into her life.

Being an enquirer also allows you to look at behaviours and consequences in a non-threatening way. If a student shares an experience where they did not make constructive choices, then the Instructor can ask questions, drawing out the experience from start to finish, pinpointing the actual moments where the definitive choices were made. The Instructor could then ask the student, 'What could you have done differently?'

Other students in the group may have suggestions. The experience, as with all sharing and discovery in Warrior Kids, becomes group learning.

Importantly, when it comes to behaviour and choices, the Instructor should focus on what to do rather than what not to do. Avoid the word 'don't' as much as possible. Instead, focus on what it is that you want the student to do. For example, if you want a student to walk, you may feel the urge to say, 'Don't' run', but in saying that you will put the image of running in the student's mind, thereby increasing the possibility that the student will run. By telling the student to walk, we are instilling the image of what it is we actually want the student to do.

Remember, if you are going to explore experiences where non-constructive decisions were made, then you also need to give experiences of constructive choices the same, if not more, attention. They are valuable points of learning too. Openly praise the students for constructive decisions and behaviour. The constructive, positive behaviour is what we are wanting and the more we celebrate, acknowledge and expect it, the more we will get it from our students.

The Instructor's turn in the sharing activities is also an opportunity to give feedback to the students, targeting specific behaviour in a respectful and non-threatening way. Here are some examples of the type of feedback I would give for a low point in the Sharing Circle.

> 'For my low point today, I felt really sad to hear that you are going through a hard time at the moment, Andrew. I like it that you spoke about it in the class today. Make sure you tell Mum and Dad if you haven't already. You are a good boy, Andrew. Sometimes we go through hard times. Remember, you are a good boy.'

Depending on the actual circumstances surrounding the difficult experience, the group may be able to discuss strategies for dealing with such experiences.

> 'I feel sad hearing about the loss in your family, Rachel. Losing someone is never easy. Sadly it is a part of life. You make sure that you do something nice for yourself today. Keep talking to Mum, Dad, Aunty or Nana about it. If you need to cry, then cry. It is good and healthy to cry.'

> 'I feel angry and sad to hear that someone treated you badly, Michael. No one should be treating you like that. It is good that you told us, you're a brave boy. Make sure that you tell

Being an enquirer means being a good listener.

> someone in your family (Mum, Dad, Aunty, Uncle, Nana) about it too.'

> 'I'm feeling angry right now. I didn't like that I had to ask people to focus so many times in class today. I like it when people are listening and doing what they are supposed to be doing in class.'

I may even target particular students who weren't behaving well and name that behaviour and focus on the behaviour that I want from students in class.

> 'I was really disappointed to hear that you have been hurting others, Thomas. I don't go around hurting others, so don't you do it either. I like it, Thomas, when you are kind and caring to others. Be kind and caring.'

> 'I was really disappointed to hear that you've been giving Mum a hard time, Belinda. We don't always get on with people in our family, we don't always get on with our mums and dads, but I do want you to respect them. Fair enough that you feel angry with Mum and Dad at times, you don't always have to agree with them. But they are your mum and dad. Treat them respectfully.'

It is important that the students understand that regardless of what someone has done to them they still have a choice about how they respond and about the sort of person they choose to be.

As for high points in the Sharing Circle, I might say something along the lines of the following.

> 'My high point is that I was really impressed with your behaviour in class today, Richard. Really good listening, really good focus. Well done, keep it up.'

> 'I feel really sad hearing that you're going through a hard time at the moment, Sally. My high point is the way that you are dealing with it. Talking to Mum and Dad, doing nice, self-nurturing things for yourself. Good on you. You are a brave girl.'

> 'I feel angry and sad to hear that someone treated you badly, Michael. My high point is that even though you felt hurt and angry you kept yourself safe without hurting anyone and without getting yourself into trouble. Great! That's a real Warrior Kid. You keep making choices like that and you'll pass your grade in Warrior Kids with no trouble at all. Well done.'

> 'Gordon, your mum spoke to me and she is really happy with your behaviour at school and at home. She says that you're making really good choices. Excellent, good boy. That is great to hear.'

> 'Matthew, I was really impressed to hear that you've been

looking after others. That's being thoughtful and caring. You are certainly a Warrior.'

I also pay extra attention to acts of caring towards the environment and nature in general, including animals.

'Rachel, I hear that you've been helping Mum and Dad at home. Good girl, that is wonderful to hear. Keep it up.'

Remember, you are not there to be a friend. You are there to be a mentor, an Instructor of Warriors; to assist the students in making constructive choices in their lives for today and for their future. Be clear, direct and nurturing. Always show the student that you have their best interests at heart.

You will notice that I explained the low point first and then the high point. When I say my low and high point in the Sharing Circle I always start with the low point. I encourage the students to do the same so that they end on a happy thought. This is important as it keeps life in perspective and allows the students to finish feeling positive.

9. Instructor Says

Recommended time allocation: 3 minutes

Moving on from the Sharing Circle, the Instructor asks the students to make a larger circle in another area of the room. The students are to stand and the circle must be large enough to allow movement. The Instructor then announces that it is time to play 'Instructor Says'.

Instructor Says is derived from the game Simon Says. However, the Instructor gets to personalise the game by using their own name, for example, I use, 'Papa Tim Says'. Instructor Says is an exciting and fun game for the students.

The way Instructor Says works is that the Instructor calls out, 'Instructor Says do this' while performing a Warrior Kids posture. The students respond by forming the same posture. When the Instructor calls out 'Do this', and performs a posture, the students **must not** form the posture. The students only form postures when they hear 'Instructor Says.' The idea is to catch students out.

In the original game of Simon Says, when students are caught out they have to sit down for the remainder of the game. In Instructor Says this does not happen.

Instead, in Instructor Says I perform postures that I am expecting the students to learn as part of Warrior Kids. I acknowledge students when they do present a posture that they are not supposed to, however they get to continue with the game.

The postures that are used in Instructor Says are part of the Constructive Response taught in Warrior Kids. The postures encourage the students to lower their centre in a relaxed manner, an essential tool for self-reflecting and creating flexibility in their personal conduct, especially when dealing with emotions or conflict.

The physical reaction to experiencing emotions is usually pretty obvious. For example, when angry, we become tense. The jaw tightens, fists clench, muscles flex, eyes narrow, brow lowers and lips tighten. Breathing becomes short and sometimes the person stops breathing altogether, holding their breath, holding the tension. People who are angry tend to get louder and expand their bodies, appearing bigger as they raise their posture.

In fear, people tend to either flinch or cower, run away or turn angry and fight. Just like anger, they restrict their breathing, limiting the oxygen flow to the brain and therefore limiting their ability to think.

Constructive Response postures programme students to react in a different manner, not only physically, but also mentally and emotionally. Through these postures students are encouraged to respond in a calm, relaxed and centred manner. This opens the path for managing emotions and making constructive choices. By practising the postures the students also get to work their bodies and strengthen their legs.

Midway through the Instructor Says game the Instructor should tell the students that they want to remember at least three of the postures as they are going to need them for the up-and-coming challenge.

Warrior Kids postures

The following are some of the postures taught in Warrior Kids.

Warrior posture

Stand upright with feet shoulder-width apart, arms at the sides. Stretch neck without tensing the muscles so that the head is slightly tilted forwards. Lower abdomen is pulled in and up. Sternum is also lifted and chest is broadened.

The warrior posture is about standing tall and confident. Students are encouraged to feel good about themselves. Confident children are far less likely to get picked on.

Relaxed responsive posture

To perform a left relaxed responsive posture the left foot is forward while the right foot is back so that the centre is angled to the right.

The relaxed responsive posture is an attentive and non-confrontational way of being in social interactions regardless of whether or not there is a threat.

Responsive posture

To perform a left responsive posture the left foot is forward, right foot is back. Left foot is pointing straight while right foot is angled to the right. Legs are bent slightly. Hands are up in a relaxed fashion with open palms facing out to act as a shield. With the left foot in front the left hand will be in front, with the right hand back. To perform a right responsive posture the right foot is forward, left foot is back.

The responsive posture is used to evade and to take control when faced with physical threats.

Rear responsive posture

The rear responsive posture is a wider and deeper posture if compared to the more upright responsive posture.

To perform a left rear responsive posture, the left foot is forward and the right foot is back. The left foot is pointing straight ahead while the right foot is angled to the rear. Knees

are bent and the centre is lowered. Hands are up in a relaxed fashion with open palms facing out to act as a shield. With the left foot in front the left hand will be in front, with the right hand back. To perform a right rear responsive posture, the right foot is forward, left foot is back.

The rear responsive posture encourages students to lower their centre, enabling them to keep a balanced posture and respond in a controlled, reflective manner. It's also a great workout for the legs.

One-knee posture

The one-knee posture is the same as the responsive posture, however it is performed on one knee. To perform a left one-knee posture, the left foot is forward and the right knee is down. The left foot is pointing straight ahead while the right knee is pointing to the right with the right foot extending out to the left. Hands are up in a relaxed fashion with open palms facing out to act as a shield. With the left foot in front the left hand will be in front with the right hand back. To perform a right one-knee posture the right foot is forward, left knee is down.

The one-knee posture is a controlled way of shifting down or up from the ground.

Starlight posture

The foot positions in the Starlight posture are the same as the rear responsive posture. Only the hand positions are different.

To perform a left Starlight posture, the left foot is forward and the right foot is back. The left foot is pointing straight ahead while the right foot is angled to the rear. Knees are bent and the centre is lowered. The left hand is held directly out in front while the right hand is held above the head as if shielding the eyes from a bright star. Hands are open with palms facing out. To perform a right Starlight posture the right foot is forward, left foot is back.

The Starlight lowers one's centre of gravity. The front arm can be used to keep an aggressor back while the rear arm position is ideal for blocking.

Central posture

Legs are apart and bent, lowering the centre. Arms are extended out to the sides and slightly bent. The central posture is used to evade and deflect strikes while allowing the student to maintain a centred posture.

Crane posture

Another common posture in the martial arts. To perform a left crane posture start by having the left foot forward and the right foot back. The right foot is angled slightly to the right. Legs are bent slightly. Hands are up in a relaxed fashion with open palms facing out to act as a shield. With the left foot in front, the left hand will be in front, with the right hand back. Lift left leg and place heel of left foot on the rear of the right calf muscle. Balance and hold. To perform a right crane posture the right foot is lifted and placed on the rear of the left calf muscle.

The crane posture is great for developing balance and self-control.

Cross-step posture

To perform a left cross-step posture, start by having the left foot forward and the right foot back. The right foot is angled slightly to the right. Legs are bent slightly. Hands are up in a relaxed fashion with open palms facing out to act as a shield. With the left foot in front the left hand will be in front with the right hand back. Take left leg across the front of the right leg and place left foot in front of the right foot. Left foot continues to point forward while the heel of the right foot is lifted as if preparing to step. Bend knees further, lowering the centre. Balance and hold. To perform a right cross-step posture the right is taken across the front of the left leg.

The cross-step posture is used to evade and again, is great for developing balance and self-control.

10. Evasion

Recommended time allocation: 10 minutes

Now it is time to put the Constructive Response postures into practice with a challenging and confronting yet fun and enjoyable exercise. In practising evasion, students gain confidence in dealing with challenging and threatening situations, they learn about distance and timing, the importance of fear and the value of self-preservation.

The Instructor has the students sit in a line facing her. She presents the padded sword. The students will respond as soon as they see the sword. They will become excited and also a little worried, some more than others. 'She's going to hit us,' is a likely comment, especially from students who have been hit by adults.

The image of the sword is deeply rooted in our psyche, originating from history, culture, myth and story. It is highlighted today in media such as art and theatre. It is an image that the students' respond to on a conscious, unconscious and even a spiritual level. It holds numerous representations and meanings.

On a psychological level, the sword can represent endings and new beginnings, life and death; the cutting away from the past of old ties, habits, ideas, beliefs and behaviours, and the opportunity for new growth.

The sword can represent the students themselves, and life and Warrior Kids represents the swordsmith, metaphorically putting the students into the fire and trials, and conditioning them for life, until they're a blade worthy of respect and honour. And the Instructor's job is to help each student make sense of this; by doing so she is, in essence, polishing the blade until the student shines bright in their mastery of the self, of behaviours and choices.

The children love the idea of training with a sword, especially boys. Rather than suppress this natural inclination towards violence, we give the students form and self-control, enabling them to explore and to make sense of this aspect of the human experience without the need to exert power over others. Children are bombarded with images of violence from books, games, television, movies, news, contact sports, toys and the playground. Much of the world is governed by violence; and violence is prevalent in many families.

Warrior Kids offers a map for students to find their way safely through this terrain, allowing them to attain self-control and respect for others while realising the benefits of constructive, peaceful choices; Warrior Kids gives them the strength to make such choices. It also gives the students the opportunity to explore swords in a fun and safe way.

Each student will take a turn to stand in front of the Instructor. The Instructor will step forwards and slowly strike at the student with the padded sword, three times. The student evades each strike by stepping into a Constructive Response posture, three postures to evade three strikes.

Survival instincts dictate that humans resort to one of two reponses when threatened: fight or flight. By using the Constructive Response postures that have been practised in the game Instructor Says, the students are learning to utilise their flight instinct in a controlled manner. As I point out to the students, 'Evasion is the best form of self-defence and keeping ourselves safe. Simply, don't be there. Your body is not designed to be hit, so don't get hit, move out of the way. It doesn't matter if it is a push, a punch, a kick, a hot pot falling from the stove or a car coming at you on the road, get your body out of the way: evade.'

Be brave, be safe

The Instructor displays the padded sword to the students, showing them that it is soft.

This is a good opportunity for the Instructor to talk about fear. I say something similar to the following.

> 'Now, you might feel fear when you come up here and stand in front of me. And you should. I'm an adult moving at you with a sword. That's scary. It is good if you are afraid, your fear will help you to get out of the way.
>
> When we are afraid our senses sharpen, the pupils in our eyes get larger to take in more visual information, our ears hear more, our nose picks up more smells, even our taste ability increases, and the hairs on our body stand up so that we can feel more. This is all about survival. Our senses sharpen to keep us alive.
>
> There are also other physical reactions to fear. We might tremble or shake; that is the adrenalin pumping through our bodies, getting us ready to move. The butterfly feeling that can happen in the stomach; that is the stomach muscles working to keep everything in order in case you need to run.
>
> When we feel fear we become focused and alert. Our body and mind are ready for action. Fear is natural and healthy. It is not a design fault; it's there for a reason. Fear can save your life. Fear is not the enemy, it is not something to avoid. Fear is something to embrace and take heed of.
>
> Fear is not telling us to curl up into a ball and get hit. That is a response to fear. We do not want to be crippled by our fear, nor do we want to jump into aggression with our fear. Instead, we can listen to our fear and be calm and relaxed and respond in a constructive manner, and our postures help us to do this. That is what this exercise is about, being brave, being safe.
>
> So, if you feel scared when you come up and face me, that is good. Respect the threat. Keep breathing, use that fear to keep yourself safe and move out of the way of the strike.'

We want to encourage our students to trust themselves, not to be afraid of fear but to utilise the strength and power of fear. They won't become crippled or overwhelmed by fear to the point that they cower, freeze or behave recklessly.

It helps if the students understand that fear is natural and that the survival instinct to flee from danger is also natural. There is nothing cowardly or belittling about it. It is simply a natural response to danger. In accepting this we can then give our instinct to fight or flight a framework of control.

One thing to note is that children who are smacked are being taught to be hit. They are taught to take impact. I have come across many children who are physically disciplined and what I have noticed about these children, and about adults who were hit as kids, is that physical discipline conditions people to being hit. Rather than heed their natural survival instincts and evade a strike or hazard, even when it is obvious, these individuals are more likely to stand still and take it. Standing still and taking it is what they are taught to do when their punishment is being handed out. And doing what they're told in that instant becomes a survival necessity. They become reliant on the inflictor to stop the punishment before inflicting any real harm. However, this faith overflows into other areas of life, such as

Session 1

standing still in front of an oncoming car in the hope that the driver will stop in time.

In Warrior Kids there is no threat of being hit, yet students with this type of background cower and prepare for the worst. From a self-defence and keeping safe perspective, this is the complete opposite to what we want children to do when faced with a threat of any kind.

In Warrior Kids I want every child to trust their intuition and their survival instincts. I want them to keep safe and I train them to this effect. In session 2 we will go through the Keeping Safe group discussion, which helps to address this further.

At this point, however, the Instructor should take note of the students' reaction and gently ease them through the exercise, assisting them to differentiate between the two types of strikes: a parent's or family member's discipline, and an exterior threat. I might even openly acknowledge it by saying, 'This is not a hiding or a smack, I would never give you a hiding, nor would I smack you. This is self-defence training, keeping safe, so move your body out of the way.'

The Instructor should be well practised in using the padded sword and demonstrate control at all times. The Instructor needs to be able to stop short of making contact with any student. Practising the eight basic sword cuts described below regularly outside of Warrior Kids is a good way for Instructors to obtain such ability and control.

Students will not respond well to being struck. As mentioned, some students may be coming from environments where they have been hit or smacked. The student's experience of Warrior Kids needs to be above this. Warrior Kids has to be a safe place where students can relax, without fear of being hurt. If a student is struck she and other students will withdraw from the exercise and possibly from Warrior Kids altogether. The Instructor will lose their trust.

The idea of this exercise is to explore fear and evasion in a fun and exciting way. So, the Instructor should take her time and move at a medium to slow pace. I say medium to slow as you do not want to give the game away. The students know that they are not under threat, yet they still like to play along with the idea and don't want it spoiled. After all, it is their experience. Some students may even request that the Instructor moves faster.

Each student should be encouraged before and during their turn, and then praised afterwards. Give out any pointers that will help a student improve for next time.

At no point should a student be at risk of being hit. No student is to be hit.

Instructors should understand that striking any student in Warrior Kids is a breach of the Warrior Kids Instructor's Code of Conduct.

The eight basic sword strikes to practise

Do not be frightened by the evasion exercise. With practice you will become more confident and find it a breeze. It is a valuable activity in Warrior Kids that the students value and benefit from.

Holding the padded sword

To begin with it will help to hold the padded sword in a simple, correct manner. The leading hand, meaning the one you write with, should be forwards on the handle, while your other hand should be at the rear or base of the handle. By having your hands apart you will have more control over the padded sword.

I practise the following eight basic cuts regularly, in the following form. When used in the evasion exercise, each cut should be performed in a very clear, deliberate manner and with a step so that the student can see exactly what is coming towards them. The cuts are described with the right hand in lead position. When the left hand is leading, perform the cuts with the opposite foot to that described stepping forward.

Practice makes perfect.

1st Cut
Thrust

Hold the sword in front of you with the tip at chest height, pointing forwards. Advance with the right foot and thrust the tip forwards.

2nd Cut
Sideways cut, left to right

Circle the sword overhead, right to left. Step forwards with the left foot and cut sideways, left to right.

3rd Cut
Diagonal upwards cut, right to left

Lower the tip of the sword, step forwards with the right foot and cut diagonally upwards from right to left.

4th Cut
Diagonal downwards cut, left to right

Step forwards with the left foot and cut diagonally downwards, from left to right.

5th Cut
Sideways cut, right to left

Raise the tip of the sword, step forwards with the right foot and cut sideways, right to left.

6th Cut
Diagonal upwards cut, left to right

Lower the tip of the sword, step forwards with the left foot and cut diagonally upwards from left to right.

7th Cut
Diagonal downwards cut, right to left

Step forwards with the right foot and cut diagonally downwards from right to left.

8th Cut
Straight downwards cut

Circle the sword from the left over head, step forwards with either foot and cut straight down.

11. Closing words

Check-out
Recommended time allocation: 1 minute

The Instructor directs students to assemble on the mats, standing in a circle, as they did at the beginning of the class.

Each member of the circle, from left to right or vice-versa, takes a turn to say one word that would describe their experience of the class. 'Say one word about how the class was for you today.' The Instructor goes last to wrap the class up.

The check-out is a conclusive way of bringing the students back together as a group. The Instructor needs to acknowledge each student directly once they have shared their descriptive word. This could simply be done with a nod.

If a student says that they were bored or they put the class down in some way, don't be offended. Simply accept the feedback. The student's comment will either demonstrate where the student is at in themselves or the student could be stating a fact, in which case we should appreciate the student's honesty and bravery. Some students will try such a remark to see how the Instructor and group members react. Remember, children don't always get many opportunities to express themselves and to be heard. If I'm going to reply to such a comment, I will say, 'Fair enough. Thank you for your honesty,' or, 'I'm sad to hear that you didn't have a good time, hopefully you'll have a better time next class.' This acknowledges the student and their feelings and demonstrates that I value what they have to say. Typically, this is all that is required.

Closing
Recommended time allocation: 1 minute

The Instructor asks for a volunteer from the group to say some words to end the class. The ending words could simply be something to the effect of, 'I had a great time and I look forward to the next class.' This should be explained clearly so that the students know exactly what is expected of them.

As with the opening words, the ending words can be in any language, especially where English is a second language. This acknowledges cultural differences and helps participants to feel that they are represented and valued in the group.

The Instructor acknowledges the speaker with appreciation and concludes with, 'Remember to take what you brought with you today: your shoes, socks, watches, water bottle, jersey, and I'll see you next time.'

Congratulations, you have just completed the first session.

Consider your accomplishment.
Consider the smiles you saw on the children's faces.
Consider what each of them achieved, the connecting, the rolls, the games, the sharing.
You gave this to them.

Be mindful of what you would do differently; your mistakes.
Most importantly, be mindful of what you did well.
Remember, practice makes perfect.

Reward yourself with some nice food and drink, and contemplate your success.

Session 2

EQUIPMENT

- 8 x gym mats, size 1200 x 1800 mm
- Koosh balls on hand for students who find it hard to sit still during the talking activities
- chairs for parents and caregivers

Introduction

In session 2 students further their understanding of Warrior Kids and continue to develop their connections with the other students. The students are also challenged further both physically and mentally with new games and activities.

Session 2 kicks off with the check-in activity, which replaces the Sharing Circle from the first session. Checking in allows each student to express and debrief events from their day or week. The Keeping Safe discussion is a major part of the second session, giving students the opportunity to talk about unsafe touching and strategies for keeping safe.

The outcomes for session 2 are that the students will:

- be able to demonstrate stretches and a sideways, forward and backward roll,
- be able to vocalise an achievement and something troublesome from their week,
- gain an understanding of keeping safe, and
- learn strategies for keeping safe.

Lession overview

1. Opening words.
2. Round of introductions: a round of names and something that each student likes to do.
3. Check-in.
4. Warm-up game: Mice, Tigers and Elephants.
5. Conditioning: stretching: 2nd form; Brain exercises.
6. Tumbling: side roll, forward roll and backward roll.
7. Keeping Safe: group discussion.
8. Monkey Tag.
9. Tumbling: handstand.
10. Closing words.

Opening words
Recommended time allocation: 1 minute

The Instructor directs students to remove their shoes and socks and to sit on the mats in a circle. Once the group is settled the Instructor has the students stand. The Instructor then asks for a volunteer from the group to say some opening words to commence the class. (Refer session 1, page 44)

2. Round of introductions
Recommended time allocation: 3 minutes

Each member of the circle, from left to right or vice versa, takes their turn to say their name and something that they like to do. (Refer Session 1, page 44)

3. Check-in
Recommended time allocation: 15 minutes

Students will often burst into the room with news, items and work to show or simply lots to say. The check-in is an activity that allows the students to share at the beginning of the class.

As with the Sharing Circle, the students come to value the check-in. The parents also appreciate the sharing activities. I've had families take the activities and put them into practice at home, sharing low and high points from their day at the dinner table. This is tremendous as it is opening up communication and constructive relating within the family and home.

The Instructor and the students sit on the mats, in a circle. Each student should be facing the centre of the circle and be clearly visible to the Instructor so that no one is in any way disassociated from the group, whether by their own positioning or by the positioning of another student. The Instructor explains the check-in. Each student has a turn to share something troublesome from their week and an achievement from their week.

The check-in is an opportunity to share.

Something troublesome is anything troubling that took place in the last seven days. It could have occurred in the classroom or playground at school, at home, or anywhere. It is completely open. It could have been an incident where the student got into trouble, but it doesn't have to be. It could be a time where the student got sick or an occasion where something simply didn't go the student's way. Maybe the student got injured, lost something, missed out on a fun event, received a poor mark at school or got into trouble for talking in class. By using the term 'trouble', the students do have an invitation to disclose any trouble that they may have gotten into without the threat of punishment. Like the Sharing Circle, the check-in is a safe place to share.

An achievement is an account of when the student triumphed. It doesn't matter how big or small the achievement. It could have happened at school in the classroom or in the playground. It could have happened at home, or anywhere. Again, it is open. It could be that the student won an award, or that they helped out at home, or maybe they landed a flip on their trampoline, or got to the next level in their game or read a book; what matters is that they felt that they achieved.

The Instructor will need to monitor time as the check-in has the potential to expand in duration

Unlike the Sharing Circle (see Session 1, page 58), a Koosh ball

Session 2

is not used for the check-in. Another difference is that, instead of saying both the low and high points on their turn as in the Sharing Circle, with the check-in the students share something troublesome and an achievement separately.

For the first round each member of the circle, from left to right or vice-versa, takes their turn to share something troublesome from their week. When everyone has had their turn the group then has a second round; this time sharing an achievement from their week.

The Instructor can query and explore experiences that are shared, clarifying information, highlighting valuable life lessons and helping students understand the relevance of action and reaction, choices and consequences. The Instructor should acknowledge each student when they have finished sharing.

The Instructor should also share something troublesome and an achievement from his or her own week. Just like the Sharing Circle, the Instructor should speak last, be conservative with their level of personal sharing, and ensure that the content of their sharing is appropriate for children. Experiences that offer insight and value to the learning of the group or that motivate students to raise questions would be of benefit. I often talk about my son and daughter and some of the things that they get up to, and I talk about how I relate to them. This will bring up questions from the students about parenting. Students want to know if I smack my children, and as I don't, they then want to know what I do instead.

As Warrior Kids is for the students, the students should not have to hear about the Instructor's personal problems or failings. The bulk of the Instructor's personal life should be kept private and separate from Warrior Kids. This is being professional and keeps the focus on the students. The Instructor should be a rock.

One other difference from the Sharing Circle is that students can pass in the check-in. If a student has nothing to share they can say 'pass'. There are exceptions to being able to pass though. Long-time students or higher-graded students shouldn't have any issue in sharing something troublesome or an achievement. As challenging as it may be for them to think of something to share on some weeks, I'm certain that they'll be able to come up with something. A further exception is when the Instructor has prior knowledge concerning a student and their week. It is not uncommon for parents or caregivers to want to speak with the Instructor before class or even to contact the Instructor during the week about their child's behaviour.

Even a sibling may have something to say and in some cases I've had other students or members of a family giving feedback about another student. For example, the father of one of my students told me that while driving his car he came across a boy he recognised from Warrior Kids walking in the middle of the road. When he drove slowly up behind the boy and tooted, the boy refused to move. It was only when the dad put down his window and called out the boy's name that the boy moved to the safety of the footpath. To address this issue I first brought it to the attention of the boy's parent. I then spoke to the boy before Warrior Kids and prepared him by saying, 'Now, we are going to have to talk about this in the class. In the meantime I want you to think of what you would like to say to me about it. I'm giving you time to prepare your words, okay?' In other instances,

Everybody is expected to share. While you are explaining what the check-in is about, students can start to think about what they might like to say.

feedback about students has come from people in the community, from schools and agencies.

If I have prior knowledge of something to do with a student, depending on what it is I might bring it up in the group. If it is a matter that could embarrass a student to their detriment then I will talk in private to that student before or after class, or I may touch on the subject during check-in. For example, I might say something along the lines of, 'Sam, you say that you haven't had anything troublesome happen this week. However, I spoke with Mum before, and there was something to do with you and your teacher at school in the classroom.' In doing this I haven't given out any great detail to the group, yet Sam will know what I'm talking about. Sam then has the opportunity to respond, either by affirming what I have said with a nod or an 'Oh, yeah,' or he may choose to deny any knowledge of the incident. If the student cannot remember or is choosing not to remember I will give out further information to help him remember. I will remind the student that he is not in trouble with me but that we need to discuss what happened. I might be disappointed and if it is something major concerning his behaviour, then it could affect his next grading. However, I will not be scolding or telling him off.

I remind the students that Warrior Kids make wise choices, choices that keep them safe and choices that bring them constructive outcomes.

Some students may need a clear, firm directive from the Instructor in front of the group. In such cases I sometimes get the student to sit in the centre of the circle. This is to remind him that as individuals we are accountable to those around us, accountable to our families, friends, school and community.

This would happen for incidents where the student:

- was gravely unsafe such as playing on the road, on the roof of a house or wandering the streets when they are supposed to be home;
- had intentionally caused harm to someone through an act of violence or had been involved in someway in someone getting hurt;
- had taken a knife or another sort of weapon to school;
- was choosing to offend his or her parents using tactics such as swearing or attacking them physically, stealing or lying.

With the last one, a student may have good reason to be angry with parents and the described behaviour can be an attempt to gain power in a situation where they feel powerless. By acting out the student is gaining attention, even if it is negative, and is signalling that things are not okay at home and in the family. It might be that the parents are arguing at home, that there is a separation in progress, that there has been a loss in the family, that someone in the house is affected by mental health issues or that abuse is happening, or that the student is being bullied at school, and so on.

When a Warrior Kids Instructor practises CPR (Consistent Positive Regard) and maintains the best interest for the student, he will be sympathetic to such issues and address any acting-out behaviour in a sensitive manner. I always stress that, 'Regardless of how someone is treating us, we still have a choice of how we behave, we still have a choice of how we respond.'

Of course, there is also acting-out due to a lack of boundaries. In families where there is one parent, typically a single mum, children will exert their independence more readily.

When students have behaved inappropriately, I plainly put to them that I do not like it. I point out that the behaviour needs to stop and I then emphasise the behaviour that I appreciate and want from the student.

Many parents have told me that they only need to mention my name at home and their children behave better. Some students have entered my classes crying and fearful of disappointing me because of something that they have done. I appreciate and value all of my students, I affirm them in every class, even when they have made mistakes, and I expect the best from each and every one of them. The majority of the time the students are very forthcoming with their mishaps: this is due to trust, trust in the CPR I uphold for them. CPR is one thing the Instructor should always strive to have for his students; it is one of the main tools in the Instructor's basket.

There are variations of the check-in. Instead of something troublesome and an achievement, the check-in could be specifically targeted towards a particular area of the student's life. For example, 'Name something good that you did at school,' which might be accompanied by, 'Who got into trouble at school this week, and what for?' Or, if the holidays have just passed: 'What was something exciting that you did in your holidays?' alongside, 'Name something that was disappointing in your holidays.' As an Instructor gains confidence and experience in running the sharing activities in Warrior Kids, that person might like to use these variations, or even develop some of his own.

In the Sharing Circle entry in session 1 (see page 58), I outlined issues that might arise. These issues also apply to the check-in. The Instructor needs to be aware of such issues and be ready to respond accordingly should this occur. The group should be contained and boundaries should be in place so that the class can flow.

4. Warm-up game

Recommended time allocation: 10 minutes

Refer to session 1 (page 45) for an outline of setting up and managing the warm-up game. The Instructor should remember to get the students to take note of their surroundings and clearly point out the perimeters of the game to ensure safety and limit any chance of injury.

Mice, Tigers and Elephants

Mice, Tigers and Elephants is an exciting and animated game that is useful for team building, strengthening interpersonal skills and developing leadership skills. It also promotes strategic thinking and thought processing.

As with all of the games in Warrior Kids, it is not about winning, it is about the students building connections, learning about themselves and having a great time. Students should be encouraged to relax and enjoy themselves.

When the Instructor calls 'Go' the students make two lines in the middle of the room, facing one another. One easy way to do this is to get the students to find themselves a partner and to face each other, with one standing either side of the centre line.

It is good if the teams are both well represented in terms of age range. Older and younger students should be mixed up, otherwise a team of older students competing against a team of younger students will naturally have an advantage. Mixing the students up will also help with the integration of the group as a whole.

When the group is in position and settled the Instructor explains Mice, Tigers and Elephants. Remember, every student needs to be giving their attention to the Instructor when he is explaining the game as this will limit the risk of injuries.

If students are unsettled, moving about and talking, then the Instructor should quietly wait until the group is ready or express his unhappiness at having to wait and make it clear that he is not prepared to start the game until everyone is ready to listen.

1. At the word 'Go' the two teams retreat to the end of the room behind them; the teams are at opposite ends of the room.

2. At each end of the room the teams make a huddle and decide whether they are going to be mice, tigers or elephants. The team can only be one of the prescribed animals. For example, a team may decide to be tigers, which means that everyone in that team are tigers. The team's choice of animal is top secret, meaning that they do not want to let the other team know what animal they have chosen.

3. Once the teams have chosen to be either mice, tigers or elephants, they return to the middle of the room and line up. The two teams are facing each other.

4. When the Instructor says 'Go', each team has to show the other team the animal that they have chosen by acting as the animal. If a team chose to be:

    a) **mice**: they put both hands beneath their chin and wriggle their fingers like mouse whiskers while making a squeaking sound.

    b) **tigers**: they raise their hands up to the sides of their head and claw the air in tiger fashion and make a roaring sound.

Session 2

c) **elephants**: they hold the end of their nose with their left hand and place their right hand and arm through the bend of the left arm to make a trunk, which they then raise up and down in elephant fashion while making a trumpeting sound.

5. When a team works out what the opposing team are they must then work out who chases who. This may prove challenging for some students. The order of chasing is:

a) mice run away from tigers;

b) tigers run away from elephants;

c) elephants run away from mice.

Or, put another way:

a) tigers chase after mice;

b) elephants chase after tigers;

c) mice chase after elephants.

For example, if one team chooses to be mice and the other team chooses to be tigers, the tigers chase after the mice and try to tag them. The mice retreat to the end of the room directly behind them. When they reach the end of the room they are safe from the tigers.

6. To begin, any student who is tagged remains with their team. However, a bit later in the game the Instructor can change this by announcing that any student who is tagged must cross over to join the other team. This should happen only if the number of students in the class are sufficient and when the students have a good grasp of the game.

Mice, Tigers and Elephants is a great game. It might take students a little while to fully understand it but that is also part of the fun as laughter is often the result of any mistakes.

7. It is common in the game for teams to choose the same animal, for example tigers end up facing tigers. When this happens no one chases anyone. Instead, the students put both feet together and bend their knees slightly. With their left hand they make a tail out their back and with their right hand a cockerel crown on top of their head. Then they dance around in a circle doing a chicken dance while making the sound of a chicken. This adds a bit more fun to the game.

8. Mice, Tigers and Elephants is played for a set amount of time then it is simply stopped. There doesn't need to be a particular outcome for the game to end.

5. Conditioning

The Instructor brings students back together to form a circle, standing up. Refer to session 1 for an outline of setting up and managing the conditioning exercises (page 48). Remember, the students should only move as far as they feel comfortable. Encourage the students to relax and soften into each stretch.

Stretching 2nd form

Recommended time allocation: 10 minutes

A simple selection of flexibility exercises.

Position 1

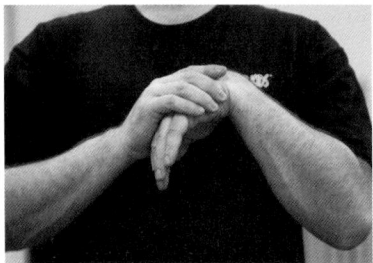

Stand with feet shoulder-width apart and legs slightly bent. Head and spine are in a straight line. The neck is stretched as the head is tilted forwards slightly, as if someone is pulling on a string attached to the crown of the head. The lower abdomen is pulled in and up. Sternum is also lifted and chest is broadened. Weight is mostly on the heels.

The left arm is in front of the chest and the left hand is allowed to hang with palm facing down. The right hand is placed on the top of the left hand and applies pressure, gently pushing the left hand in towards the left wrist.

The Instructor tells the students to breathe in slowly through the nose, then to breathe out slowly through the mouth. Feel the stretch up through the body, feel the spine lengthen, and feel the stretching of the left wrist.

Position 2

Remain standing in the same position. Left hand flexes backwards so that the palm faces up. The right arm reaches underneath the left arm or in front of it, takes hold of the left fingers and gently pulls down, stretching the left wrist. The Instructor gives the breathing commands, telling the students to 'breathe in' and then to 'breathe out'.

Position 3

Still standing with feet shoulder-width apart, this time the right arm is in front of the chest and the right hand

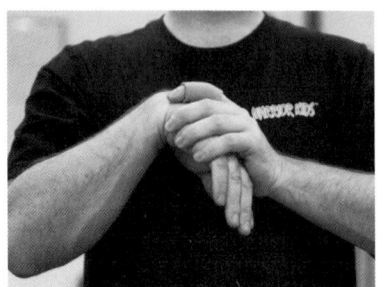

Position 3 is the opposite to position 1.

allowed to hang with the palm facing downwards. The left hand is placed on the top outside of the right hand and applies pressure, gently pushing the right hand in, towards the right wrist.

The Instructor asks the student on his left to take the class through the breathing commands by telling everyone to 'breathe in' and then to 'breathe out'. From session 2 onwards each member of the circle, from left to right or vice-versa, is given a turn to say the breathing commands for the class. The breathing commands can be said in any language, especially where English is a secondary language.

The pace of the breathing should be the same as performed by the Instructor in position 1.

By allowing the students to say the breathing commands, we further build their confidence, encourage clear communication and allow them to take charge and have further ownership of Warrior Kids. Some students may not feel ready to say the commands openly in the group. If this happens the Instructor should relieve the student of any pressure by moving to the next student in line.

Position 4

Position 4 is the opposite to position 2.

Still standing in the same position, the right hand flexes backwards with the palm facing up. The left arm reaches underneath the right arm or in front of it, takes hold of the right fingers and gently pulls downwards, stretching the right wrist. The Instructor looks to the next student on his left and asks that student to give the breathing commands.

Position 5

Remaining in the same standing position, the left arm is bent and placed behind the head. The right hand is placed on the left elbow and gently applies pressure, pushing the left arm downwards. The head should be kept upright and the weight of the left arm should be kept off the head so that there is no pressure on the neck.

The Instructor looks to the next student along in the circle and asks that student to take the class through the breathing commands.

Position 6

Opposite to position 5. The right arm is bent and placed behind the head. The left hand is placed on the right elbow and gently applies pressure pushing the right arm downwards. The head should be kept upright and the weight of the right arm should be kept off the head so that there is no pressure on the neck.

The next student in the circle takes the class through the breathing commands.

Position 7

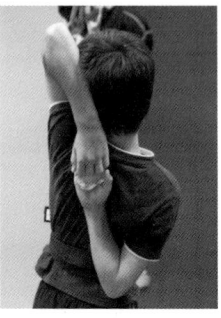

Remaining in the same standing position, the left arm reaches over the left shoulder and down the back. The right arm reaches up behind the back. Both hands reach for one another, stretching the arms and chest. Some students may even be able to connect the hands. However, this is something that is worked towards over time and doesn't have to happen immediately.

The next student takes the class through the breathing commands.

Position 8

Position 8 is the opposite to position 7.

The right arm reaches over the right shoulder and down the back. The left arm reaches up behind the back. Both hands reach for one another, stretching the arms and chest.

The next student takes the class through the breathing commands.

Position 9

The left arm is extended across the chest and out to the right. The right arm is bent upwards and in towards the chest, pulling the left arm further across the chest, stretching it more.

The next student takes the class through the breathing commands.

Position 10

Opposite to position 9. The right arm is extended across the chest and out to the left. The left arm is bent upwards and in towards the chest, pulling the right arm further across the chest, stretching it more.

The next student takes the class through the breathing commands.

Position 10 is the opposite to position 9.

Loosening-up exercise 1

At this point in the conditioning it is good to loosen the arms and shoulders with a gentle exercise.

Gently swing the arms forwards and up to just above the head, then allow gravity to let the arms drop, swing down and out behind the body. Find the natural rhythm of this exercise and repeat 8–12 times.

The Butterfly

Now it is time to stretch and loosen up the lower region of the body. Sit down and bend the legs, bringing the soles of the feet together. Keeping the back straight, hold the ends of the feet with the hands. Raise the knees up and down together like the wings of a butterfly. Do this at a steady pace, 30 times.

Sharing opportunity
During the butterfly exercise I sometimes ask each student to name a place where they would like to fly to.

Position 11

Remain seated with the back straight and the soles of the feet together. Hold the ankles with both hands and lower elbows on to the knees. Gently apply pressure with the arms, pushing down on the knees. This will extend the inner legs.

The next student takes the class through the breathing commands.

Position 12

Remain in the seated position with a straight back and the soles of the feet together. Grasp the ends of the feet and gently pull the feet upwards while easing the knees closer to the floor, without using the elbows.

The next student takes the class through the breathing commands.

Position 13

Staying seated, cross the legs. Instead of having the legs tucked in, shift them out so that they are straight across the front of the body. Keep the back straight, place fingers on the floor in front and walk the fingers out, extending the arms. Bend at the waist and take the chest towards the floor. The buttocks remain on the floor throughout the stretch. Reach out as far as able and then hold for the breathing.

The next student takes the class through the breathing commands.

Position 14

Opposite to position 13, meaning that the legs are swapped around. If the left leg was in front for position 13, now put the right leg in front. Place fingers on the floor in front and walk the fingers out as far as able, then hold for the breathing.

The next student takes the class through the breathing commands.

Loosening-up exercise 2: stirring the pot

Turning to the side, extend the legs out wide, making the sideways splits. Hands are together, one hand holding the back of the other. Rotate upper body from left to right reaching out over the floor in front with the chest and arms.

As the rotation returns back over the body, bring the hands closer to the chest and then reach back out when the rotation continues forwards, as if stirring a large pot. After 8 rotations change direction, rotating right to left.

> **Sharing opportunity**
> When stirring the pot I ask each student what they are stirring in their pot.

Position 15

Relax and soften into the stretch.

Remain seated with the legs outstretched. Sit upright with the back straight and legs stretched out to the sides. Relax and soften into the stretch.

The next student takes the class through the breathing commands.

Position 16

Remain seated with legs outstretched. Place the fingers on the floor in front and walk the fingers out, extend the arms, bend from the waist and lower the chest towards the floor. Reach out as far as able, then hold the position for the breathing.

The next student takes the class through the breathing commands.

Loosening-up exercise 3: massage the legs

Still seated with legs extended out to the sides, gently beat the inner legs with the edge of the hands. The massage runs the length of the inner leg to the knee, avoiding the groin area.

Repeat position 16.

Loosening-up exercise 4

Bring straight legs together and in front of the body. Alternate lifting the right knee and the left knee up and down to loosen the legs.

Position 17

Moving up on to the knees, the left hand reaches back to grasp the left heel and the right hand reaches back to grasp the right heel. Arch the spine, and push the stomach outwards, tip head backwards to look up at the ceiling and hold.

The next student takes the class through the breathing commands.

Position 18

Sit down and bring legs together in front of the body. Inhale and raise the arms sideways and upwards, above the head. Breath out and stretch forwards, bending from the waist. Reach out with the hands as far as able and grasp the legs or feet. Legs should be fully extended. Hold the position, relaxing and softening into the extension.

The next student takes the class through the breathing commands.

Stand and shake the body to loosen. This ends the 2nd form of stretching.

Brain exercises

Recommended time allocation: 3 minutes

Standing as part of the circle, the Instructor leads the students through the first set of brain exercises. Refer session 1, page 51.

6. Tumbling

Recommended time allocation: 10 minutes

Refer to session 1 for the outline of setting up and managing the tumbling exercises (page 52).

Remaining in the circle, the Instructor looks around the group and chooses two students who have role-modelled appropriate and constructive behaviour. Acknowledging their behaviour to the class, the Instructor leads both students to the front of the mats and has them sit down, with ample space between them. The Instructor then tells the remaining students that at the command 'Go' they are to line up behind one of the two leaders to make two lines, then sit down. The Instructor should ensure that no one moves until he says go.

Once all the students are lined up and the lines are as even as possible, the Instructor introduces the next activity and goes on to explain and demonstrate the first tumble.

Side roll from the Crouching Frog posture

Revisit and run through the side-roll techniques explored in session 1 (see page 53). Each line of students should do the exercise twice.

Forward roll from the Crouching Frog posture

On completing the side roll, revisit the forward-roll techniques explored in session 1 (see page 54). Each line of students should do the exercise twice.

Back roll from the Crouching Frog posture

The Instructor demonstrates and explains the back roll. The students are given two ways to perform a back roll. They can give both ways a go or just choose one. The back roll can be more challenging for the students than the side and forward rolls as they have to get used to the idea of going backwards.

During the practise the Instructor may need to use his hands to support students to help the children turn over the correct way. But don't overdo it or the student will become reliant on you. Students need to be able to explore the roll on their own and find their way.

Assisting students with the back roll

Some students will have never performed a back roll and may benefit from some hands-on assistance from the Instructor. As with the side and forward rolls in session 1 (page 53), when physically touching students the Instructor should always be aware of appropriateness and safety: appropriate and safe areas of the body to touch, and appropriate and safe ways of touching.

The student crouches in position, ready to attempt the roll.

The Instructor says, 'As you roll on to your back, I'm going to hold your lower legs and help you over.'

The Instructor's hands should be on the back of the calf muscle or on the ankle. The Instructor should ensure that he directs the student to roll backwards over the shoulder as explained on the next page for the 1st back roll. This helps to avoid neck and back injuries.

1st back roll: over the shoulder

Rolling back over the shoulder is an effective, easy and safe way to start rolling backwards. It builds the students' confidence and prepares them for the back roll over the centre.

Start from the Crouching Frog posture. Sit down on the buttocks and lean back, rolling up the length of the spine.

A good preparation exercise for the back roll is to repeat rolling up the length of the spine and then rewinding and rolling back down again. There is a natural rhythm in this movement. The students can practise this exercise on the mats before attempting the back rolls.

The students need to understand that when doing the back roll it is important to use momentum, so once they start, by sitting down on to their buttocks, they should keep moving, rolling up the length of the spine, tilting the head to the side and rolling over the shoulder and up on to the feet.

It is important that the students are careful with the head and neck when rolling backwards. If a student is tilting his head to the right he needs to be rolling over his left shoulder. If a student is tilting his head to the left, then he needs to be rolling over his right shoulder.

It is good to get the students to place their hands above the head and to push off the floor, or to hold a fixed position with the hands and arms, in order to support the head and neck when rolling over. This also leads to more advanced rolling abilities.

The back roll is concluded by returning up onto the feet in the Crouching Frog posture.

Another way of doing the back roll over the shoulder is to get the students to come out first and perform a forward roll over the shoulder, as outlined in session 1 (page 54). Then push rewind, rolling back the way they have come. In doing this the students get used to the idea of tilting the head to the side and using the shoulder.

2nd back roll: over the centre

Start off in the Crouching Frog posture. Sit back on to the buttocks and use the momentum of this action to lean back and roll up the length of the spine. Place the hands above the head on to the floor and push off, or hold the hands and arms in a fixed position and roll over the centre on to the feet, returning to the Crouching Frog posture.

The centre back roll is often more challenging for the students than the shoulder roll.

Some students may choose to give the shoulder roll a few goes before attempting the centre roll. Other students may already be familiar with the back centre roll and not so familiar with the shoulder roll.

As with the side and forward roll, the students should go through twice. Afterwards the Instructor can have them race through, allowing the students to loosen up and enjoy the exercise.

7. Keeping Safe:
group discussion

Recommended time allocation: 15 minutes

Note The content of the Keeping Safe discussion should be appropriate for children. The Instructor should be aware of language and keep the discussion simple and straightforward. Anything explicit or of a sexual nature beyond what is outlined below is not appropriate.

Question 1

When it comes to touching between people, what sort of touching is safe touching?

The Keeping Safe group discussion is an integral part of the holistic tapestry that is Warrior Kids. In session 2 the Keeping Safe discussion is about safe physical interactions and keeping safe around angry adults.

The students value the opportunity to discuss and explore this topic and the Instructor should be comfortable and confident in discussing such issues. If the Instructor finds the discussion uncomfortable or even threatening, then it would be wise for the Instructor to seek support in the way of professional supervision before conducting this activity.

It is normal for discussions of this nature to be uncomfortable. No one likes the idea of a person breaching boundaries and touching a person inappropriately, whether it be through acts of violence or indecency. However, children and young people struggle with it too, and it is up to adults to support children and assist them in understanding and preventing inappropriate touching in their lives. It is up to us to help children to keep safe.

To assist with the Keeping Safe discussion, the Instructor should be guided by the same principles as for the Sharing Circle outlined in session 1 (see page 58), and the methods of addressing the various issues that may arise.

The Instructor and the students sit on the mats in a circle. Each student should be facing the centre of the circle and be clearly visible to the Instructor so that no one is in any way disassociated from the group, whether by their own positioning or by the positioning of another student.

Once the group is settled, the Instructor explains to the students that in Warrior Kids there are all sorts of different activities and challenges, and sometimes there is sitting down and talking, which is what the group will be doing now. The Instructor then goes on to announce that, 'Today we are talking about keeping safe — safe around touching.' It is good to point out that Warrior Kids originated from the martial arts and that martial arts are about self-defence or self-protection.

The Keeping Safe discussion is generated by questions.

Students who wish to answer raise their hand and the Instructor elicits the answers from the group. To start with students might talk about touching that is soft and gentle. They then may go on to the rules of games such as rugby and netball, and what is regarded as safe touching or tackling when playing. I ask the students if hugging is safe. Mostly they agree it is. I ask if it is safe to hug just anyone. They say, 'No' and we discuss who is safe to hug: Nana, Papa, Aunty, Mum, Dad, friends and so on.

It is important to stress that it is good to hug people that you trust and feel safe with. This statement is inclusive of family members. It is a sad fact that children that are abused are typically abused by those close to them: family and friends.

I ask the students if tickling games are safe. Again, they mostly agree that they are, but as with the hugging it is only safe to play tickling games with people who they trust and feel safe with.

Other forms of touching, such as massage, would be included in this category. In some families the children may rub or massage Mum

and Dad's shoulders. This is wonderful and should be encouraged. Sadly though, for an offender of child abuse, massage could be used as part of the grooming process. So again, 'people who you trust and feel safe with' is an important concept to advocate.

There are no easy answers when it comes to abuse. The Instructor has to remember that as much as he may want to protect the students, the chances are that he won't be there when a student faces abuse. The Keeping Safe discussion will help to illuminate early warning signs for the students, and the Instructor should encourage each student to trust their intuition and instincts when it comes to keeping safe.

The reality is that we do not live in a perfect world. As much as people try to make the world safe for children the truth is that government and social services are overstretched. Students will come and go in Warrior Kids, and children who have been removed from an abusive environment are commonly placed in another abusive environment or before long are put back in the original one.

Children who have been abused are conditioned and vulnerable to further abuse; that conditioning and vulnerability makes them a target unless their experience of abuse is addressed, which is what Warrior Kids and the Keeping Safe discussion is all about.

Question 2

What sort of touching is not safe?

Again, the students put up their hands and the Instructor elicits answers. The students will tend to recite a long list of different types of striking such as kicking, punching, slapping, head butting, as well as striking with objects. There will also be choking, scratching, pushing, and so on. These are all good examples, as they are not safe touching, and it is good for the students to clearly know this. It means that if someone touches them or someone else in a manner the students know is not okay, they will know that something should be done about it. Understanding this empowers the students.

Students may mention that smacking as a punishment is not safe touching. Literally to smack is to strike and I can't condone one form of striking and reject another. I encourage discussion on smacking and many students are keen to know how I deal with my son and daughter, as my children have never been smacked. It is interesting and valuable for students to explore alternatives to smacking. Just because things were done a certain way in the past doesn't mean that it needs to be that way in the future.

Once the students have exhausted all the different types of striking and other aggressive methods of physical interaction, and if it hasn't already been raised, the Instructor should talk about the touching of 'private parts'.

At the mention of private parts, it is common for there to be some sniggers from students in the group and that's okay. I say that, 'we can laugh about it, but sadly it does happen.'

I go on to say that, 'private parts are just that, private. Apart from Mum, Dad or a doctor when we are sick, there is no reason for anyone to be touching you there.'

I stress that it's not okay and it is not safe.

I also mention that it's not safe or okay if someone tries to get you to touch their private parts. This tactic of manipulating the victim into doing the touching is commonly used by offenders.

Sometimes there can be episodes of touching among children at schools or at home. Curiosity is natural and children do wonder about their bodies. However, it is the responsibility of adults to

Session 2

uphold boundaries of appropriate conduct and to teach children that private parts are private, and that it is not okay for anyone to touch them or for them to be touching anyone else's private parts.

While such play among children can be innocent, it can also be an indication that a child has been or is being abused and is in need of intervention. Instructors should tread carefully and avoid making any accusations until all the facts are clear. The Instructor should interact with community or government agencies or health professionals to gain support and resources in dealing with such issues.

During the discussion with the students the Instructor should also mention 'uncomfortable touching'. Uncomfortable touching is not necessarily touching that hurts or the touching of the private parts, but it can certainly be a warning that something's not right. To explain this further I tell of an experience that a friend of mine had when she was a girl. When attending a birthday party at a neighbour's house, a man, who she didn't know, sat down beside her, placed a hand on her leg and told her that she was a pretty girl. Rightfully, the girl felt uncomfortable. She said she had to go because her mother was waiting for her and ran home as quickly as she could. This is an example of uncomfortable touching and it demonstrates early warning signals. Early warning signals are conscious and unconscious signals one receives when faced with a threat. They are signs that trigger our primal fear and our survival instincts. The girl felt and identified the early warning signals that she wasn't safe. She took heed of the signals and responded accordingly.

To take this even further, the Instructor can also use the phrase 'touching in an adult way'. For children who have been brought up in an abusive environment, 'uncomfortable touching' may not be so uncomfortable. Children who are abused are usually confused about their feelings and find comfort in being wanted and touched. Some may even know that it is inappropriate, but for them the abuse may be construed as love.

The Instructor can explain 'touching in an adult way' as the 'type of touching that adults do.' This means touching that adults consent to and that is part of an intimate relationship between adults. It is touching that is not appropriate when it involves children and includes, for example, touching such as stroking of legs, buttocks and the genital region. The Instructor should stress that this sort of touching of children is not okay. It is not love. I also say, 'No one should treat you like this.'

When incidents of abuse are mentioned I share my feelings about it, whether they be sad or angry, and I state that it's not okay.

Sharing of experiences

When it comes to talking about inappropriate touching, whether it is aggressive touching or sexual touching, the students may have experiences to share. They may even choose to disclose abuse. The content of the experiences may not be appropriate for others in the group to hear. This has been covered in the issues that may arise section of the Sharing Circle in session 1 (page 58).

The Instructor should remain calm and flexible. If experiences are shared, the majority of the time they are completely appropriate and of great value to the group. The Instructor can use the opportunity to highlight constructive behaviour and unconstructive behaviour. The Instructor should be open and clear to students about what is not okay and what is okay.

The students should be encouraged to share. If the content of their experience is not appropriate for others in the group to hear,

Exercise: understanding personal space

the Instructor can stop the student and get him to talk to him at the end of the session.

If the Instructor has experiences that offer insight and value to the Keeping Safe discussion, then he can share them. However, the Instructor should be restrained when it comes to sharing personally in the group. Remember, the class is for the students.

The Instructor talks to the students about personal space, the area directly around them that people who we know and trust may enter but others should not. To help with this, the Instructor performs a simple demonstration.

The Instructor picks two volunteers from the class, a boy and a girl.

1. The boy stands about five metres from the Instructor, out in front of the class. The boy faces the Instructor.
2. The Instructor asks the class, 'How close is too close?' and slowly walks towards the boy, who remains still.
3. When the gap between the boy and the Instructor closes to about two metres, the Instructor pauses, looks to the class and asks, 'Is this too close?' The Instructor elicits opinions from the class.
4. The Instructor continues to step closer to the boy until the space between them is reduced to about one metre. The Instructor pauses, looks to the class and asks, 'Is this distance okay?'
5. The Instructor looks to the boy and asks him, 'Is this too close for you?'
6. The Instructor steps forwards, closing the gap further. 'Is this too close?' he asks the class.
7. When it is clear to the Instructor that he is too close, he stops.
8. Now the Instructor asks the boy to turn side on to him. 'What about now?' the Instructor asks the class. 'Is this distance too close?'
9. The Instructor asks the boy to turn around so that his back is facing the Instructor. 'What about now?' the Instructor asks. 'Is this too close?'
10. If it is obvious to the Instructor that he is standing too close, he says, 'Nobody should be standing this close to you, unless they're someone that you feel safe with such as Mum, Dad and certain others such as friends and family.'
11. The Instructor thanks the boy and asks him to rejoin the class and sit down.
12. The demonstration is repeated with the girl.
13. In conclusion, the Instructor points out any differences in individual responses between the first demonstration with the boy and the second demonstration with the girl.

He might say, 'Some of you may not like anyone getting a bit close to you, some may not mind, however, no one should be coming right into your space. And if you ever feel uncomfortable with how close someone is then that is your body's way of telling you that you need to move away.'

Session 2

14. The Instructor points out that there are times in life when people do stand close, such as on a train or in a crowd. 'There are times that being in a crowd might not feel safe. What do you do in those situations? Stay close to family and friends.'

Question 3

If someone is trying to touch you in a way that's not safe, whether they're trying to hurt you, trying to touch your private parts or trying to get you to touch theirs, or are touching you in a way that's uncomfortable, or touching you in an adult way, it is not okay. So, what should you do about it?

The answers given can be explored by the class to determine their effectiveness, appropriateness and safety. I query responses that are far-fetched, unsafe or simply not wise; other students in the group tend to set it right. Typical answers the students may give are:

○ Say, 'Stop it, I don't like it.'
○ Shout, 'No! Leave me alone!'
○ Defend yourself.
○ Run away or get away if need be. I always stress 'get away' as this encompasses all sorts of strategies, for example the trickery used by the girl at the party telling the man that her mother was waiting for her.
○ Use a big voice to attract others.
○ Tell somebody about it.

When 'telling somebody about it' is raised, the Instructor should pause the group discussion and ask each member of the circle, from left to right or vice versa, to name an adult that they could talk to. I stress that it has to be an adult. By all means the students can tell a friend or a family member closer to their age, but it's important that the students think of an adult that they trust, someone who is a position to do something to address the unsafe conduct.

The Instructor should go first, telling the students that it's just as important for him to talk to someone if a person was trying to touch him in an unsafe way. The Instructor explains that he can certainly look after and protect himself, but it wouldn't be right for him to beat people up in defence as that would just get him into trouble. The Instructor would need to respond in a safe manner and, by talking with another adult, the Instructor would be able to work out the appropriate and constructive steps that needed to be taken.

The Instructor then turns to the student beside him. This student takes his turn to name an adult that he could turn to. The Instructor acknowledges every answer, either with a verbal response or a nod. The Instructor should clarify any answers that are unclear.

After naming a safe adult the Instructor can point out that talking to an adult is also a wise thing to do if the students become aware that someone else has been or is being touched in an unsafe way. Following the discussion the Instructor can bring the focus back to what else students could do if someone was trying to touch them in an unsafe way, and take any last answers.

It is important to stress to the students that they need to be careful how they touch others. It is not uncommon to have children attending Warrior Kids who have issues with boundaries and inappropriate touching, especially when they have witnessed family violence or have been abused. By talking to all the students about ensuring that they are safe with others, we are indirectly reaching out to those that have issues in this area.

Another aspect for discussion is about girls inadvertently putting themselves at risk by seeking the attention of older males. This behaviour can mistakenly be read as flirtation, which it is not. Certainly these girls may be exploring or experimenting with social interactions, however, they have no understanding of the implications or the risk of such behaviour.

Again, some may have already been abused and be set in a pattern of behaviour, which makes this part of the discussion even more important. These children need to understand and get a clear message that they need to keep safe with their bodies and keep safe in their interactions with others.

To introduce this issue the Instructor could ask, 'Who is it safe to hang around with?'

Question 4

How do you keep safe around angry adults?

The Instructor should ask the students to think about this question for a moment and then repeat it: 'How do you keep safe around angry adults?'

The students usually centre this discussion on the home and family, where the range of adult anger covers quiet brooding, heated discussions, yelling, the banging or throwing of things and, sadly yet commonly for some, physical violence and abuse. Again, the answers come from the student themselves.

When students ask me what they should do in any given situation in the home, I put it back to them, saying that as much as I would like to be there to help, the fact is I'm not going to be, so what can they do to keep themselves safe? The students are clever. The person the student most needs to believe in is him or herself.

I often say to the students that I wish I was a superhero, I wish that I had a cape, wore tights and had a pair of fancy underpants. Then I could fly around the world and keep everyone safe. But I don't have a cape, tights or fancy underpants, so it is up to the students to keep themselves safe.

Answers that students have given for keeping safe around angry adults include:

- Don't get involved — it's adult business. It's not a child's job to try and stop it or to try and protect a parent.
- Stay away from the angry adult.
- Go outside or to the bedroom. (I point out that they should take any younger children with them and even pets.)
- Do something nice for Mum or Dad such as make them a cup of tea or a card. (Only older students should be making cups of tea.)
- Don't do anything that will make them angry at you. Sound advice. Not a good idea to give cheek or answer back.
- If they're arguing, tell them to stop it. This will work in some families, in others it won't be safe. With such answers I say, 'If it's safe for you to do that then do it. If you know that it's not safe, then don't do it.'
- Talk to Mum and Dad about it. If not at the time of the incident, then later, when they are calmer and the mood has changed.
- Go next door to the neighbour's or to a friend or relative that lives close by. However, it is important that the child does not get into trouble for leaving the property and if they do go, then they go safely.
- If the situation is getting scary they could phone Nana, Uncle, Aunty or a friend of the family. The children can also phone the police, but only if it's safe to do so. If it's not safe then maybe they could get a friend or relative to phone the police on their behalf.
- If Mum or Dad wants you to do a task, such as the dishes, then do it.
- If need be, be tricky. Some children have spoken about discreetly hiding the car keys when Mum or Dad is angry and drunk. My only concern is that the children may get caught in the act. However, I'm not there at the time and the children know the situation better than I do. I reiterate that

Session 2

they need to keep safe. There are many other strategies that the students can use, such as finding a place to hide.

I commend all the constructive and safe answers and query any that aren't safe or appropriate.

Some students may share experiences at this point. As previously mentioned, the Instructor needs to be conscious of disclosures and can refer to the outline given in the Sharing Circle in session 1 (page 58).

Often the focus of the shared experiences is on parents having arguments, outbursts or making mistakes. I explain to the children that life is not always easy and that there are a lot of pressures and that mums and dads have a right to feel angry at times. I get angry, we all do. There's nothing wrong with feeling angry, it's what we do with the anger that determines if we're safe or not.

The fact is that the majority of parents who bring their children to Warrior Kids are good, open, caring and supportive. After all, they have made the effort to have their children in the class. Discussing Keeping Safe strategies with the students prepares them for everyday life, as well as for their future.

You will notice that the answers for the Keeping Safe discussion are generated by the students as opposed to being from the Instructor. This is important in Warrior Kids. By allowing the students to come up with the answers we are empowering them and demonstrating that they have good survival instincts and above all else, commonsense and wisdom.

If a student is faced with an unsafe situation we will not be there. They are on their own. I certainly encourage and steer the discussion, pointing out important facts and responses, and I can add my own answers, but ultimately the process and the discussion belongs to the students.

The Instructor thanks the students for their efforts. The Instructor should pay extra attention to students who contributed greatly or to any who gave tremendous answers. The Instructor can point out that Keeping Safe is something to think about and that the students might come up with other ideas for keeping safe later on at home. Stress that it is important to keep safe and that no one has the right to hurt or to touch them in a way that is unsafe.

It is also good to point out that it is not okay for the students themselves to hurt others or touch others inappropriately. Keeping Safe works both ways, it is about making sure that we touch others in a safe way and that others touch us in a safe way.

The parents benefit by being present during the Keeping Safe discussion. I have had parents come to me at the end of the class with much to say about their life and what the discussion brought up for them and their child. For some parents it has been a catalyst for change.

It is good to remember that the Keeping Safe strategies are going home with each student and their family. Not only will the students be thinking about it, but also the parents.

Parents and caregivers may be sitting at the side in the room and they will have their own reactions and responses to the Keeping Safe discussions. At times parents and caregivers have had something to offer to the discussion and it has been appropriate. However, the Instructor should ensure that the parents and caregivers do not monopolise the time and attention. Warrior Kids is for the children.

8. Monkey Tag

Recommended time allocation: 5 minutes

Moving on from the Keeping Safe discussion and with the aim of lifting the energy in the room, it is time to play a game. At the word 'Go' students find themselves a partner and then find a space somewhere in the room for the pair to sit down.

Refer to session 1 for the outline about setting up and managing the warm-up game as it applies here (see page 45).

The Instructor should remember to get the students to take note of their surroundings and clearly point out the perimeters of the game to ensure safety and to limit any chance of injury. The play space for Monkey Tag can be made larger or smaller to make it more or less challenging

Monkey Tag is a fun and exciting game that is about evasion and awareness. The best way to keep safe is simply not to be there, to get away.

One of the first lessons ever taught to the famous Ninja warriors of Asia was that when faced with a threatening confrontation, the best thing to do was run away. There was no room for ego or saving face. Their families and associates relied on their behaviour in terms of remaining inconspicuous. I share this with my students. Many of the children and adolescent participants in Warrior Kids find this surprising. It shatters the image of the ninja they have come to know from movies and video games.

Monkey Tag

1. The Instructor asks for one person in each pair to put up a hand.
2. The person with their hand up is either deemed the *chaser* or the *evader*. This gives the Instructor choice and means that he can decide what would work best for each pair. For example, an active student maybe better to start as the chaser in order to get a not-very-active student moving.
3. The Instructor moves the *evader* across the room, away from their partner, and gets the *evader* to sit down. This is done for every pair.
4. At the word 'Go' the *chaser* pursues the *evader*, who tries to keep away.
5. The name of the game is Monkey Tag, therefore all students must move around on all fours, that is on their hands and feet, like a monkey. The students cannot stand.
6. If the *chaser* tags the *evader* they switch roles, meaning the *evader* becomes the *chaser* and the original *chaser* must now evade.
7. The new *chaser* counts to 20 to allow the *evader* a chance to get away.
8. Everyone else is off-limits. The students are only allowed to touch their own partner. Students cannot touch, in any way, any other student other than the one that they are chasing, even by accident. If they do touch another student, even by accident, then they have to sit down and stay where they are until the Instructor releases them.

Monkey Tag is a tiring game as it is hard work running around on all fours. Some students may not be able to play for too long and some may even find it a challenge to begin. However, Warrior Kids is all about being challenged.

9. Tumbling

Recommended time allocation: 10 minutes

Refer to session 1 for an outline of setting up and managing the tumbling exercises (page 52).

The Instructor chooses two students who have shown appropriate and constructive behaviour, no matter how small that behaviour may have been, and acknowledges their behaviour aloud to the class.

The Instructor then leads both students to the front of the mats where they sit down, with ample space between one another. The Instructor then tells the remaining students that at the command 'Go' they are to line up behind one of the two leaders to make two lines, and sit down.

Once all students are lined up and the lines are as even as possible, the Instructor introduces the next activity and goes on to explain and demonstrate handstands.

Handstands

Encourage the students to relax and enjoy themselves.

As with the rolls, I offer the students two ways of performing a handstand. They can give both ways a go if they want or just choose one.

The students stand up in their lines. The student at the front of each line steps to the centre of the mats. This is important as it creates distance from the line of students directly behind and means that no one will get kicked when the student raises his legs.

Each student should have two attempts at a handstand then move to the back of the line so that the next student can have their turn.

Balance is important when it comes to handstands. Students may reach out too far with their hands to begin with or even reach too short. They may throw their legs over as opposed to lifting them up. It takes time and practice.

The Instructor should remind the students that they practised rolling in the first and second classes of Warrior Kids. Therefore, if they feel that they are falling when attempting a handstand they can tuck up and roll, creating a safe and soft landing.

However, the Instructor should point out that they are practising on mats so if a student does fall, they will be safe.

Assisting students with the handstand

Some students will never have performed a handstand and may benefit from some hands-on assistance from the Instructor. As with rolling, when physically touching students the Instructor should always be aware of appropriateness and safety; appropriate and safe areas of the body to touch, and appropriate and safe ways of touching.

The Instructor should first ask a student if they want help. If the student does want assistance then the Instructor verbally declares, 'I'm going to get you to lift your legs up and I'm going to take hold of your ankles and hold you up so that you can experience what a handstand feels like.'

The Instructor has the student place both hands on the mats and lift both legs up behind him. The Instructor catches the student's legs by the ankles and holds them up, allowing the student to establish a sense of the posture.

1st Handstand

The 1st Handstand is a good start for students who haven't performed handstands before or who haven't done a handstand for some time. It leads them slowly and without pressure into handstands and builds their confidence.

The student stands with one leg forward and hands raised above the head. Bend forwards and place hands on the mats in front. Keeping the arms straight, raise legs up behind a small distance from the floor and back down again.

2nd Handstand

This is taking the handstand further. Stand with one leg forward and hands raised above the head. Bend forwards and place hands on the mats in front. Keeping arms straight, raise legs up behind until the body is vertical and hold the position, balancing on the hands. To finish, lower the legs, place feet on the floor and return to standing.

Give any pointers that may help a student improve and encourage and praise each attempt at a handstand. Practice makes perfect.

Run the lines through the handstand practice 2 or 3 times.

Regardless of how their handstand may look, the students achieve by just giving it a go.

10. Closing words

Check-out
Recommended time allocation: 1 minute

The Instructor directs students to assemble on the mats, standing in a circle as they did at the beginning of the class.

Each member of the circle, from left to right or vice-versa, takes their turn to describe in a few words how the class was for them today.
If need be the Instructor could go first, but, it would be more beneficial to go last to wrap the class up.

Closing
Recommended time allocation: 1 minute

The Instructor asks for a volunteer from the group to say some words to end the class.
Once the closing words have been said the Instructor acknowledges the speaker with appreciation and concludes with, 'Remember to take what you brought with you today: your shoes, socks, watches, water bottle, jersey, and I'll see you next time.'

> You have completed session 2. Well done!
>
> The classes will be challenging at times, not only for the students, but also for you as Instructor.
> Students may present difficult behaviours, or you may become aware of struggles that they are facing in their lives.
>
> Breathe, always breathe.
> In and out, and as you do, let go.
>
> As an Instructor, be a rock. You cannot be a rock if you are burdened and buried beneath the challenges and troubles of others. Practise the art of detachment. Think of a large rock. That rock is the same whether you are holding on to it or if you are miles away from it. Even though all things are connected, we may cling to the rock but it is still physically separate from us, and because of this the rock can be a truer support.
>
> As an Instructor we are constantly training.
> Training to let go.
> Training to be detached.
> Training to be a rock.
> Training is practice, and practice makes perfect.

Session 3

> **EQUIPMENT**
> - 8 x gym mats, size 1200 x 1800
> - 1 x Koosh ball
> - chairs for parents and caregivers

Introduction

In session 3 the intensity of the programme changes and the students are pushed further with two confronting challenges: Carry the Log and Warrior Kids Wrestling. Team-building, playing nicely, supporting others, self-control and trust are the themes for this session. Students are introduced to the Warrior Deflector Shield and a couple of students will be given the chance to explore their leadership qualities. Bump, one of the most popular games in Warrior Kids, kicks the session off and the students have the opportunity of expressing their high and low for the week later in the session with the Sharing Circle. Great fun.

The outcomes for Session 3 are that the students will:

- understand the value of team work,
- further develop their ability to relate to others,
- understand the concept of safe play,
- learn how to look after and care for others,
- begin to understand the concept of the Warrior Deflector Shield.

Lesson overview

1. Opening words.
2. Round of introductions: a round of names and an animal that stands out for each student today.
3. Warm-up game: Bump.
4. Conditioning: Stretching 3rd form; Brain exercises.
5. Carry the Log challenge.
6. Warrior Kids Wrestling.
7. 2nd breathing exercise: activating the Warrior Deflector Shield.
8. Sharing Circle.
9. Closing words.

1. Opening words
Recommended time allocation: 1 minute

The Instructor directs students to remove their shoes and socks and to sit on the mats in a circle. Once the group is settled the Instructor has the students stand. The Instructor then asks for a volunteer from the group to say some opening words to commence the class. Refer to session 1 (page 44).

2. Round of introductions
Recommended time allocation: 3 minutes

Each member of the circle, from left to right or vice-versa, takes their turn to say their name and to name an animal that stands out for them at that moment. It could be the student's favorite animal or the first animal that comes to mind. Refer Session 1 for the set-up of introductions (page 44).

3. Warm-up game
Recommended time allocation: 10 minutes

Refer to session 1 for the outline of setting up and managing the warm-up game (page 45). The Instructor should remember to get the students to take note of their surroundings and clearly point out the perimeters of the game to ensure safety and limit any chance of injury.

Bump

Bump is a fast, action-packed game that is very popular with the students. It highlights the importance of playing fair and allows the students to practise their evasive skills.

This game requires a large play area. As with all of the games in Warrior Kids, it is not about winning, it is about the students building connections, learning about themselves and having a great time while physically warming up. Students should be encouraged to relax and enjoy themselves.

When the Instructor calls 'Go' the students find a partner and they stand side by side, shoulder to shoulder, somewhere in the designated game area. The pairs should be spaced around, allowing room for movement. When the group is in position and settled the Instructor explains Bump.

Remember, every student needs to be giving their attention to the Instructor when she is explaining the game as this will limit the risk of injuries. If students are unsettled, moving about and talking, then the Instructor should quietly wait until the group is ready, or express her unhappiness at having to wait and make it clear that she is not prepared to start the game until everyone is ready to listen.

1. One pair of students is split up, one student being deemed the *chaser* and the other student deemed the *runner*.

2. When the Instructor calls 'Go' the *chaser* must pursue the *runner* and tag her. The *runner* must evade the *chaser* by moving around the pairs of waiting students.

3. The *chaser* and the *runner* cannot run between any students standing side by side, as this would cause a pair to part. This is not allowed.

> Often in a group there can be a small number of children that form their own subgroup. This subgroup can have a controlling influence on the other students and on the overall programme. The Instructor should look to prevent this.
>
> Often in a warm-up such as Bump the subgroup will attempt to play the game by themselves, bumping only members of the subgroup, thereby disassociating the other students. At times I pause the game and ask for students that haven't had a turn to raise their hand. I then emphasise that everyone needs to have a turn and to make sure that the people with their hand up get bumped. I will intervene further during the game, if need be, by stopping a student from bumping one pair and telling them to bump another pair. Or, I may announce a new rule. People cannot return to the pair that they were just bumped from. They must choose a new pair.
>
> As soon as I prevent a subgroup forming during a game the dynamics change and the class returns to being one cohesive group. The subgroup is an attempt to push at the boundaries and to differentiate a pecking order. There is nothing wrong with the students forming their own particular friendships but it is essential that all students are included and made to feel a part of the class, and that they are conscious and careful in their treatment of others. Therefore, I always make a point of mixing the class so that students get to know everyone and barriers are broken down.

4. The *runner* can get safe from the *chaser* by standing at the end of any pair and crying 'Bump!' The student at the opposite end of the pair becomes the *runner* and must evade the *chaser*.

5. There is only one *runner* at a time and only the *runner* can bump people. The *chaser* cannot bump.

6. If the *chaser* tags the *runner*, the *chaser* and the *runner* then swap roles. The *runner* becomes the *chaser* and the *chaser* becomes the *runner*.

7. Even though the game is called Bump, the students do not physically bump into others. To bump a student off the end of a pair they simply stand at the opposite end of the pair and in a loud voice say 'Bump!' The Instructor should explain this clearly.

8. Any student who physically bumps into a pair may require a warning or even have to sit the remainder of the game out. As with all activities, safety is essential.

9. The *chaser* should also be tagging appropriately. The Instructor can have a student demonstrate an appropriate tag when explaining the game. This way the students know exactly what is expected of them and it's clear that rough play won't be tolerated. Remember, the students are trusting the Instructor to control the class and to keep them safe. A student who is hit in the game may withdraw and lose confidence as a member of the class.

10. Another good rule to have is that the *runner* should avoid bumping any pair that are not standing shoulder to shoulder. This is good for when a student has an issue with another student in the class and the two of them end up paired together, for example, boys and girls who don't want to stand next to each other. These two students are expected to get over their differences and play the game.

11. Also, the *runner* should avoid bumping any pair that are calling out to be bumped. It is important that everyone is involved in the warm-up game and that everyone gets a turn.

12. The more turns each student gets to have at being the *runner* or *chaser* within the allotted game time, the more successful the game.

13. Bump is played for a set amount of time then simply stopped. There doesn't need to be a particular outcome for the game to end.

4. Conditioning

The Instructor brings students back together to form a circle, standing up. Refer to session 1 for the outline of setting up and managing the conditioning exercises (page 48). Remember, the students should only move as far as they feel comfortable. Avoid injuries. Encourage the students to relax and soften into each stretch.

Stretching 3rd form

Recommended time allocation: 10 minutes

This is a simple selection of flexibility exercises.

Position 1

Stand with feet shoulder-width apart. Head and spine are in a straight line. Lower abdomen is pulled in and up. Sternum is also lifted and chest is broadened. Weight is mostly on the heels.

The left arm is bent and placed behind the head. The right hand is placed on the left elbow and gently applies pressure, pushing the left arm downwards. The head should be kept upright and the weight of the left arm should be kept off the head so that there is no pressure on the neck.

The Instructor says the breathing commands, telling the students to breathe in slowly through the nose, then out slowly through the mouth. Students should feel the stretch up through the body, feel the spine lengthen and feel the stretching of the left arm and shoulder muscles.

Position 2

This position is the opposite to position 1.

The right arm is bent and placed behind the head. The left hand is used to gently push the right arm downwards. The head should be kept upright and the weight of the right arm should be kept off the head so that there is no pressure on the neck.

The Instructor tells the students to 'breathe in' and then 'breathe out.'

Position 3

Remaining in the standing position, the left arm is extended across the chest and out to the right. Right arm is bent upwards and in towards the chest, pulling the left arm further across the chest, stretching it more.

The Instructor looks to her left or right and asks the next student along to take the class through the breathing commands. Refer to session 2 for the outline of the students taking the breathing during the conditioning exercises (page 84).

Position 4

Opposite to position 3. The right arm is extended across the chest and out to the left. Left arm is bent upwards and in towards the chest, pulling the right arm further across the chest, stretching it more.

The next student along takes the class through the breathing commands.

Position 5

The Instructor announces to the students that she is now going to test their balance and see how much self-control they have. Throughout the next position the students cannot move or make noise. They must demonstrate

Keeping the torso upright, hold and balance in position to stretch the right thigh.

the utmost self-control, otherwise the position may need to be started again. Some students will find keeping this position challenging, but the Instructor should encourage the students to do it properly, otherwise they could lose focus.

Raise the lower right leg so that the right heel is pressed against the right buttock and the right calf muscle is against the rear of the right thigh. The right hand grasps the right foot, holding the leg in place.

The next student along takes the class through the breathing commands.

On conclusion of this position keep the right leg up, ready for position 6.

Position 6

Keep the right leg up, with the right calf muscle pressed against the right thigh. Bring the right leg up to the front and grasp it with both hands towards the chest while keeping the torso upright. Hold and balance.

The next student along takes the class through the breathing commands.

Position 7

Opposite to position 5. Raise the lower left leg so that the left heel is pressed against the left buttock and the left calf muscle is against the rear of the left thigh. Use left hand to grasp left foot, holding the left leg in place while keeping the torso upright. Hold and balance.

The next student along takes the class through the breathing commands.

Position 8

This position is the opposite to position 6.

Keep the left leg up with the left calf muscle pressed against the left thigh. Bring the left leg up to the front and grasp it with both hands and pull towards the chest. Keep the torso upright. Hold and balance.

The next student along takes the class through the breathing commands.

Position 9

Stand with legs apart. Both legs are straight and feet are in line, pointing forwards. Arms are raised sideways to shoulder level and are in line with each other. Palms face down as the arms are outstretched. Looking straight ahead, lift the chest.

Turn the right foot slightly towards

the left. Then turn the left foot out to the left. Keeping the legs straight, breathe out and bend the torso sideways to the left, taking the left hand down towards the floor. The left hand can grasp the left knee or ankle or, if able, place the left palm on the floor behind the left leg.

The right arm is kept in line with the shoulders and the left arm, and will be pointing upwards. Head is turned right to look up at the right thumb.

The next student along takes the class through the breathing commands.

Position 10

This position is the opposite to position 9.

Return to standing, with legs apart and feet in line and pointing forwards. Arms are shoulder level and in line with each other. Palms face down.

Turn the left foot slightly towards the right. Then turn the right foot out to the right. Keeping the legs straight, breathe out and bend the torso sideways to the right, taking the right hand towards the floor. The right hand can grasp the right knee or ankle or, if able, the student should place the right palm on the floor behind the right leg.

The left arm is kept in line with the shoulders and the left arm, and will be pointing upwards. Head is turned left to look up at the left thumb.

The next student along takes the class through the breathing commands.

Position 11

Repeat position 9.

The next student along takes the class through the breathing commands.

Position 12

Repeat position 10.

The next student along takes the class through the breathing commands.

Position 13

Bring legs together, raise them individually and shake to loosen. Lie on the mats on the stomach. Elbows are bent and hands are placed on the floor beneath the shoulders. Breathing in, slowly push down with the arms to raise the head and chest up, arching backwards, away from the floor. Arch the back as far as possible by raising chest and abdomen. Roll the head back and look up.

The next student along takes the class through the breathing commands.

Position 14

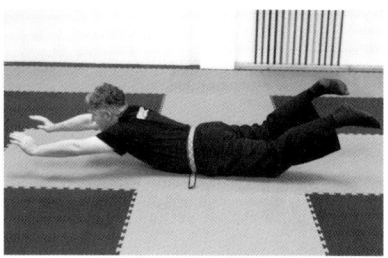

Return to lying on the mats, stomach on the ground. Looking forwards, extend arms out in front. Breathing in, raise the chest, arms, and both legs (including the thighs) off the floor. Hold the position.

The next student along takes the class through the breathing commands.

Position 15

Lying face-down, bend the knees and reach back with arms to grip both ankles with hands, the left hand grasping the left ankle and the right grasping the right. Breathe in and raise the head, chest and legs as far as possible. Hold the position.

The next student along takes the class through the breathing commands.

Position 16

Turning over, sit up, extend the left leg straight out and tuck the right leg inwards, with the right foot touching the inside of the left thigh. Breathing in, raise both arms upwards and straighten. Breathing out, bend forwards from the hips, stretch the arms towards the left foot and, if possible, grasp the foot with both hands. You can also try to take the forehead down to the left knee; however, ensure the torso is eased down towards the waist to relax the spinal muscles. Relax into the position.

The next student along takes the class through the breathing command.

Position 17

This position is the opposite to position 16.

Extend the right leg out straight and tuck the left leg inwards, the left foot touching the inside of the right thigh. Breathing in, raise both arms upwards and straighten. Breathing out, bend forwards from the hips, stretch arms towards the right foot and, if possible, grasp the foot with both hands. You can also try to take the forehead down to the right knee; however, ensure the torso is pushed down towards the waist to relax the spinal muscles. Soften into the position.

The next student along takes the class through the breathing commands.

Position 18

Remaining in the seated position, put both legs out straight. Bending the right knee, lift the right leg over the left thigh and place the right foot flat on the floor on the outside of the left knee. Place right hand behind on the floor, with the right arm straight. Twisting to the right, take left arm around the right knee and, if possible, press the left hand against the outside of the left knee and look behind. Relax into the position.

The next student along takes the class through the breathing commands.

Position 19

This position is the opposite to position 18.

Put both legs out straight. Bending the left knee, lift the left leg over the right thigh and place the left foot flat on the floor on the outside of the right knee. Place left hand behind on the floor, with the left arm straight. Twisting to the left, take right arm around the left knee and, if possible, press the right hand against the outside of the right knee and look behind. Soften into the position.

The next student along takes the class through the breathing commands.

Position 20

Lie on your back with legs out straight. Extend your arms out to the sides at shoulder level and in line with each other. Bend both knees and bring them up and over the abdomen. Twist, taking the bent legs to the left side and hold them just off the floor while turning the head to the right. Relax into the position.

The next student along takes the class through the breathing commands.

Position 21

Opposite to position 20. Lie on your back with both knees bent and over the abdomen. Twist, taking the bent legs to the right side and holding them just off the floor while turning your head to the left. Relax into the position.

The next student along takes the class through the breathing commands.

Position 22

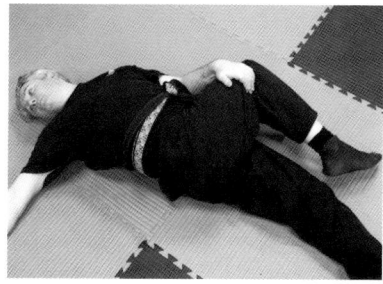

The same as position 20, however this time the left leg is extended out straight and only the right leg is bent over the abdomen. Take hold of the right leg with the left hand and pull the right leg over to the left while turning the head to the right. Relax into the position.

The next student along takes the class through the breathing commands.

Position 23

This position is the opposite to position 22.

The right leg is extended out straight and the left leg is bent over the abdomen. Take hold of the left leg with the right hand and pull the left leg over to the right while turning the head to the left. Relax into the position.

The next student along takes the class through the breathing commands.

Position 24

Lie on your back with legs extended straight out and together, arms at the sides. Keep the head in line with the body. Slowly and gently, roll the head from left to right, as if saying no. Soften the body and relax into the movement. Roll the head from side to side for one minute.
The next student along takes the class through the breathing commands.

This concludes stretching 3rd form.

Brain exercises

Recommended time allocation: 3 minutes

Standing as part of the circle, the Instructor leads students through the brain exercises. Refer to session 1 (page 51).

5. Carry the Log challenge

Recommended time allocation: 20 minutes, including processing time

The Carry the Log challenge is an activity that emphasises the value of teamwork while also encouraging and supporting students to look after and care for others. It requires students to trust one another. Trusting others can certainly be challenging and scary. Accepting challenges and facing fears is all part of being a Warrior.

It is good to point out with the Carry the Log challenge that there are different types of fear. There is fun fear, such as taking a ride on a rollercoaster. There is fear where we are challenged personally to perform, such as in giving a speech, and then there is the fear of danger where there is a high risk to our safety or the safety of others. In other words, our survival is under threat; in essence this is the root of all fear.

It is up to the students how they perceive the Carry the Log challenge, but the Instructor should certainly encourage them to relax and give it a go. It is the set-up of the challenge that will enable students to feel confident. The Instructor should put a lot of emphasis on the rules, promoting teamwork and the looking after and taking care of others.

Remaining in the circle, the Instructor looks around the group and chooses two students who have role-modelled appropriate and constructive behaviour. She acknowledges their behaviour aloud to the class.

The Instructor announces that these two students will be the leaders for the next challenge and leads both of them to an appropriate space where they sit down with ample space between them. The Instructor then tells the remaining students that at the command 'Go' they are to line up behind one of the two leaders to make two lines, and sit down. The two lines should be as equal as possible in numbers.

The gym mats are laid out in two straight lines, one line of gym mats in front of each leader. The Instructor could pick two to four students to help her set up the gym mats while the other students wait quietly.

Once everyone is seated, settled and ready to listen, the Instructor explains the Carry the Log challenge.

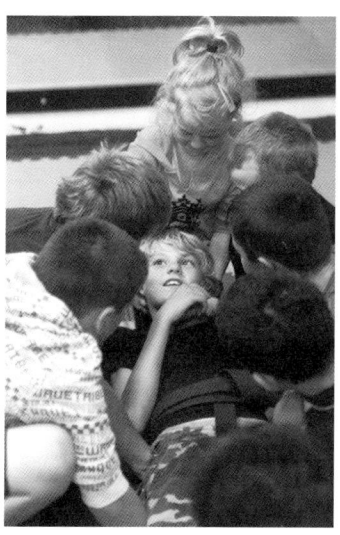

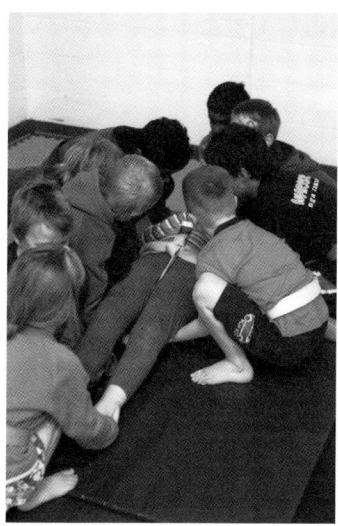

The role of the team leader

To help explain the challenge the Instructor should ask for a volunteer. The volunteer comes to one end of the gym mats in front of the teams and lies down on her back. The volunteer's head should be directly in front of a team leader. The Instructor tells the student to put her legs together and to press her arms against her sides so that she is imitating a log of wood.

Once she is lying down, the remainder of her team will move around her and lift her up, carry her to the end of the mats and put her down.

On reaching the end of the mats the team, including the student being carried, return to the start to carry another team-mate. Every student will have a turn at being carried.

1. A member of each team will have to look after the head of the student being carried. Their hands will have to go under the student's head and lift, being careful of the student's hair.

2. Remaining members of each team will line up on each side of the student. I point out that the torso is going to be the heaviest part to carry, so if you're feeling strong then that's where you will need to be lifting. It is important that there are two or more team members on each side of the upper torso placing their hands underneath the back. One person should focus on lifting the upper back while the other should focus on lifting the lower back.

3. Those team members not lifting the back will carry the legs and feet. The team members who are carrying the legs should ensure that the legs are kept together.

4. The student who is carrying the feet has an important job as she will set the pace for the team. She is the one who ensures that the team walks at an appropriate speed: not too fast, not too slow.

The Instructor should stress that the student being carried has to be able to trust their team, and each member of each team must show the student that they are trustworthy. This is not a time to act up or to be silly. No one is allowed to get hurt.

The team should be respectful of the student who is being carried and should carry them in an appropriate manner with their hands on appropriate areas of the student's body.

It is important to stress that when preparing to lift the log, the students lifting should bend their legs and not their backs. The Instructor should demonstrate the correct way of bending the legs and lifting. It should also be pointed out that the teams are lifting the whole body, that they are not lifting the person by their arms or by their clothes. The carrying hands must go underneath.

When the Instructor has finished explaining the Carry the Log challenge, each team will stand and make a huddle to decide who will be carried first. The leader has the overall say; she can choose anyone. This is important as teams may get lost in discussion and debate over who should have their turn when.

I point out to the leaders that if there is someone in their team

> For the larger part the Instructor should let each team work the challenge out for themselves. The Instructor should refrain from organising a team and allow the students to learn and benefit from their own planning and decisionmaking. Even when it is obvious that something is not going to work, the Instructor should allow the students to find out for themselves.
>
> The Instructor should only intervene when safety is an issue, when time is running out for the challenge or when a student is feeling uncomfortable because their team is having difficulty carrying them.
>
> At no point though should an Instructor help to carry. The challenge is for the students. The Instructor can help organise the students to enable them to amplify their strength as a team and gear them up with some encouraging words. I might query why clearly strong and able students are carrying the head or feet when it is clear that the team would benefit from them helping to carry the torso.

who is jumping in wanting to be carried first, then the leader shouldn't pick that person to have a go until everyone else has had their turn.

If there is someone who is wanting to go after everyone else has had their turn then the leader should make that person be carried first. It is better for those who have trepidation to get it over and done with, rather than allowing it to build into an impossible mountain in their minds.

The team leader can also arrange the team in terms of positions when lifting and carrying a student. The leader can choose who carries the head, the torso, the legs and the feet.

Out of respect for the team, each team leader will be carried last; and when it is the team leaders turn to be carried the Instructor will choose another student from each team to be the leader.

The following rules should be stated clearly to the students:

1. During the explanation of the challenge the Instructor should ask the class, 'When you lift your team-mate, are you going to run to the other end of the mats?' The answer that we are seeking from the students here is 'NO.' The Instructor asks, 'How are you going to move then?' The answer this time should be 'WALK.' The Instructor should affirm this.

2. The Instructor should then ask the students, 'When you have carried your team-mate to the end of the mats, are you then going to simply let her go?' Again, the answer that we are seeking is 'NO.' The Instructor then asks, 'What are you going to do then?' The answer should be, 'PUT THE PERSON DOWN SOFTLY.'

3. The Instructor should also state that when lifting and carrying the student, her head and feet should be in line.

    a) If the student's head is higher than her feet then the team will have to stop, lay her down and start again.

    b) If the student's feet are higher than her head, then the team will have to stop, lay her down and start again.

    c) If a team carrying a student starts to stumble, putting the student at risk, then the team will have to start again.

4. The challenge is about teamwork, so if someone in the team isn't helping to carry the student or if someone lets go before the student has been laid down softly, then the team will have to start again. The entire team should be in physical contact with the student being carried from the moment of lifting until after the student has been gently put down.

5. If the team carry the student right to the end of the mats, lower her down and at the last moment let go so that her buttocks hit the floor, then the team will have to start again. The student must be lowered down gently.

6. The Instructor should explain that this challenge is about looking after people. 'We all know how to hurt people, I want to see if you know how to look after and care for people.'

Sensitivities

Students should understand that they attend the class to take part, to be challenged and to be confronted — not to sit and watch others do the class.

In saying that, there will be issues of sensitivity that arise with various challenges; sensitivities to which the Instructor will have to be sympathetic. Some students may have issues around touch; some may have been abused. While the Instructor should certainly encourage every student to have a turn at being carried, they should also be aware that it would be detrimental to force students to have a turn against their will. I encourage my students to give everything a go, but if a student becomes emotionally stressed or starts to withdraw I will let them off having a turn at being carried. Being sensitive to students' needs will serve to build trust. Often the student will usually have a turn at being carried the next time we do the challenge.

It is important to remember that students' behaviours and perceptions have been built over many years. Changes will not happen overnight. Changes will also take time to develop. A gentle, consistent approach will be beneficial for the student and for the Instructor.

Another point of sensitivity concerns students who feel uncomfortable with their bodies. Some students will be overweight. When organising the class into teams at the beginning of the challenge, I make sure that each team is manageable in terms of the members being able to lift and carry each other. The teams could be mixed, with a range of ages, sizes and shapes, or I may put older students in one team and younger students in another. I look for what will work. However, it is not about making it too easy: the challenge should still be a challenge. One aim of the challenge is to have students working together as a team: many hands make light work.

If I have a student who is clearly much larger than the other students in the class, then I will enrol that student as an assistant Instructor at the beginning of the challenge, protecting them from any shame. This student's role will be to monitor a team and ensure that they are doing the challenge properly. This student will not be expected to lift, carry or to be carried. If it is obvious that a team working together could lift a larger student, then that student should have a turn at being carried. The Instructor will need to ensure that

Session 3

respect is maintained throughout the challenge. The students are supposed to be demonstrating their ability to look after and care for others. They may need reminding of this, especially when the challenge becomes harder for all of them and they find it difficult to lift one of their team-mates.

I have found that the challenge isn't usually physical, but rather psychological. If a team-mate is larger, the team tend to assume that it is going to be too difficult or even impossible to carry them. The Instructor should watch for put-downs and cutting remarks about a student's appearance or size. Any such remarks should be addressed. At no point should a put-down or cutting remark be dismissed or ignored. It is a great learning opportunity for the class. Nor should a student be able to make excuses for their put-down or cutting remark.

The students need to understand that the challenge is about teamwork and demonstrating their ability to look after and care for others. Words can hurt, so students need to be responsible and careful about what comes out of their mouths.

Teams having difficulty carrying a student, if left to their own devices, will often get themselves into a state of reluctance, and simply give up, or their repeated attempts to lift the student will become lame and without effort. If so, the Instructor should intervene. It is good to make the team aware of how they are making the student feel, and that rather than giving up, the team may need to reorganise themselves and work better together. I often say, 'What if there was a fire and you had to get this person out? You wouldn't even think about it, you would just do it. Imagine that there is fire now and lift this person and carry them to safety.'

The Instructor should acknowledge each team when they carry a student successfully to the end of the mats. There will also be opportunities to acknowledge students who are making an outstanding contribution and demonstrating teamwork. Also acknowledge obvious displays of care and consideration of others.

The challenge isn't a race. However, I don't tell the teams that. Teams will often think that it is a race and this will help to keep them on task so they complete the challenge in appropriate time. The Instructor should make sure though that the teams do not get carried away with racing each other. Teams need to walk when carrying a student and to lift and lower a student carefully. Ultimately, the overall goal for each team is to complete the challenge within the outlines given.

Processing the Carry the Log challenge

On completion of the Carry the Log challenge, each team should sit down in their line to demonstrate to the Instructor that they have finished. If one team is some distance ahead of the other, the Instructor may like to allow the finished team to go again, giving members the opportunity to be carried again.

Some teams of older students may request the opportunity to carry the Instructor. If the other team isn't finished, the Instructor could make the most of this opportunity to bond further with the students and to demonstrate a willingness to trust them. Both teams may request to carry the Instructor.

When both teams are finished and are sitting quietly in their lines, the Instructor can begin to process the challenge. Processing will allow the students to identify points of learning and achievements and validate the challenge as a beneficial experience. It will also allow the class to address any issues that may have

Session 3 — arisen during the challenge and any lingering feelings of resentment between students.

Step 1

Whenever the Instructor speaks to the class, she should ensure that she is clearly visible to each student. This is respectful to the students and means that each student is visible to the Instructor.

For step 1 of the processing, the Instructor should look to the leader of one of the teams and ask her to stand and step to the side, inadvertently facing the class through facing the Instructor. This is a non-threatening way for the student to speak to the whole class.

Question 1

The Instructor asks the student standing what was it like to be the leader. For example, 'Mary, you were the leader of your team, how was it being the leader?'

Of course this is a closed question, meaning that the student will probably reply with one word such as good, great or cool.

This is perfect as it is a way of warming the student and allows the Instructor a doorway to deepening the process. If Mary says that it was cool then I will ask her, 'What was cool about it?'

Now we are starting to open. If Mary simply replies by saying, 'Everything,' I will encourage her to be specific by asking, 'What parts of the challenge were cool in particular, Mary?'

Once Mary realises that she isn't going to get out of answering that easily she'll start to think. For some students this question may prove a challenge in itself, and that's perfect. Give the student time to gather her thoughts and to come up with an answer. If it is obvious that she is having difficulty putting her experience into words, then the Instructor can help by going on with the next question.

Question 2

'How was your team?' Again, a closed question, but the student will now be aware that she'll be expected to give a full answer. If Mary was to say, 'Good,' I would ask, 'What was good about them?' or, 'What did the team do that was good?'

Question 3

'Were there any problems in your team, Mary?' Here, Mary gets to talk openly and freely about behaviour of individual students that made her role as team leader difficult. This is great feedback from a peer and is valuable for other students to hear.

While the majority of the feedback will be valid, there are times when a leading student may have an issue with another student or,

- a fellow student's perceived disruptive behaviour may be exaggerated,
- the behaviour could be due to a student being much younger than the others in the team,
- the student in question may be facing external or internal issues in their lives.

The Instructor should be aware of any issues and sensitive to the needs of each student. One of my own experiences involved a boy who was being too rough. Many of the students complained about him. The Warrior Kids class was being conducted as part of a school programme and it was the first session of the school day for the students.

I paused the class and settled everyone. Then I looked at the boy. It was obvious that he was distressed. I gently said his name and asked how he was feeling today. He was quick to say that he was fine. I remarked that he didn't appear to have a lot of self-control this morning and that he didn't seem himself. The boy looked downwards.

'What happened this morning?' I asked. The boy's eyes started to water. 'My dad gave me a hiding for no reason,' he said.

Instructors should be aware that this is what a percentage of their students will be facing in their lives. This boy was nine years old and a hiding for him wasn't a smack on the bum. A hiding for him involved fists. Dad had been in a bad mood that morning and the boy had copped it.

I told the boy to come over and stand beside me. Then I put an arm around his shoulder and pulled him in close to my side, giving him a hug. I explored the events of the morning with him, allowing him to talk. The other students were all a part of this and it was important that they were. It made some of them see the boy differently and allowed them to feel empathy. For some it related to their own experiences. I was open with my anger. I said to the boy that I felt angry and sad that he had been hurt, and I told him that I was angry at his father for hurting him. After some comforting I asked the boy if there was anything else he needed in order that he felt understood and acknoweldeged. Openly talking about it had done it. We briefly talked about strategies of keeping safe around angry adults, in particular about keeping safe around Dad.

I then encouraged the boy to enjoy his Warrior Kids class. I told him that Warrior Kids was his time, time to enjoy himself. I told him not to let his bad experience that morning rob him of having a good time. The boy rejoined the class and from that moment on he was lighter and his smile had returned. This whole process took no more than five minutes. Throughout the class I continued to check in with him or simply gave him a touch on the shoulder or a rub on his back when I passed by.

Boundaries need to be reiterated in the class, but the Instructor must always be aware that there are reasons for behaviour. When a team leader reflects disruptive behaviour in her feedback the Instructor should manage it appropriately. If a student was clearly being silly and pushing at the boundaries, then the Instructor should remark about how sad it is to hear about that behaviour. If a student was actually doing better than usual even though they were still being disruptive, then the Instructor should openly acknowledge this and encourage the student to keep going with her improvements. The example I used above is a way of addressing such issues.

Another question the Instructor can ask the team leader is, 'Did your team listen to you?'

On completion of Step 1, the Instructor moves on to Step 2.

Step 2

Mary, the team leader, remains standing while the Instructor turns her attention to Mary's team and asks the team how Mary did as a leader. Constructive, positive feedback for the leader is the aim here. Members of the team raise their hand if they have something to say about Mary's performance and the Instructor elicits the comments.

At times there will probably be one-word answers as mentioned above, such as 'good', 'okay', 'great'. The Instructor can deepen these answers with further enquiry. 'What did Mary do well as a leader?'

There should be no negative feedback, even if it is perceived as constructive. If there had been any obvious issues with the team leader during the challenge then the Instructor should have dealt with them and offered any correcting directives during the challenge. The Instructor should keep the focus on talking up the leader's strengths and achievements. For many students a role as leader may be their first. Positive encouragement and affirmation in front of their peers will deliver the greater benefits.

Constructive feedback would be appropriate. Comments such as, 'She didn't speak much,' or 'I couldn't hear her,' would allow the Instructor to boost Mary with encouragements about her being clever and that what she has to say is valuable. Point out that the team were wanting to hear their leader. 'You have a wonderful voice and wise things to say, so use your voice.' Other remarks might be, 'She let others take over,' or 'She only listened to her friends'; again, these are opportunities for the Instructor to give specific, uplifting encouragement.

The Instructor might have some feedback of her own to offer the leader. The Instructor may even have feedback for individuals of the team or for the team as a whole. This would be a perfect time to express this feedback.

Step 3
Identifying feelings

The Instructor asks the team and their leader to raise their hand if they felt they could trust their team during the challenge. This question allows the students to identify their feelings during the challenge. There is no right or wrong answer. Nor is there any reason for the Instructor to query or explore the answers. Just simply let the experience of each student be what it is.

The Instructor then tells the students to lower their hands and says, 'Raise your hand if you enjoyed the challenge.' Again there is no right or wrong answer, we are simply allowing the students to identify and openly acknowledge their experience and their feelings.

The Instructor thanks the leader and their team for their participation. The team leader sits back in line with her team. The Instructor turns her attention to the second team and repeats steps 1 through 3.

There may appear to be a lot to cover in the explanation of the processing, yet it is straightforward and over time it will become natural to the Instructor, enabling it to flow at a steady pace. Processing is important and shouldn't be ignored.

6. Warrior Kids Wrestling: safe play

Recommended time allocation: 20 minutes

There will always be a few in our society that are physically aggressive, but the rest of us just want to get along and this is reflected by the students' enjoyment of Warrior Kids Wrestling.

Warrior Kids Wrestling, or WKW for those students who are keen on professional wrestling, is an exploration of safe play. It allows the students to continue working together and to continue looking after and caring for others, while at the same time being physically challenged and having fun.

All of the activities in Warrior Kids are designed to get reactions, instigate and bring behaviours and issues to the forefront, and WKW does just that.

Like the Carry the Log challenge, WKW can be confronting and scary. The Instructor should refer to the evasion challenge and the discussion on fear from session 1 (page 72). There is nothing wrong with feeling scared. This should be stressed to the students. The students should be encouraged to relax and simply give WKW a go. Emphasise that no one is allowed to get hurt. As with the Carry the Log challenge, it is the set-up of WKW that will enable students to feel confident. The Instructor should put a lot of emphasis on stressing the rules of WKW and promoting safe play and the looking after and taking care of others.

With the students sitting in their two lines from the Carry the Log challenge, the Instructor enlists the aid of two to four students to put the gym mats together, creating one large, matted space. Once this is done, the Instructor then announces that at the word 'Go' the class is to make a circle around the outside of the gym mats and sit down.

Control is essential here: control in terms of group management and in terms of students demonstrating self-control as this sets up the right environment for Warrior Kids Wrestling.

Once all the students are sitting around the outside of the mats, and are quiet, settled and ready to listen, the Instructor declares that it is time for WKW. Such an announcement usually gets a cheering response from the class. However, some students may groan and look away.

The Instructor goes on to explain the rules of Warrior Kids Wrestling. By using the labels 'Warrior Kids Wrestling' or 'WKW', we are clearly stating that the wrestling is going to be different to any other form of wrestling which indeed it is; and the students who are feeling reluctant about having a go will be thankful to learn this. Even keen wrestlers, used to being bumped and jostled, will appreciate WKW's message that people don't like being hurt or the threat of getting hurt.

For Warrior Kids Wrestling all students remain seated around the gym mats. As with the Roll Tiggy game in session 1, the Instructor tells the students to move back from the gym mats, creating a buffer space as a safety precaution. The Instructor can walk around the gym mats to ensure that there is a clear path. The presence of the group around the edges of the wrestling mats serves to provide a visual containment of the rules of WKW.

The Instructor should pick a student and enter the middle of the mats with this student to demonstrate the rules of Warrior Kids Wrestling using visual examples.

The set-up of Warrior Kids Wrestling

1. Two students go to the centre of the gym mats.
2. The two students will be on their knees and remain on their knees throughout the challenge. At no point during the wrestling can a student stand. If a student does stand the match should be stopped immediately, both students should return to the centre of the mats, be reminded that they have to stay on their knees and then be allowed to resume.
3. When the students are on their knees in the centre of the mats and all students are quiet and settled, the Instructor will call 'Go'. The two students will then wrestle, each trying to get their opponent down.
4. Once a student gets her opponent down she must then pin him so that he cannot get back up.

Clear rules for Warrior Kids Wrestling

The rules for Warior Kids Wrestling create the boundaries for safe play while allowing room for each student to be challenged. These rules must be adhered to at all times throughout the challenge.

At any point during a match where a rule has been breached the match should be stopped immediately, both students should return to the centre of the mats, be reminded of the rule that was breached and then be allowed to continue. It is the Instructor's responsibility to ensure that a high level of safety and respect is maintained throughout the challenge. Clear rules for the wrestling are:

- The main rule for Warrior Kids Wrestling is to have fun. WKW is not about 'winning' over others or getting hurt. If students want to win at WKW then they should simply relax, have fun and finish their turn with no one hurt and smiles on both faces. This is a win/win outcome.
- At this point I would usually query the students on how often they've played a game with other children and the game turned serious. I talk about WKW being about safe play and having a good time. It is no fun when someone gets hurt.
- Every student must be quiet and settled before the Instructor can say 'Go' and start a round of WKW. This will help with the management of the class and the containment of the wrestling. Control of the challenges and the class is essential to the success of any class.
- Practise safety at all times.
- In an in-school programme, boys wrestle boys and girls wrestle girls. There should be no mixed-gender wrestling. Often there are fewer girls in a class and this will help them to feel comfortable. Of course this does depend on numbers and the overall make-up of the group. In a community-based class it could be entirely appropriate to have a girl wrestle a boy in session 3. The students in a community class are less likely to have previous history and know each other.
- There are to be no wrestling moves that students may have seen on television. Students cannot attempt any move that they have seen in professional wrestling or on film.
- There is no touching or holding around or above the neck.
- There is no striking of any type, such as punching, kicking, etc.

Session 3

- When being pinned, a student can use her feet to gently press against her opponent and push them off; however, kicking is not allowed. This should be clearly explained.
- There is no hair-pulling or pinching. Students with long nails will need to make sure they don't scratch.
- Students will need to be careful of one another's clothes. We don't want anyone going home and getting in trouble for ripped clothing.
- In WKW students can tickle. Tickling is great as it lightens up the challenge. However, students must not dig their fingers into their opponent. Also, students must be respectful of each others' bodies and tickling, as with all touching during wrestling, should be in appropriate places of the body. The Instructor can refer to the Keeping Safe discussion the class had in session 2. I will often demonstrate safe areas for tickling on a student. I will ask the student to raise her arms and without physically touching her I will indicate appropriate areas to tickle which are:
  - under the ribs on either side of the torso,
  - the tummy,
  - under the arms, and
  - under the feet.
- Students should also be mindful of one another's heads. They can get so caught up in the action that they forget what their upper bodies are doing and as a result can end up banging heads.
- When a student is pinned by another student there is no counting. The Instructor will not be announcing winners in this fashion. The conditions for succeeding at WKW have been made clear. If a student gets pinned they are expected to get themselves out of it. The Instructor should encourage the students to 'Wriggle, don't giggle!' Often when students are pinned they curl up into a ball and simply giggle. Some students will curl up into a ball straight away, even without being pinned. Encourage students not to give up, not to give away their power. Encourage them to wriggle and to wrestle their way to freedom.
- Everyone gets a turn.
- Wrestlers must stay on the mats throughout the match.
- Everyone must listen to the Instructor. If at any point the Instructor says stop, every student must stop what they are doing and give their full attention to the Instructor.
- Students around the outside of the mats are allowed to talk quietly to the person next to them during the wrestling as this will help them to pass the time. However, they are not allowed to move around or make excessive noise during the wrestling. The attention of every student must be on the Instructor when she is talking.
- It is good for the Instructor to point out that wrestling is not all about muscle power; it is mostly about brain power. Students should be encouraged to strategise and be tricky. The right attitude is also helpful. I have had a smaller student

grab a larger student by the foot and tickle him. The larger student was laughing so much that he wasn't able to wrestle.

- If at any point a student is purposely being unsafe or is persistently unsafe after repeated warnings, then she is out of the game and must return to sitting at the side of the mats.

Sensitivities

As with the Carry the Log challenge, there may be issues of sensitivity that arise during Warrior Kids Wrestling. While the Instructor should certainly encourage every student to have a go at WKW, the Instructor should also be aware that it would be detrimental to force students to have a turn. I encourage my students to give everything a go, but if the student becomes emotionally stressed or starts to withdraw I will let them off.

Emotional stress is very different from emotional manipulation. Some students may be in the habit of using their emotions to manipulate situations in order to get what they want. When this is obvious the Instructor should challenge such behaviour and clearly state that he does not like it.

Further points

Often in the mix of students that make up a class in Warrior Kids there will be children who have issues around being safe with others and those who have issues feeling safe around others. WKW is a way of exploring these issues.

1. It's an opportunity to address bullying behaviour

If I have a student who I know isn't safe with others, who may have a history of hurting or bullying children, then I will have him wrestle a younger student.

With both students kneeling in the centre of the gym mats, and with all students being quiet and settled, I speak directly to the

Session 3

student with the bullying behaviour. To begin with I will ask the student to look at me; then I will simply ask, 'Can I trust you, Greg? Can I trust you to be safe?'

I might make reference to any known accounts of bullying that Greg has been involved in, yet I would not do this in a way that would embarrass Greg in front of the other students. Greg has an opportunity to change and behave differently here. Shaming him will keep him in negative behaviour. Accounts of inappropriate behaviour can be raised subtly with clues that Greg will be aware of but the other students in the class won't understand. 'Can I trust you to look after your wrestling partner, Greg? Can I trust you to be safe with Michael?' 'Yes,' is the only answer that will mean that Greg gets to have a turn at WKW because, as I've made clear, 'Only safe students get to do Warrior Kids Wrestling.' I will encourage Greg to relax, have fun and keep safe.

If I have two students that I know don't get on, I will pair them up for wrestling. For the majority of the time throughout WKW I will be sitting to the side of the gym mats with the other students. However, there are times when I will stand and walk out on to the gym mats to monitor and ensure that the wrestlers are keeping safe and practising self-control. This would be one of those times.

When all the students are quiet and settled, I will look at the two students on their knees in the middle of the mats. I will start by openly acknowledging the animosity between them. I will inform the two students that it is actually due to that animosity that they are wrestling each other. Their match is not about the two of them sorting one another out, it is about them forgetting their differences and getting along. As I did with Greg, I will speak directly to both students, one at a time, and ask them if I can trust them to be safe. I will ask the exact same questions that I asked Greg, and the two students will have to convince me and the class as a whole that they can be trusted.

It is also common in a group to have some students who have been victims of bullying. Rightfully, such students will have grave concerns about entering a wrestling match. However, there is great value in these students having a go. The Instructor will need to convince worried students that she will ensure that they will be safe. The Instructor can stress the point that no one is allowed to get hurt.

The Instructor could even have a private word with a worried student before their turn and ask them who they would feel comfortable wrestling. Choice would give the student some empowerment. As Warrior Kids is made up of a mix of children with a mix of issues, there will be safe and non-threatening students in the class that the student might choose, or the Instructor could recommend.

Warrior Kids Wrestling can allow victimised children the opportunity to explore safely being different in physical interactions. This will build their confidence. Encourage all students to, 'Be brave, be safe.'

2. Peer pressure

Some students around the outside of the gym mats may resort to yelling out during a wrestling match, or remarks may be made before a match gets started. These should all be addressed.

I would stop everything and wait for the class to be quiet and settled. I would then talk about the playground and how, when I was at school and students fought, other students would stand around cheering and encouraging them to fight. I will then look around the Warrior Kids students and say, 'I'd hate to think that any of you would do that.' I pause to give the comment effect. I then ask, 'What should you do when you see people fighting at school?' I elicit answers from the students, acknowledging appropriate ones and questioning inappropriate ones.

In Warrior Kids Wrestling the students on the outside of the mats are allowed to support and encourage the students wrestling in the middle of the mats; however, they must openly support both students and help monitor to ensure that the wrestling is safe. Those supporting cannot use loud voices as the students wrestling need to be able to hear the Instructor. Maintaining a low level of noise helps to control and contain the group.

Before a wrestling match begins there may be comments from the side such as 'Sonja's going to get wasted,' or 'You're going to lose,' or 'Waste him, Eric.' This language is inflammatory and pressures students to fight as opposed to wrestling safely and having fun. The students who make such remarks are usually the ones who will instigate altercations in the classroom and in the playground, therefore it is essential that their remarks are addressed.

When addressing such behaviour I usually ask the student in question to stand up and face me. This is about the student being responsible and accountable to the group. If they choose to behave in such a manner they need to be able to explain why. I will remind the class that Warrior Kids Wrestling is about challenging one another in a safe, fun way, while demonstrating that they can each look after and care for others.

I will then explore the remarks with the student, asking them:

a) Why are you wanting to see a certain student get wasted or hurt?

b) Why are you wanting a student to get into trouble for hurting another?

c) Why do you feel the need to make such remarks?

I will state that I don't like that behaviour and that I don't like those remarks. 'Remarks like that are not about looking after or caring for others.' I will say to the student that when they choose to behave like that they are lowering themselves, they make themselves small. I remind the student that they can be better than that and that they should always be better than that. I will then ask the student in question if we can now continue and get on with the wrestling without them making any more unconstructive remarks. When the student says yes they can then sit down.

There can also be comments from male students towards the female students. A boy might comment that a wrestling match between girls is a catfight or that girls are too weak to challenge boys or that boys are superior. It is important that a high level of respect is upheld throughout the class, so as with all remarks or undermining comments, these should be explored too.

Over the years I've had a number of girls attend Warrior Kids that have demonstrated as much skill and determination as any boy. In fact, at times the boys in a class have been scared of certain girls, especially when it came to wrestling. I've had a girl wrestle two boys her age and pin them both down at the same time. I share this with classes when belittling remarks are made about girls' abilities. Usually there is a girl in the class who is wanting to have a go with the boys and prove them wrong anyway. But, as previously explained for the in-school programme, boys wrestle boys and girls wrestle girls.

3. Students getting rough

The Instructor's full attention should be on the students wrestling in the middle of the mats at all times. If for any reason the students on the side need to be addressed, then the Instructor should pause the wrestling match to do so. Sometimes when I sit among the students there can be a few who think that it is an ideal opportunity to speak to me. I tell these students that my attention needs to be on the two wrestlers.

Some students will get rough during their wrestling match. Wrestlers should be able to be rough as long as they are both safe. At times, some boys will exert a lot of energy and throw each other around the gym mats. This will be a great release of tension for them and if they are listening to the Instructor and enjoying the experience then there is nothing wrong with it.

However, sometimes students will get carried away due to the pressure to perform or to appear strong in front of the other students. With older students a boy may also want to impress a girl in the group. Issues between students arise. These are cases where the rough play may become of concern as there is a higher risk that someone could get hurt. The Instructor should pause the wrestling match and speak openly of what she is seeing. As the reasons for such behaviour cannot always be openly announced as they might shame the student in question, the Instructor can certainly acknowledge the pressure to perform.

Students need to know that the Instructor is in control, that she is the boss and that her authority overrides any pressure to behave inappropriately or unsafely.

4. Acknowledge every student

Warrior Kids Wrestling provides an opportunity for the Instructor to assess where students are in terms of behaviour, self-image and relating socially.

There will be students who follow others in terms of remarks, there will be students who are victims of peer pressure, there will be students who are aggressive and there will be students who are passive. It can also be interesting to see the reactions of various family members who may be present and watching from the side.

As with all of the activities, every student should be acknowledged for their efforts. This is extremely important in WKW. Students should be openly acknowledged for playing safe, for looking after and caring for their wrestling partner. This should be done during a wrestling match and immediately after each wrestling match. To acknowledge students at the end of a wrestling match I usually get the class to be quiet and settled. I then ask the students in the middle of the mats to stand and face me. To begin with I will ask each student how the wrestling match was for them, and did they enjoy it? I will then ask each of them how their body feels and if they are hurt anywhere. Then, with everyone listening, I will thank both students for modelling safe play and acknowledge their efforts. In particular, I will praise demonstrations of care and consideration in a match. I will also praise any good wrestling tactics or moves that I saw, especially when it could be helpful for self-defence. I will praise their smiles and the fun that they were having.

Of course, some pairs or some students in particular may require encouragement to relax and enjoy themselves and not to take it all so seriously. Others may need to be uplifted, acknowledging how brave they were to go into the middle of the mats to give the wrestling a go and that they deserve to feel proud about their efforts.

7. 2nd breathing exercise: activating the Warrior Deflector Shield

Recommended time allocation: 3 minutes

The 2nd breathing exercise gives the students a further opportunity to refocus and channel their energy. The 2nd breathing exercise is used to activate and strengthen the Warrior Deflector Shield, an imaginary force-field generated from the constructive and positive beliefs and memories of a student's life. The shield is used to deflect negative, unconstructive remarks and gestures and to prevent such messages from getting in. The Warrior Deflector Shield is a means to increase a student's fortitude and resilience in the face of adversity.

To generate a powerful shield, students remember:

- that they are loved and treasured,
- the people and animals who believe in them,
- their achievements and successes,
- what they are good at, and
- that they are clever and can do whatever they set their mind to.

In presenting the Warrior Deflector Shield, the Instructor can make reference to the *Star Wars* and *Star Trek* movies, with which the students maybe be familiar. These movies feature deflector shields and mentioning them is a good way of engaging the students' interest.

The Instructor has the students form a circle, standing around the outside of the mats. The Instructor leads the students, demonstrating and talking them through the 2nd breathing exercise and activating the Warrior Deflector Shield.

Activating the Warrior Deflector Shield Part 1

Arms are crossed over the chest. Hands are open, with palms facing the chest. Breathing in slowly through the nose, lower the arms down past the stomach and out to the sides to full extension. Continuing to breathe in, raise the arms with the palms facing out to the sides with the fingers pointing down. Cross the arms above the head.

Activating the Warrior Deflector Shield Part 2

Reverse the movement by turning the palms outwards. Slowly exhale through the mouth, lowering the arms back out to the sides with the fingers pointing upwards. Bring arms inwards and cross while drawing them upwards to return to the chest.

While performing this movement the students imagine creating a circular energy field around their body so it becomes encased. Ask the students to visualise the shield. Ask them, 'What colour is your shield?'

Repeat the movement five times. To conclude, the students step back into the Starlight posture (page 71). Run through the 2nd breathing exercise twice.

Have the students imagine that their Warrior Deflector Shield is on all of the time, protecting them from negative attitudes and intentions. The 2nd breathing exercise can then be used to strengthen their shield. Acknowledge those students who are demonstrating good self control and focus.

As an alternative, students can both inhale and exhale through their nose as opposed to in the nose and out the mouth.

8. Sharing Circle

Recommended time allocation: 15 minutes

The Instructor and the students sit on the mats in a circle. Each student should be facing the centre of the circle and be clearly visible to the Instructor so that no one is in any way disassociated from the group, whether by their own positioning or by the positioning of another student.

The Instructor presents the Koosh ball and announces that it is time for the Sharing Circle, where each student will have a turn to share a low point and a high point from their week. Refer to session 1 (page 58) for more on the Sharing Circle.

9. Closing words

The Instructor directs students to assemble on the mats, standing in a circle as they had at the beginning of the class. Refer to session 1 (page 76).

Check-out

Recommended time allocation: 1 minute

Each member of the circle, from left to right or vice-versa, takes their turn to say one word that describes how the class was for them today. If need be the Instructor could say theirs first, however it is more beneficial to go last in order to wrap up the class.

Closing

Recommended time allocation: 1 minute

The Instructor asks for a volunteer from the group to say some words to end the class.

When the closing words have been spoken the Instructor acknowledges the speaker with appreciation and concludes by saying, 'Remember to take what you brought with you today, your shoes, socks, watches, water bottle, jersey and I'll see you next time.'

> You have completed session 3. Well done!
>
> Today we focused on working with others and looking after and being careful with others.
> We also explored allowing others to look after and care for us.
>
> While you are supporting and assisting your students, allow yourself to be supported and assisted by others too. It is essential that you have support, and not just in a spiritual sense.
> Attend classes regularly with a more experienced Instructor.
> If you are not able to do this then find external supervision in the form of a counsellor.
>
> The struggles and concerns of the students and their families are a heavy burden. It would be damaging to your health, mentally, emotionally, physically and spiritually, to bear this burden on your own. It would also be damaging to your relationships with your family and those close to you.
>
> You too are a warrior in training. As you seek to bring peace to the lives of your students and their families, seek to have peace in your own life.
>
> Peace is ultimately where we are heading:
> peace of mind, peace of heart,
> peace of body, peace of spirit,
> peace with nature, peace with the world.
>
> Peace is what every Instructor should cultivate in their lives.

Session 4

EQUIPMENT

- 8 x gym mats, size 1200 x 1800 mm
- 1 x Koosh ball
- chairs for parents and caregivers

Introduction

Session 4 is about anger. Students are given the opportunity to explore anger in safe, controlled and fun ways. Each student is able to express their anger physically within the confines of the wrap-up challenge. The group discussion on anger allows the students to identify triggers and experiences that they feel angry about, to be aware of the varying sensations of anger in their body, and to find constructive ways to manage their anger. The session starts off with the Melting Candles game, which makes the overall class experience valuable and rewarding for all.

The outcomes for session 4 are that the students will:

- be able to identify anger physically and mentally,
- learn healthy, safe and constructive ways of managing and expressing anger, and
- be able to help others to manage their anger.

Lesson overview

1. Opening words.
2. Round of introductions: a round of names and a way that each students helps his or her family at home.
3. Warm-up game: Melting Candles.
4. Conditioning: Stretching 1st form; Brain exercises.
5. The wrap-up challenge.
6. 3rd breathing exercise.
7. Group discussion: anger.
8. Melting Candles.
9. Closing words.

1. Opening words

Recommended time allocation: 1 minute

The Instructor directs students to remove their shoes and socks and to sit on the mats in a circle. Once the group is settled the Instructor has the students stand. The Instructor then asks for a volunteer from the group to say some opening words to start the class. Refer to session 1 (page 44).

2. Round of introductions

Recommended time allocation: 3 minutes

Each member of the circle, from left to right or vice-versa, takes their turn to say their name and to describe a way in which they help their family at home. Maybe they help with the dishes or the cleaning. Maybe they make their bed and get themselves ready for school. There could be all sorts of ways that the students help out at home. Refer to session 1 for the set-up of introductions (page 44).

3. Warm-up game: Melting Candles

Recommended time allocation: 10 minutes

Refer to session 1 for the outline of setting up and managing the warm-up game (page 45). The Instructor should remember to get the students to take note of their surroundings and clearly point out the boundaries of the game space to ensure safety and limit any chance of injury.

Melting Candles

Melting Candles is a quick game to play and gets the students moving. They get to practise their awareness and evasion skills while also having a great deal of fun.

The Instructor tells everyone to take a few steps back, increasing the size of the initial circle. When the group is in position and settled the Instructor explains Melting Candles.

1. The Instructor chooses three or four students and tells them to stand in the middle of the circle. These students are *chasers*. The number of *chasers* chosen depends on the total number of students in the class and their ability.

    If there are 12–14 students in the class, four *chasers* should be chosen. If there are 10–12 students in the class, then there should be three *chasers*, and so on. The number also depends on the ability of the students. If there are a large number of young ones in the class then a higher number chosen to be *chasers* may work better.

    The Instructor can change the number of *chasers* at any time during the game. This will help to keep the game running smoothly.

2. The Instructor tells the students forming the circle to take a good look at the *chasers* in the middle. This is so they know who will be chasing them. At the word 'Go' the *chasers* will pursue the other students and tag them.

3. When a *chaser* tags a student he must say, 'Tagged!' in a loud voice so that the student knows that he has been tagged. If a *chaser* does not say 'Tagged!' when tagging then that tag does not count.

4. When a student is tagged he becomes a melting candle. To do this he stands still with his feet together. He places his hands together above his head to make a flame and then

sways his body in dance as he slowly 'melts' like a candle and lowers his body towards the floor.

5. Melting students can be saved. Any student who is not a *chaser* and is not melting can run up to a melting candle, tag them and say, 'Saved!' If a student does not say 'Saved!' when tagging then her tag does not count. A student who is saved stops melting and returns to evading the *chasers*. If the student melts all the way to the floor so that he ends up sitting then he is out of the game.

6. The object of the game is for the *chasers* to tag all of the students. If all the students are tagged and are melting then there will be no one to save them. This means the *chasers* have won.

7. The game is played in short bursts. The Instructor stops the game every couple of minutes and has the class return to the initial circle where the Instructor will then choose new *chasers*. Every student should be given a turn to be a *chaser*.

8. Students should be tagging appropriately. The Instructor could have a student demonstrate an appropriate tag when explaining the game. This way the students know exactly what is expected of them and that rough play won't be tolerated.

9. Melting Candles is played for a set amount of time then simply stopped. There doesn't need to be a particular outcome for the game to end.

4. Conditioning

The Instructor brings students back together to form a circle, standing up. Refer to session 1 (page 48) for the outline of setting up and managing the conditioning exercises. Remember, the students should move only as far as they feel comfortable. Avoid injuries. Encourage the students to relax and soften into each stretch.

Stretching 1st form

Recommended time allocation: 8 minutes

Refer to session 1 (page 49) for the stretching 1st form positions. Each member of the circle, from left to right or vice versa, is given a turn to say the breathing in and breathing out commands for the exercises, as explained in session 2 (page 84).

Brain exercises

Recommended time allocation: 3 minutes

Standing as part of the circle, the Instructor leads the students through the brain exercises. At this point in the programme it is good to alter the exercises in order to bring an extra challenge and to take the students further.

Exercise 1
Crossovers. Raise the left knee and touch it with the right hand. Then swap over and raise the right knee and connect it with the left hand. Alternate sides for 20 seconds.

Exercise 2
Now reaching behind, the right hand connects with the raised left heel. Swapping over, the left hand connects with the raised right heel. Alternate sides for 20 seconds.

Combine exercises 1 and 2
Raise the left knee and touch it with the right hand then, without putting the left leg down, put it behind the right leg and touch the left heel with the right hand. Swap over and perform the same movement with the right leg and left hand. Alternate sides for 20 seconds.

Exercise 3
Slowly turn the left arm around to complete a circle forwards on the left side of your body, with the arm passing your left ear. Continue to turn your left arm forwards and, at the same time, start turning your right arm backwards in a circle on the right side of your body. Your arms should now be making circles in opposite directions. Do this for 20 seconds.

Exercise 4
You can add exercise 4 at this stage. Exercise 4 is about activating what are commonly known as 'brain buttons'. On either side of the sternum there is a spot of soft tissue where a pressure point can be located. Using the thumb and forefinger of one hand, massage these two points. At the same time place the free hand on the stomach and rub in a clockwise direction. It is important that the circular action is from left to right as this is the natural directional flow of the digestive system. Do the exercise for 20 seconds, then swap hands and repeat the exercise for another 20 seconds.

While the stimulation of the brain buttons increases the flow of oxygen to the brain, the massaging of the stomach helps to stimulate and enhance the digestive system. The massaging of the lower abdomen in a circular fashion from left to right is an exercise that the students can practise when they are feeling unwell in their stomach as it encourages bowel movement. Massaging the stomach from right to left is going the opposite direction to the digestive system and can induce vomiting; which can also be useful when one is feeling unwell.

5. The wrap-up challenge

Recommended time allocation: 30 minutes

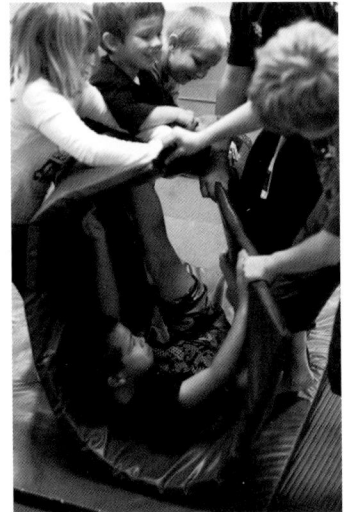

The main aim of the wrap-up challenge is to allow students to explore anger in an open, safe and fun way. The wrap-up is an engaging challenge that allows students to work in teams and gives each student the opportunity to support others and to be supported by others while dealing with their anger.

As with previous challenges, the wrap-up can be scary for students; however, accepting challenges and facing fears is all part of being a Warrior. The Instructor can refer to session 1 and the evasion challenge (page 72) and the discussion on fear if need be.

Trust is a key word when doing the wrap-up challenge. Much like the Carry the Log challenge and the Warrior Kids Wrestling in session 3, students need to be able to trust their team-mates. Therefore, the Instructor should put a lot of emphasis on stressing the rules, promoting teamwork and looking after and taking care of others.

With the class standing in a circle, the Instructor looks around the group and chooses two students who have modelled appropriate and constructive behaviour, and acknowledges their behaviour aloud to the class. The Instructor announces that these two students will be the leaders for the next challenge and leads both of them to an appropriate space and has them sit down with ample space between them. The Instructor then tells the remaining students that at the command 'Go' they are to sit with one of the two leaders to make two groups. The two groups should be equal in number or as close to equal as possible.

The Instructor sets up two groups of mats in two different areas of the room in the following fashion. Two gym mats (1200 x 1800 mm) are placed side by side on the floor. Another gym mat of the same size is placed on top of the bottom two mats. The top mat should be horizontal to the bottom two, with one side of the top mat flush with one of the ends of the two bottom mats. (Different-sized mats should be used in a similar way.) The Instructor could pick two to four students to help set up the gym mats while the other students wait quietly for them to finish.

Once everyone is seated, settled and ready to listen, the Instructor explains the wrap-up challenge. The Instructor ensures he faces everyone so that no student is behind him. This is respectful to all students and means that each individual student is visible to the Instructor. As with all of the activities and challenges in Warrior Kids, the attention of every student needs to be fixed on the Instructor while the challenge is explained.

The Instructor announces, 'Today we are going to have fun with anger.'

It is important to keep the discussion on anger at a level that the students can understand and to which they can relate. I start by talking about the two most common ways that people deal with anger:

1. People exert their anger externally, outwards, putting their anger on to others, on to nature or objects. They might yell, take unreasonable risks, hit, smash things, be openly negative and critical of others, threaten, intimidate, abuse and be violent. They try to use their anger to control situations. The

Session 4

outcomes of this are that people get hurt, get into trouble, and lose the trust, friendship and love of others.

2. The second common response to anger is to turn it inwards. The person might blame themselves for everything that goes wrong, be negative and critical about themselves out loud or in their mind, get frustrated with themselves, isolate themselves from others, not care about themselves, overeat or adopt another or a number of similar addictions or behaviours, spend most of their time avoiding reality. The outcomes of this are that the person's body will harbour stress and tension that can lead to serious health problems. They will get sick, feel depressed and have a negative outlook on life.

I continue by saying, 'Today we're going to look at other ways of dealing with our anger; healthy, safe ways. Ways that don't get us into trouble and don't harm us.' I point out to the students that: 'we are all experts when it comes to anger. We've been feeling and dealing with this emotion since we were born. We are all experienced when it comes to anger.' This is important to stress as people tend to feel that they are inadequate, unskilled or uneducated in dealing with their anger; that the management and understanding of anger is for experts such as psychiatrists and psychologists.

Physical release of anger is often regarded as cathartic and some believe that it can induce dormant memories and cause further anger and emotional hurt. I find this idea amusing, especially since people are already having outbursts and rampages. My students are already having tantrums. The majority of the time people already demonstrate management and control with their anger. They choose where and when they display their anger, they choose who they put their anger on to and they choose the way in which they exert their anger. This is calculation and control.

Students can behave one way at home and another way at school. Adults do the same when it comes to work and home. Anger is rarely wild and unpredictable. It is usually the opposite, very controlled and very predictable. It's just that people don't always choose to control their anger in a safe and mature way. Instead, anger is often used to gain power and control over a given situation or an individual.

Whenever I have worked with people and their anger I have been able to track their anger and demonstrate to them the level of control that they have had over it. I show them how there are certain times that they choose to act out their anger, towards certain people and in certain environments. More often than not it has become habitual, but it is still controlled. There are certain unwritten rules and other controlling factors that the person will abide by, even in the throes of their rage.

Abusive partners will typically do so behind closed doors or in an environment where they feel confident that they'll get away with it. It is the same with adults who abuse children: typically they will choose their time and place and usually they will strike areas of the body where bruises and marks are easy to conceal.

Even our anger can be held with a heart of kindness.

— Buddha

Session 4

People who use intimidation and acts of violence when out and about in public choose their times, choose the environment and choose their targets. They may even dress up for the occasion, consciously choosing to wear clothes that help them to appear menacing. People who have outbursts will usually do so in front of some people but not in front of others. These examples all demonstrate calculation and control.

Like all emotions in the human experience, anger is healthy and natural. Anger defines boundaries, instils motivation and can be extremely useful when used to protect ourselves or others. It is a basic emotion that is wired to our will to survive. Anger by itself is not negative, however, the way people choose to behave with their anger may be constructive or non-constructive.

The focus on anger through out the wrap-up challenge should be held lightly. It shouldn't be too serious as anger is typically an overly tense emotion as it is. I point out to the students that I 'love anger.' It's such a wonderful and powerful emotion. We can use our anger in positive and constructive ways. If someone is picking on you or someone else at school, by all means be angry. Show them your anger and firmly tell them to, 'Back off!'

However, hitting or beating someone is not an appropriate way of expressing anger. This I make clear to the students.

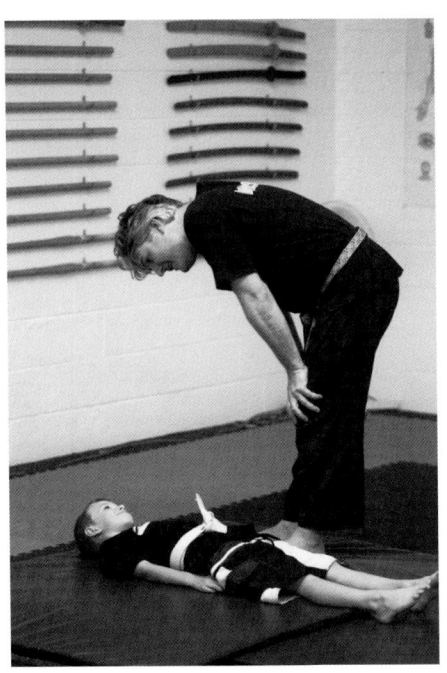

To begin the wrap-up challenge I say, 'If we feel the urge or need to express our anger, then we have to do so in a constructive, safe way. Today we are going to practise expressing our anger in a safe way. We are going to do this with a challenge called the wrap-up.'

At this point the Instructor asks for a volunteer. The volunteer lies down on his back at the centre of the top gym mat, with his head resting near the edge of the mat. His head must be on the gym mat. If at any point during the challenge his head moves off the gym mat, the challenge should be stopped immediately so that he can reposition himself.

Safety is the key to all of the activities in Warrior Kids. A student's head cannot be allowed to hit the floor. The team leader or Instructor can put their hands underneath the student's head if they see that it is going towards the floor.

The leader of the team that the volunteer was chosen from sits on the floor at the volunteer's head. The Instructor goes on to explain the wrap-up challenge.

1. Each member of each team will have a turn to lie down at the centre of the top gym mat, as demonstrated by the volunteer.

2. The remaining members of the team stand along either side of the gym mats. There should be the same or nearly the same number of students on both sides.

3. The students at the sides of the gym mats crouch down and lift the edges of the top gym mat. Both edges are lifted until they meet, making a cylinder around the student lying down in the centre.

4. The edges of the gym mat are held in place by the students. Some gym mats have Velcro. The Velcro should not be used

as it requires a tearing action to get apart. A pushing action is more appropriate for this exercise.

5. The team leader, sitting at the head of the volunteer, should be able to look through the cylinder. This means that the edges and sides of the gym mat should be kept off the volunteer, giving him room to move.

6. It should be stressed to all that the volunteer should be able to trust his team. Team members must demonstrate that they are trustworthy. There should be no falling on to the mat or pushing the gym mat down on to the volunteer, no tickling of the volunteer's feet, nor any kicking of the sides of the gym mat. Anyone choosing to behave in this manner could miss out on having a turn in the centre.

7. When the team is ready and the Instructor has given his okay to start the challenge, the team leader tells the volunteer to 'breathe in through the nose and out through the mouth. Breathe in.' On the second in-breath the volunteer should start to think of a time when he felt angry. He should think about what he felt angry about, where he was at the time and who was involved. The volunteer is encouraged to feel that anger now. When the team leader says 'Go' the volunteer gets to let loose.

8. When the volunteer hears the word 'Go' he can then exert his aggression on to the mat. In other words, the student can have a tantrum, a controlled tantrum. Remaining on his back, the volunteer must use his feet and hands to try and force the sides of the gym mat open. The volunteer can push, kick or hit the mat. However, he cannot slide out of the end of the mat, cannot turn around or get on to his knees.

9. When pushing at the sides of the mat, the volunteer must have contact only with the mat. It is important that he understands that under no circumstances is he to strike the hands or bodies of the students holding the edges of the gym mat.

10. The students lining both sides of the mat and holding the edges offer resistance to the volunteer, giving something for him to push against.

11. Apart from the team leader and the volunteer, all of the team should be participating in holding the gym mat and supporting the volunteer.

    a) The students can verbally encourage the volunteer. However, their voices should not be loud as the team leader and the Instructor need to be heard.

    b) The students should understand that it is not a time to be joking around or laughing. Their focus needs to be on supporting the volunteer to express his anger.

12. The students holding the gym mats should keep safe by keeping their faces back from the mat and the active limbs of the volunteer. The students should also avoid standing at the end of the mat for two reasons. One, the team leader has

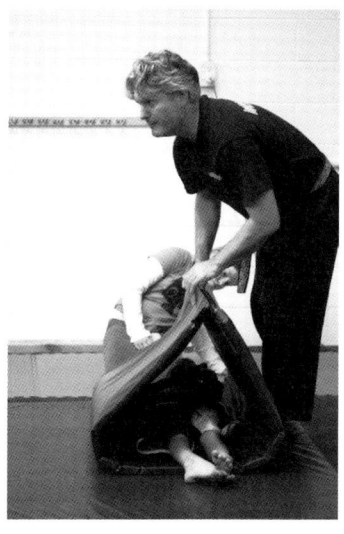

Session 4

to be able to see through the cylinder as he needs to stop the activity if he sees that safety is becoming an issue. Secondly, a student standing at the end of the mat could receive a kick from the volunteer.

13. While exerting physical energy is certainly an outlet for anger, the voice is also a powerful outlet. When people get angry they tend to be loud. I want the students to use their voices to express and release anger. However, if I explain to the students that the voice is a great outlet for releasing anger, they won't be so keen to try it. Instead, I tell them about Warrior Spirit, telling them that their Warrior Spirit is a power that they all have.

   a) The voice can be a powerful tool when it comes to self-defence and keeping ourselves safe. Earlier I explained how a child might show their anger and tell someone to back off if they are being picked on at school. I tell the students that this is their Warrior Spirit and that during the wrap-up challenge I want to see and hear their Warrior Spirit. I want them to roar.

   b) It is important that the students roar rather than using particular words or phrases. Some students might try to bring attention to themselves by yelling out a swear-word or an insult. The class should know that this is unacceptable.

14. While the team leader is monitoring his team and ensuring that everyone is safe, he will also be counting to 25. Once the team leader has reached this number he uses his hands to signal to the team to let the gym mat go. This allows the volunteer to break free.

   a) The volunteer may force the mats open on his own. However, if he does so too quickly, he won't have had the full benefit of the opportunity to express his anger. In this case he should start again.

   b) One way the Instructor can assist the volunteer to break through the gym mat is by removing one or two of the students holding the edges of the mat. The Instructor can give further assistance by removing more students.

15. When the volunteer is free from the gym mat he then sits up. If the volunteer is the first in his team to have a go at the wrap-up then the team leader will sit on the mat facing him and take him through the 3rd Warrior Kids breathing exercise:

   a) The team leader faces the volunteer and tells him to breathe in slowly through his nose and out slowly through his mouth.

   b) A second time the team leader tells the volunteer to breathe in slowly through his nose and breathe out through his mouth.

   c) The third time the team leader tells the volunteer to breathe in slowly through his nose, then to hold the breath.

   d) After a short time the team leader tells the volunteer to slowly breathe out of his mouth.

It is important that the pairs have plenty of space around them that allows some privacy for their sharing.

Session 4

After explaining the 3rd breathing exercise to the class, I will ask the students why they think we do it following each wrap-up. The students are usually quick to respond with answers such as 'To calm the person down,' 'To make sure that the person is okay,' and 'To make sure that the person isn't angry anymore.' These answers are all perfect.

Further to this, the breathing exercise also teaches the students a method of managing their anger through breathing and slowing down. When people get angry the breath typically shortens in length, escalating the anger and limiting the person's perspective and their ability and flexibility to respond.

Because the team leader is the first person to take someone through the breathing exercise, the first student through the wrap-up will be the second person to take someone through the 3rd breathing exercise. By following this order of students, everyone will get to have a turn at supporting a fellow student in calming.

16. Team leaders will go to the centre of the gym mat last, allowing their team-mates to go before them. When the team leader takes his turn in the centre another able student should be made team leader, taking his place and sitting at the head of the student in the centre.

17. The team leader chooses the order of students to have a turn at the wrap-up challenge. Everyone has a turn.

18. The team leader should ask for the Instructor's assistance if any issues arise during the wrap-up challenge. This includes problems with team-mates behaving inappropriately, undermining the team leader's position or refusing to comply with the team leader's requests.

19. Throughout the wrap-up challenge the Instructor and any supporting staff should be overseeing and making sure that the challenge is running smoothly and within the conditions laid out in the explanation of the challenge.

20. The Instructor and any supporting staff should be actively and verbally encouraging each student in the middle of the gym mat to express their anger, and also encouraging each student working as a team member by holding the mat. Team leaders should also be encouraged and supported by the Instructor.

Students will often ask for another go at the wrap-up challenge. However, this is dependent on time as the debrief of the wrap-up challenge is essential and cannot be missed. Community-based classes allow students to keep revisiting and going over the various challenges and exercises of Warrior Kids as well as exploring new ones. However, school-based programmes are limited and those attending will usually get exposure to only 10 classes before new students are given a turn.

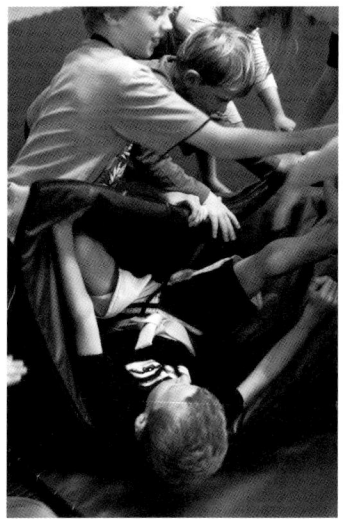

Often children will compare the wrap-up challenge to being born. I openly acknowledge this insight, as it certainly adds further depth to the activity.

The key to the wrap-up challenge is the safe expression of anger. The Instructor should stress that he has to be able to trust

Session 4

each student; trust them to be safe with their anger throughout the challenge. The students must demonstrate self-control and abide by the rules set out for the wrap-up challenge. Any breach of these conditions will mean that the student or students in question will not be able to have a go at being wrapped in the mat. The Instructor can remind the students that no one is allowed to get hurt in Warrior Kids.

While the focus on anger should be light, the boundaries must be clear with the wrap-up challenge. Each student must be able to trust their team-mates and know that they will be supported and safe from harm. As with Warrior Kids Wrestling and Carry the Log and other similar challenges in Warrior Kids, issues can arise. However, clearly defined boundaries and prominent leadership from the Instructor will limit the possibility of issues arising. If issues do arise then they should be addressed immediately. Instructors should refer to the set-up of Carry the Log challenge and Warrior Kids Wrestling in session 3 (pages 106 and 114) and other similar challenges, to be aware of issues that may arise.

On completion of the wrap-up challenge the mats are returned to the set-up that was in place at the beginning of the class.

This would be a good time for the students to have a water break.

6. 3rd breathing exercise

Recommended time allocation: 3 minutes

The Instructor has the students form a circle, sitting down on the mats. The Instructor leads the students, demonstrating and talking them through the full 3rd breathing exercise.

The 1st and 2nd breathing exercises taught in Warrior Kids are great for centring and calming one's self and re-focusing; however, it is not always appropriate for students to perform these exercises in the varying environments and situations in their life, such as in the classroom or when being spoken to by an adult or in front of their peers.

The full 3rd breathing exercise is subtle and private, making it a perfect technique for public situations. It doesn't involve standing or the use of hands. Others will have no idea when a person is doing it. I explain this to the students when introducing the full 3rd breathing exercise.

The 3rd breathing exercise

The 3rd breathing form involves a three-step cycle.

1. Sitting in a relaxed posture (preferably cross-legged) and keeping in time with the Instructor, the students slowly breathe in deeply through the nose, then slowly breathe out through the mouth.

2. A second time the students slowly inhale deeply through the nose, and slowly exhale through the mouth.

3. The third time the students slowly inhale deeply through the nose and hold their breath for five seconds. Then slowly exhale through the mouth.
   a. Run through the cycle again, however, at step 3 hold the breath for 6 seconds.
   b. Run through again, however, at step 3 hold the breath for 8 seconds.
   c. Repeat the cycle again, however, this time the cycle is shortened to two steps.

Step 1

The students slowly breathe in deeply through the nose, and slowly breathe out through the mouth.

Step 2

The second time the students slowly inhale deeply through the nose and hold their breath for 8 seconds. Slowly exhale through the mouth.

Repeat twice.

Repeat the cycle again, however, this time the cycle is shortened to one step.

Step 3

The students slowly inhale deeply through the nose and hold their breath for 8 seconds. Slowly exhale through the mouth.
Repeat three times.

Variation

The Instructor could have the students close their eyes during the exercise. The students should be encouraged to pay attention to what's going on inside their bodies and minds as they do the exercise. The Instructor will need to talk the students through as they will not be able to utilise visual guides.

The Instructor should encourage the students to practise the breathing exercises in their day-to-day life. Breathing exercises are something that the students can utilise when they feel angry, annoyed, sad, scared, ashamed, stressed, anxious, restless or unsettled, or even if they're laughing too much.

7. Group discussion: anger

Recommended time allocation: 25 minutes

The instructor should ensure that the group discussion is age-appropriate. Keep control of the language and keep the discussion simple and straightforward.

As a parent observing, I have learnt also.

— Warrior Kids parent

The Instructor and the students remain seated in a circle on the gym mats. Each student should be facing the centre of the circle and be clearly visible to the Instructor so that no one is in any way disassociated from the group, whether by their own positioning or by the positioning of another student. The Instructor acknowledges everyone's effort in the wrap-up challenge. The Instructor could even ask for a show of hands from those who enjoyed it.

From this point the Instructor leads the students in a discussion about anger by asking some simple questions.

To assist with the group discussion, the Instructor should be familiar with the set-up of the Sharing Circle outlined in session 1 (page 58) and of the methods of addressing the various issues that may arise that are described there. This will help to contain the group discussion and allow it to flow.

As with the Sharing Circle, the Instructor should simply elicit the answers from the students with minimal response, meaning that each answer does not have to be elaborated on, unless of course it has clear learning potential for the class and therefore warrants extra attention.

When the students answer the questions, they won't just be giving answers that relate to themselves. They will be reflecting on what they witness and experience from the people in their lives; predominantly their parent figures. As our group discussion is an exploration into anger and the choices that people make when feeling angry, it is entirely appropriate and of great value to allow the students to give answers that relate to the people in their lives. Sometimes it may be a case of learning what not to do.

If students fail to bring up certain answers from the following questions then the Instructor can give the answers himself for the benefit of the group.

The Instructor should make a point of directing the questions to the older students from time to time. Often, in the classroom at school, some students will only answer questions if they have to. Otherwise, they are quite happy to skip by. Many students are worried and self conscious about giving an incorrect answer. In Warrior Kids there is no such thing as an incorrect answer; rather, there are experiences and ideas, inappropriate and appropriate, that we share and discuss as a group in order to make constructive choices in our lives.

Parents, caregivers and family members present in the room during the group discussion on anger are always very interested too. This is an opportunity for them to explore anger and the issues surrounding it, from the safety of the sideline. With the focus and attention being on their child, parents and caregivers will be able to learn, consider and take on aspects of identifying, managing and addressing their own anger and the anger within the family. They will be able to safely consider their own behaviour and gain strategies for making constructive choices with their emotions.

The students will often use the term 'you' rather than 'I' when talking about anger and behaviour. Talking in the third person will allow students to disclose their less-than-desirable behaviour without openly being judged or condemned for it; which means that it is safer for them to share. At times I will encourage students to own their behaviour by getting them to use the term 'I'. However, in this instance the use of 'you' is completely acceptable.

Question 1

When do you feel angry?
or
What sort of things do you feel angry about?

Anger is often very serious. Ensure that the discussion is light and moves at a steady pace.

Question 1 is about identifying triggers and events or situations that we feel angry about. This is the first step to learning how to manage anger and stress.

The students should follow the normal conduct in Warrior Kids group discussions by putting up their hand to answer the question. The Instructor elicits answers from the students.

There are numerous reasons as to why children may feel angry at any given time. It is important to remember that anger is a defence mechanism and therefore a survival mechanism. Anger is a secondary emotion, meaning that the person feeling it initially feels another emotion that is rooted in sadness, hurt or fear. These base emotions can stem from situations where one is faced with change or feels threatened, and feels that the situation is beyond their control.

Answers that may be given to question 1 involve experiences of feeling sad, scared, shame, guilt, regret or frustration, such as:

- teasing,
- put-downs of an individual or their family,
- bullying,
- broken promises,
- being ignored,
- not being heard,
- being excluded,
- friends not wanting to play with you,
- being blamed for something you didn't do,
- people talking behind your back,
- cruelty to animals,
- mistreatment of nature,
- mistreatment of others,
- making a mistake,
- changes,
- death,
- fighting between others: verbal or physical,
- not getting your own way: for example, Mum and Dad saying 'no' to something that a student may have wanted. I always point out that the students are entitled to feel angry when Mum and Dad say no, however mums and dads are supposed to say no and they should. When a parent says no the child can certainly feel upset, yet the child has to accept and respect their parent or parents' authority. Children also have to know that they cannot have everything, nor can they do everything that they may want to do,
- things simply not working out: students may have been working hard on a project at school or a hobby at home and it simply doesn't work out the way they wanted. This leads to disappointment and frustration.
- failing or the fear of failing,
- past hurts and fears that have manifested in the body and mind that can be triggered. Especially poignant for students who have experienced abuse, domestic violence, the break-up of a family, the death or suicide of a family member or even having been severely shamed or isolated and so on.

- depression, whether experienced firsthand by the student or through a family member,
- discrimination, marginalisation and oppression where there is a clear rejection of the self, a clear message that you are not okay, which leads to a loss of autonomy, freedom and expression of the self. Situations where there is power-over tactics and manipulation being used also relate to this.
- injustice or unfairness,
- restriction of the self, where circumstances are or seem to be beyond one's control and when one feels unable to change their circumstances and imprisoned by them; which again leads to a loss of autonomy, freedom and expression of the self,
- confusion and powerlessness leading to frustration,
- feeling undervalued and not respected,
- seeing someone that you care about being hurt, and
- events in the world: war, starvation, inequality, the state of the environment.

It is important to acknowledge that tiredness, hunger, a lack of time and space for processing and other stressors can be factors in feeling anger, and that when we are not feeling well or good we need to be extra careful with our anger and the choices that we make. When combined with one or more of the reasons to feel angry listed above, these factors could result in anger escalating to a point that the student feels limited in their ability to manage.

Of course, sometimes it is the little things that really seem to upset people, such as an item not being put back in the right place, or someone using something without asking. However, the feelings over little things tend to be a manifestation of underlying emotions that are due to something more serious. We just don't always see it at the time.

Anger for all of these reasons is justified. We cannot say that a person's anger itself is right or wrong. Their anger is simply what it is. Anger is a natural and healthy response. Constructive anger and constructive use of anger can bring about change.

When people in New Zealand got angry about the Springbok rugby tour of New Zealand in 1981 because of the team's association with apartheid in South Africa, most of them responded with non-violent action: they marched on the streets and staged sit-ins on the rugby fields. This was a constructive use of anger. These acts resonated around the world and were later acknowledged by South African statesman, President Nelson Mandela, who had learned of the New Zealanders' actions while imprisoned with other leading African National Congress Members.

When people in New Zealand got angry about nuclear ships and weapons they marched on the streets and took their boats on the water to stop those ships from entering the harbour. This led to a nuclear-free New Zealand, a stance to which it remains committed. Again, this was constructive use of anger.

It was my anger and frustration at the lack of preventative programmes for children that largely led me to create Warrior Kids.

Anger becomes an issue when people don't allow it to shift, instead they hold on to the anger by thinking negatively and losing

Session 4

sight of the bigger picture. Anger becomes an issue when people choose to express it through violence, abuse and destructive acts.

During the sharing the students will feed off one another, relating and identifying with similar experiences. This and the sharing itself validates these experiences.

Question 2

How do you know that you feel angry?
or
What happens in your body when you feel angry?

The second question is about identifying anger in our bodies and becoming aware of early warning signs. Being able to identify stress and anger in the body means a student can take steps to manage, de-escalate or make allowance for it.

Answers commonly given for question 2 are:

- the body goes tight or tense,
- your hands make fists,
- you feel bigger and stronger,
- the face goes red,
- you feel all hot,
- the face gets all scrunched up,
- the brow drops and you look mean,
- the jaw clenches,
- you feel sick in the stomach or the stomach feels knotted,
- you start thinking angry thoughts,
- you only think about the bad things and forget everything else,
- you get loud, start to bang things around and slam doors,
- you start answering back to people,
- you don't want to do anything fun,
- you want to be left alone, and
- you feel like you're going to lose control.

Question 3

What sort of things do people do when they feel angry?
or
Not what people should do when they feel angry, but what do they do?

Question 3 is about the behaviours that people would be best to avoid when angry. Often this question is misinterpreted as asking what people should do when they are feeling angry. You might have to make this distinction clear for the students. You will notice that a number of the answers will relate to adult behaviour that the students may have witnessed.

Answers commonly given for question 3 are:

- say things they don't mean,
- say things they shouldn't,
- make inappropriate gestures with their hands or fingers,
- they answer back,
- they throw things,
- they smash or break things,
- they trash their room,
- they hit people,
- they yell or scream,
- they run away,

Session 4

- they threaten,
- they hurt and abuse people, animals or nature,
- they don't listen,
- they ignore people,
- they sulk,
- they drive fast,
- they drink, and
- they do drugs.

Question 4

What happens to us if we choose to behave this way? If we choose to hurt and abuse others, smash things or yell and scream?

Question 4 explores consequences. Answers commonly given to this question include:

- we get into trouble,
- we get a detention,
- we have to sit outside the principal's office at lunchtime while our friends get to play,
- we get grounded by our parents,
- people won't want to be our friend,
- people won't want to play with us,
- people won't trust us,
- our Mum and Dad will be disappointed,
- if we smash or break something then we'll have to pay for it, or our Mum or Dad will have to pay for it,
- if I trash my room I'll just have to clean it up later,
- if I break my toys then I won't have them any more,
- we may get a reputation and be blamed for other things, and
- other people might want to hurt us.

I also add to question 4:

'And what about me, I'm an adult, what if I chose to behave like that? What could happen to me?'

- I could get arrested,
- I might have to pay money,
- I might go to prison, and
- I might lose my family, my wife and children.

Question 5

So, how do you look after yourself when you feel angry, what do you do?

The aim of question 5 is to elicit safe, constructive and practical answers from the students, which they can use in real, everyday situations to manage, de-escalate, channel and process their anger.

Anger is a powerful energy that can be used in a positive and constructive way. Families could be encouraged to practise these responses with the student. I have had this happen and it's great. This is changing the family, the home and the students' lives for the better.

Appropriate answers commonly given for question 5 include:

Session 4

Hitting a rolled-up mat is another activity that can be used for expressing and working with anger.

- If someone is calling you names at school, you could walk away.

    Walking away is a common response that children are encouraged to use at school. Not always easy though, especially if the person insulting you follows.

- Hit your pillow or something soft that won't break.

    Students should be encouraged to hit their pillow in the privacy of their own room. Hitting people, animals or nature is not appropriate and not okay. Hitting walls, anything breakable or anything that could harm them is inappropriate and not okay. If students feel the need to hit then they should hit their pillow. Students could use a punching bag.

- Smash an unwanted item.

    Some of my students have been able to break up or smash old, unwanted furniture at home as an outlet for their anger. However, this has been under the supervision, direction and approval of their parents. Some students have even been lucky enough to be a part of demolition projects.

- Do vigorous exercise.

    Anything physical is great, especially if the student is extremely agitated. Burn off the anger and excess energy. Go for a run or a bike ride. Other physical activities can include helping out with work around the house such as mowing the lawn, vacuuming the floors or weeding the garden. Students could also kick a ball around, climb a tree or dance to loud music. The Instructor should stress that it has to be a safe activity where the student and others are not in any danger. Students should check with their parents before leaving their property.

- Build something.

    Some students like to go into the shed or into the backyard and build something with their hands. Arts and craft; I've worked with boys who like to make bead necklaces when they felt stressed. They found it calming.

- Yell or scream into your pillow.

    Again, something that is best done in the privacy of a bedroom. Some students may have access to a large space such as a park, where they can be loud without scaring the neighbours.

- Wrestle with Dad or your dog.

    As long as no one gets hurt, including the dog, then this is a perfect outlet for anger.

- Draw a picture.
- Write an angry letter then rip it up.
- Rip up some old newspapers.
- Sleep.
- Go for a swim or have a shower.

    In other words, cool down. With anything relating to water and children, adult supervision is vital. The Instructor should stress this in the group.

Session 4

- Have a drink of water.
- Wash your face.
- Have some Self Time: time alone with yourself.

    Self Time is what I use instead of Time Out. Time Out tends to be allocated or enforced by an authority figure such as a parent or teacher. Self Time is about the person themselves choosing to take time just for them without having to be told to. Self Time is going in to a quiet space such as a bedroom, a hut or a tree, where one can be alone and gather their thoughts.

- Breathe in and out.

    When people get emotional, whether it be angry, sad, scared and so on, they tend to breathe shallow, taking small breaths in and out. Some people even hold their breath. By consciously taking deeper breaths we alleviate the emotion, allowing the feeling of it to shift. When we breathe shallow or hold our breath, we hold on to the experience of the emotion. Breathing in and out is also useful in the classroom where a student can't get up and walk out when they feel angry or frustrated. Thinking of an X at the same time can also take it further as it stimulates both sides of the brain, the left and the right, and further alleviates the emotion.

    It should be pointed out to the students that they have now practised three different breathing exercises in Warrior Kids that they can use at times of stress.

- Counting to ten.

    If it works, count to 100.

- Pray or talk to God.

    Depending on the student's particular belief.

- Talk to someone.

    An adult, a friend, someone that the student feels safe with and can trust. They could even talk to their pet or an imaginary friend.

- Think about the good things in your life.

    Widening one's perspective, looking at the bigger picture rather than at the little picture. Remembering that people love us, believe in us and value us.

- Activate your Warrior Deflector Shield as explained in session 2 (page 122).
- Get a hug from someone you trust and feel safe with.
- Eat some fruit or other healthy food.

    This is especially important for students who eat when they get emotional. When some people get emotional they can crave comfort food out of habit. Comfort foods tend to be foods that are high in fat, sugar and salt; these are not a constructive choice for one's health.

- Go for a walk and get some fresh air.
- Practise your moves from Warrior Kids.

    For example, rolling, handstands and cartwheels.

Session 4

○ Enjoy the great outdoors, be with nature.

○ Get involved with a group or groups who represent your opposition to an issue; social, environmental or otherwise. Choose a group that uses non-violent, constructive action to instigate change.

In Warrior Kids, shinai (bamboo practice swords) are used to work with anger. However, the Instructor must be correctly trained in the use of the shinai.

Some students may suggest methods for managing anger that are not so appropriate, such as video games. However, one of the aims of video games is mentally to challenge the person playing. This type of mental challenge when a person is feeling angry will only escalate aggression.

This understanding has come from the students themselves, with numerous accounts of how they smashed their game consoles out of anger because they couldn't get past the next level. Of course, sometimes the anger has been turned on other areas of the home, even on to mum, who was just trying to find out what was going on.

The Instructor acknowledges the students' efforts and participation in the group discussion.

8. Melting Candles

Recommended time allocation: 5 minutes

Time to shift the energy and allow the students to move on from anger. The Instructor and the students form a circle and start another round of Melting Candles, as played earlier in the session (page 125).

9. Closing words

The Instructor directs students to assemble on the mats, standing in a circle as they were at the beginning of the class. Refer to session 1 (page 76).

Closing

Recommended time allocation: 1 minute

The Instructor asks for a volunteer from the group to say some words to end the class.

When the closing words have been spoken the Instructor acknowledges the speaker with appreciation and concludes with, 'Remember to take what you brought with you today, your shoes, socks, watches, water bottle, jersey and I'll see you next time.'

Session 4

> You have completed session 4. Well done!
>
> Having explored anger in the class, you have been given the opportunity to consider your own anger and the behaviours that you choose when feeling angry.
>
> Many mistakes can be made because of the mismanagement of anger. You may be aware of regrets from the past when you dealt with your anger, there may even exist issues that are still present, behaviours that you would like to change.
>
> This is not a weakness, nor is it a fault. It does not make you unfit to be an Instructor. Such awareness is a strength; such desire to improve one's self is a blessing.
>
> Our students and their families are not perfect.
> We are not perfect either.
> The practice of this consideration is humility.
>
> By questioning, addressing and changing our behaviours, we are seeking our authentic self.
> So question, address and change the behaviours in your life that are not constructive.
>
> Every morning we are blessed with a new day, a new beginning, a new start.
> No matter what we were or what we did yesterday, we can start afresh today.

Session 5

> **EQUIPMENT**
> - 12 x gym mats, size 1200 x 1800 mm
> - Koosh balls (one for each student)
> - chairs for parents and caregivers

Introduction

Having had two intense and confronting activities in session 3 with the Carry the Log and Wrestling challenges, followed by session 4 and the focus on anger, session 5 is designed to be light and playful.

The students' fifth time together starts with the Rats and Rabbits game. Students have the opportunity to practise their tumbling ability further with a new version of Roll Tiggy, and then there is opportunity for students to affirm themselves in the One 2 One activity where they identify and share their good qualities. The Sharing Circle concludes the session. Have fun!

The outcomes for session 5 are that the students will:

- be more confident and able when rolling,
- be able to identify three or more attributes that they like about themselves and express them,
- be able to demonstrate reflective listening.

Lesson overview

1. Opening words.
2. Round of introductions: a round of names and each student says what they think makes them a Warrior Kid.
3. Warm-up game: Rats and Rabbits.
4. Conditioning: Stretching 2nd form; Brain exercises.
5. Roll Tiggy, 2nd version.
6. 1st breathing exercise.
7. One 2 One: What do you like about yourself?
8. Sharing Circle: a low and high point.
9. Closing words.

1. Opening words

Recommended time allocation: 1 minute

The Instructor directs students to remove their shoes and socks and to sit on the mats in a circle. Once the group is settled the Instructor has the students stand. The Instructor then asks for a volunteer from the group to say some opening words to commence the class. Refer to session 1 (page 44).

2. Round of introductions

Recommended time allocation: 3 minutes

Each member of the circle, from left to right or vice-versa, takes their turn to say their name and say what makes them a Warrior Kid. They may choose to say something awesome about themselves. Perhaps they will announce that they are really good at something or that they did something really nice for someone or they may choose to acknowledge an admirable trait in their personality. The answers to what makes a Warrior Kid are open. Refer to session 1 (page 44) for the set up of introductions.

3. Warm-up game: Rats and Rabbits

Recommended time allocation: 10 minutes

Refer to session 1 (page 45) to read the outline of setting up and managing the warm-up game. The Instructor should remember to get the students to take note of their surroundings and clearly point out the boundary of the game to ensure safety and limit any chance of injury.

Rats and Rabbits

Rats and Rabbits is a simple, fast-paced game that the students enjoy. It gets the students moving straight away, allowing them to burn off troubles from their day and any accompanying tension. Rats and Rabbits is full of fun and laughter. It is also a game that allows the Instructor to have some play with the students.

When the Instructor calls 'Go' the students make two lines facing one another in the middle of the room. An easy way to do this is to get the students to find themselves a partner and for those partners to face one another in the centre of the room, one either side of the centreline. When the class is in position and settled the Instructor explains Rats and Rabbits.

1. In Rats and Rabbits the students are split into two teams, two lines opposing one another. It is good if the teams are both well represented in terms of age as this will help with the continued integration of the group.
2. One team is named *rats* while the other team is named *rabbits*. The two teams stand facing one another, just out of arms' reach.
3. The Instructor calls either *rats* or *rabbits*.
    a) If the Instructor calls *rats* the Rats team must retreat to the wall or a designated line directly behind them, while the *rabbits* chase and tag them.
    b) On reaching the wall or designated line, the *rats* are safe from the *rabbits*.
    c) When pursuing, the *rabbits* must tag as many *rats* as possible.
    d) If the Instructor calls *rabbits* the *rabbits* must retreat to the wall or a designated line directly behind them, while the *rats* chase and tag them.

4. At the beginning of the game nothing happens when a student is tagged. This gives everyone a chance to gain a sense of how the game works. However, a short time into Rats and Rabbits the Instructor can announce that *rats* who get tagged become *rabbits* and vice-versa.

5. A fun way to keep the students on their toes and to test their listening early in the game is for the Instructor to call out '*Radishes!*' Some students will run, some will stay.

6. The Instructor can further trick the students by physically pointing or running in the opposite direction to the team that he calls out. For example, I will call out *Rats!* but run and point in the direction that the *rabbits* would use to retreat. After using this method of trickery a couple of times I will then mix it up and actually run in the direction of the team I call.

7. When the students have a good grasp of the game the Instructor can change the game further by having both teams start off on their knees. In this case, when the Instructor announces *Rats!* or *Rabbits!*, both teams jump to their feet and either chase or retreat.

8. After starting off on their knees a few times the Instructor can then take the students to the next level by having them lie down on their stomachs and reach behind to hold both feet with their hands.
   a) This time the Instructor announces that he will whisper either *Rats* or *Rabbits*, which means the students have to be listening very carefully.
   b) When *Rats* or *Rabbits* is called the students jump up on to their feet and either chase or retreat.

9. If a whole team is tagged the Instructor then has the option of starting the game again. This depends on time.

10. Rats and Rabbits is played for a set amount of time. There doesn't need to be a particular outcome in order for the game to end.

Keep the game moving along.

4. Conditioning

The Instructor brings students back together to form a circle, standing up. Refer to session 1 (page 48) for the outline of setting up and managing the conditioning exercises. Remember, the students should only move as far as they feel comfortable. Avoid injuries. Encourage the students to relax and soften into each stretch.

Stretching 2nd form

Recommended time allocation: 8 minutes

Refer to session 2 (page 84) for the stretching 2nd form positions. Each member of the circle, from left to right or vice versa, is given a turn to say the breathing in and breathing out commands for the exercises, as explained in session 2.

Brain exercises

Recommended time allocation: 3 minutes

Standing as part of the circle, the Instructor leads the students through the brain exercises described in sessions 1 (page 51) and 4 (page 127).

5. Roll Tiggy, 2nd version

Recommended time allocation: 20 minutes

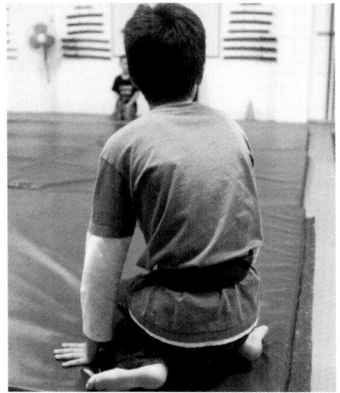

Roll Tiggy is an opportunity for the students to practise and perfect their rolls, enabling them to further develop their motor skills and self-control. Most importantly, Roll Tiggy is about having fun.

The students sit down and wait as the Instructor organises the gym mats into a large square the equivalent of 12 mats (each 1200 x 1800 mm). The Instructor may like to have a couple of the students assist with the setting up of the gym mats.

When the gym mats are set up the Instructor tells the students that at the word 'Go' they are to sit around the outside of the mats. Once the students are in place, the Instructor ensures that there is a buffer space around the outside of the gym mats. This is a safety precaution as students will be rolling over the mats and could knock or kick into anyone sitting too close. To create a buffer space the Instructor tells the students to move back. The Instructor then walks around the gym mats, ensuring that there is a clear path.

1. Four students are on the mats at a time; one student in each corner of the square, forming the Crouching Frog posture. If the mat space is smaller than the area described above, Roll Tiggy can be played with two students on the mats at a time.

2. The Instructor chooses a student from among those sitting around the outside of the gym mats. This student gets to nominate one of the four students crouching on the mats to be the *chaser*.

3. When the Instructor calls 'Go!' the *chaser* rolls after the other students on the mats in order to tag one of them.

4. The four students on the gym mats, including the *chaser*, can only move by rolling. They can roll forwards, backwards, sideways and diagonally as long as they remain on the mats.

    a) Students on the mats must remain in the Crouching Frog posture throughout the game. They cannot stand.

    b) Students on the mats cannot move by sliding, crawling or shuffling. They must roll.

    c) Rolls should be clean. Bodies need to be tucked up. There is no rolling with the body straight.

    d) If a student rolls off the mats, that student becomes the *chaser*.

At the word 'Go!' the chaser sets off to tag opponents.

Session 5

Evasion is the key to not getting tagged.

5. When a student on the mats is tagged, she becomes the *chaser*. Immediately following the tag she must remain still and count for 15 seconds, allowing the original *chaser* a chance to get away. The new *chaser* then rolls after the other students on the mats to tag one of them.

6. Students should be careful when tagging and practise the utmost self-control. Tags should be soft, whether with the hand, foot or other part of the body. Tags must also be to appropriate areas of the body. Anyone not playing in a safe manner may need to be removed from the game. No one is to be hurt or to be touched inappropriately.

7. Every student on the mats should get a turn at being the *chaser*.

8. Some students may not be confident with their rolling ability and may require support from the Instructor during the game. Refer to assisting students with the rolls in sessions 1 (pages 53 and 54) and 2 (pages 87 and 88).

9. The Instructor should openly acknowledge the rolling attempts of each student.

10. When the four students on the mats have had 3 or 4 minutes of playing Roll Tiggy, the Instructor gets them to stop and to move off the mats. It might be possible to allow these students to go and get a short drink before joining their fellow students sitting around the outside of the mats.

Students should be careful not to get cornered!

11. The Instructor then chooses four more students to go on the mats and play Roll Tiggy.

Session 5

Watch for students that might be dizzy.

Every student gets a turn. If a student does not want to have a turn but they are physically able, remind them that, 'You come to Warrior Kids to do Warrior Kids, not to watch others do Warrior Kids.' Encourage the student as much as possible. If they are still resistant to having a go, ask them to think about who they would like to play the game with out of the students in the group. This will give them some power because they have choice.

Of course this should be done tactfully and the student should not be made to feel embarrassed or ashamed. It can be done discreetly,

with the Instructor sitting alongside the student as some of the students are playing the game. However, the Instructor's attention should also be on the game. If the student is still resistant, tell them, 'I'm going to let you off today, but next time I want you to do it, okay?'

The Instructor should refrain from taking part in the game as her attention needs to be on the class as a whole: Warrior Kids is for the students.

If the last round of Roll Tiggy requires someone to have another turn due to numbers, the Instructor can ask the students to raise their hand if they'd like to have another turn. From there the Instructor can choose a suitable student or students if need be.

In the interest of reinforcing appropriate behaviour, it would be wise to choose someone who has been a model student, or there might be someone who didn't get much of a turn the first time and deserves another go.

The Instructor needs to ensure that a high level of respect is held throughout the game. This is a good opportunity to pick up on language and comments from students. Every student in Warrior Kids should feel safe to play Roll Tiggy, regardless of their ability or level of skill. The game is not about winning, it is about having a go, practising tumbling, building confidence. Most of all, it is about having fun. Address any put-downs or belittling remarks. Encourage students who are out to win to relax and enjoy themselves.

6. 1st breathing exercise

Recommended time allocation: 2 minutes

The Instructor has the students form a circle, standing around the outside of the mats. The Instructor leads the students, demonstrating and talking them through the 1st breathing exercise. Refer to session 1 for the outline of the 1st breathing exercise (page 57).

7. One 2 One: what do you like about yourself?

Recommended time allocation: 20 minutes

The One 2 One activity is an opportunity for the students to further build their connection with fellow students and to practise their communication and interpersonal skills, while also enabling them to share on a deeper level. The One 2 One activity features more in future sessions of Warrior Kids and focuses on a number of topics.

The Instructor informs the students that at the word 'Go' they are expected to find a partner and to find a space in the training area of the room and sit down. The training area is the designated space of the room in which the class is run. It is important that no one moves until the Instructor announces 'Go'. Some students may rush to partner up with a certain person in the group, which encourages others to do the same.

For the first One 2 One activity it is important that the students are partnered up with someone that they feel comfortable with. However, it is also important that no one is left out or made to feel isolated. Therefore, in some instances the Instructor might have to aid the students by designating a partner for them. This is beneficial when there are students who already have a strong connection with their chosen partner. As I've said before, 'I love friendship in Warrior Kids, however friendship becomes a problem when it disrupts the class.' There may be students who are too familiar with one another and who play and talk when they are together. Such students will need to partner up with somebody else.

This is also the case with students who have a long history with Warrior Kids. Rather than have them choose to be with students that they already know, I will encourage them to find someone that they do not know so well. This strengthens the overall group and widens the family feeling.

Common feedback from some students who have attended Warrior Kids four or five times is that while they don't have any friends at school, they do have friends at Warrior Kids. This is great, this is Warrior Kids serving its purpose and doing what it is supposed to. After further involvement with Warrior Kids these same students tend to become more confident and self-assured and start to implement what they have learnt at school, developing further friendships.

In choosing a space some pairs may try to take prime areas such as the gym mats. It would be wise to say that the gym mats cannot be used, or to separate the mats, allowing each pair to use one. Another way would be to see who rushes for the gym mats and then to swap them around with pairs who quietly opted for the floor.

It is important that the pairs of children have plenty of space around them to allow privacy for their sharing.

1. One person in each pair is chosen to speak first. One way to do this is to ask for a person in each pair to put up their hand. The Instructor can then choose the student with their hand up or choose the student with their hand down to speak first. The latter is great for dealing with students who have pressured their partner to put their hand up in order to avoid going first.

2. The student speaking first has three minutes to tell their partner what they like about themselves or, as it would be put to them, 'What do you like about yourself?'

Koosh balls

If there are enough Koosh balls on hand, one could be given to each student to hold throughout the activity. The Koosh ball is an effective textile focal point that stimulates the brain and aids the student in finding the words to share with their partner.

The use of Koosh balls can become a problem if they are not managed with clear guidelines. Before handing the Koosh balls out I explain the rules:

- You cannot pass your Koosh ball to another student.
- You cannot swap your Koosh ball with another student.
- While you can turn the Koosh ball over in your hands or bounce it in your hands, you cannot throw the Koosh Ball up high.
- Do not bang the floor with the Koosh ball to make noise.
- Do not tie the Koosh ball in knots or damage it in any way.

If anyone breaches these rules then they may have their Koosh ball taken off them. Newer or younger students, or even students who have learning difficulties, may be given a couple of warnings first before their Koosh ball is taken away.

a) This question is designed to foster confidence and self-worth by having the student openly acknowledge and own their positive attributes and qualities.

b) It can help to give the students a set number of attributes that they must share. For example, the sharing student might have to say at least five or ten things that she likes about herself. The student listening can help by counting with their fingers each time their partner says something nice about herself.

3. To assist the students in understanding the One 2 One activity, the Instructor should model by answering the question first, openly saying what she likes about herself to the group. The Instructor should even designate a student to count for her so that the activity is modelled in its entirety. This is great for the students to witness and also for the parents and other family members on the side to witness.

4. It is important that the students understand that it is what they like about themselves as opposed as to what they like to do. Directly using names during the explanation can help. For example, 'What does Jane like about Jane?' or 'What does Michael like about Michael?' The students could be encouraged to pretend that they are talking about one of their friends, saying what they like about that friend. They are then talking about themselves in the third person.

5. The partner of the student speaking just listens. They do not say a thing. Older or more confident students can be given the Instructor's approval to encourage or assist their partner verbally. However, it is important that the focus is on the student sharing.

6. The Instructor should be on hand to assist students who have trouble with this activity. Some students may have trouble understanding what they are supposed to do, while others may simply find it difficult. When assisting, the Instructor could openly acknowledge what she likes about the student, to spur the students on.

7. When three minutes have passed, the listening partner is given two minutes to repeat to their partner what they heard them say. It doesn't have to be word for word, they simply do their best to repeat what they heard.

By having their partner repeat what they have said, students can reflect on and clarify what they have shared.

It is important to stress that it is not the quantity of what is shared that is important, but the quality of what is shared.

a) This close feedback enables the student who shared the opportunity to reflect and clarify what they said.

b) Some students may not have been listening to their partner. They now have the insight of this and have the opportunity to work on their listening in the future. The ability to listen to others is the prime prerequisite of good communication.

8. After the partners have had two minutes of giving feedback, it is time to swap roles. The listening student says what she likes about herself and her partner listens and counts.

9. If students finish parts of the activity early, they must wait for the remainder of the class and for the Instructor's okay before moving on to the next part. If this occurs, the Instructor has the opportunity to increase the expectations of the students: instead of sharing 10 things about themselves, they could share 15.

10. When both students have had a chance to share, listen and give feedback, they thank one another. This signifies the end of the activity. The Instructor collects the Koosh balls or has some students collect them.

Homework

Every now and then I set the students homework, a task that they are expected to do outside of class. This is to take the learning beyond the session. There is no marking of this homework, no pass or fail; it is simply a task that I expect the students to accomplish.

The homework for session 5 is for the students to ask Mum or Dad five things they like about themselves. This could be done in the car on the way home from Warrior Kids. The sooner the better, as it will still be fresh in the student's mind.

By openly announcing the homework task to the class, I am, by implication, requiring the parents watching from the side to participate. And you will know that the parents have heard you when they smile or look to one another.

There is no pressure on the students or the parents to perform the homework task. It should simply be a task actioned lightly. If students or parents feel pressured then they might feel that the Instructor is looking down on them; that is not in the spirit of Warrior Kids.

The task is simply a way of students sharing an activity with their parents and it allows the parents to be a part of their child's Warrior Kids experience.

8. Sharing Circle: a low and high point

Recommended time allocation: 15 minutes

The Instructor and the students sit on the mats in a circle. Each student should be facing the centre of the circle and be clearly visible to the Instructor so that no one is in any way disassociated from the group, whether by their own positioning or by the positioning of another student.

The Instructor presents a Koosh ball and announces that it is time for the Sharing Circle, where each student will have a turn to share a low point and a high point from their week. Refer to session 1 for the outline of the Sharing Circle (page 58).

9. Closing words

The Instructor directs students to assemble on the mats, standing in a circle as at the beginning of the class. Refer to session 1 (page 76).

Closing

Recommended time allocation: 1 minute

The Instructor asks for a volunteer from the group to say some words to end the class.

When the closing words have been spoken the Instructor acknowledges the speaker with appreciation and concludes with 'Remember to take what you brought with you today, your shoes, socks, watches, water bottle, jersey and I'll see you next time.'

You have completed Session 5. Great work!
You are halfway through the 10-week programme.

During this session you were expected to share what you like about being you.
What was that like? Was it easy or a challenge?

While external factors certainly play a part in the success of a Warrior Kids programme, the overall success is determined by the Instructor. If the Instructor hasn't got it together then the programme will fall short in its delivery.

Here is an exercise that you can try.
Take a pen and a piece of paper. Put the title 'Qualities that I bring to Warrior Kids' at the top of the page and date the page.
Beneath the title and date, number 1 to 10 down the left side of the page. Then list 10 personal qualities that you bring to Warrior Kids. Be honest.
Put your list of qualities on the wall in a place where you can see them and be reminded that you are a person who can do this.
Value these qualities. Strengthen them. Address what you need to in order to be the best Instructor that you can be.

Every day, tell yourself that you are a great Warrior Kids Instructor.
Use the words 'I am a great Warrior Kids Instructor.'
Say it over and over again, for four minutes every day.
Such focus will help you become a great Instructor.

Session 6

> **EQUIPMENT**
> - 8 x gym mats, size 1200 x 1800 mm
> - 1 x Koosh ball
> - chairs for parents and caregivers

Introduction

In session 6 the theme is Constructive Response and Assertiveness when dealing with bullying. The students start by practising their evasive skills in the warm-up game, Hospital Tag. A group discussion about the ways people can be mean prepares the students for the Constructive Response and self protection exercises that follow, where each student gets to stand up to bullying and further develop their Warrior Spirit. The class gets to practise activating and strengthening their Warrior Deflector Shield. The session concludes with an exploration into ways of constructively and safely dealing with and addressing bullying.

The outcomes for session 6 are that the students will:
- be more confident in dealing with bullying and aggressive behaviour,
- be equipped with tools and skills for dealing with bullying and aggressive behaviour,
- understand that no one has the right to hurt them.

Lesson overview

1. Opening words.
2. Round of introductions: a round of names and who or what each student thinks they represent.
3. Warm-up game: Hospital Tag.
4. Conditioning: Stretching 3rd form; Brain exercises.
5. Constructive Response: self-protection.
   a) Group disussion.
   b) Constructive Response.
   c) 2nd breathing exercise: activating the Warrior Deflector Shield.
   d) Group discussion: recap.
6. Closing words.

1. Opening words
Recommended time allocation: 1 minute

The Instructor directs students to remove their shoes and socks and to sit on the mats in a circle. Once the group is settled the Instructor has the students stand up. The Instructor then asks for a volunteer from the group to say some opening words to commence the class. Refer to session 1 (page 44).

2. Round of introductions
Recommended time allocation: 3 minutes

Each member of the circle, from left to right or vice versa, takes their turn to say their name and to say who or what they represent. Refer to session 1 (page 44) for the set-up of introductions.

The students can represent their families, their group of friends, their schools or their communities. They can represent an ethnicity. They might represent a cultural group or a tribe. They may also represent a sports team, a hobby group, club or church. Each student chooses one thing to say that they represent.

When each student has said their name and who or what they represent, the Instructor talks about the responsibility of representing others and what happens if we behave in a non-constructive way that will impact on who and what we represent. For example, if a student chooses to get into trouble at school, the consequences of that trouble may have a negative impact on the student's family. If a student chooses to do well at school the consequences may impact on the student's family in a positive way.

Keeping in mind who or what we represent can help us make constructive choices for our lives and those around us.

> If we are rewarded, our family is rewarded.
>
> If we are celebrated, our family is celebrated.
>
> If we are punished, our family is punished.
>
> You represent your family,
> the past, the present, the future.
>
> You represent your community,
> you represent yourself.
>
> Make your loved ones proud.
> Make yourself proud.

3. Warm-up game: Hospital Tag
Recommended time allocation: 10 minutes

Refer to session 1 (page 45) for the outline of setting up and managing the warm-up game. The Instructor should remember to get the students to take note of their surroundings and clearly point out the boundary of the game to ensure safety and limit any chance of injury.

Hospital Tag

Hospital Tag is a fast, action-packed game that keeps the students on the move. Hospital Tag fits in with the self-protection aspect of session 6 as it focuses on body awareness and evasive skills. Hospital Tag is also a great deal of fun.

When the students are settled and ready to listen the Instructor explains Hospital Tag.

1. In Hospital Tag every student is a *tagger*. When the Instructors starts the game by calling out 'Go', the students race about, tagging one another.

2. When a student is tagged he loses the use of one of his limbs.

   a) When a student is tagged the first time, he loses the use of one of his arms. The student puts the arm behind his back and keeps it there as he continues with the game, using his remaining limbs to tag the other students.

   b) When a student is tagged a second time he loses the use of his other arm. The student puts his arm behind his back so that now both arms are out of action. The student continues with the game, attempting to tag the other students with his legs and feet.

   c) It is important to stress safety at this point when explaining the game. Students can only tag other students softly, with their legs or feet. There is no kicking in the game. All tagging should be of a safe nature. Any student not playing the game appropriately may need to sit on the side until the game is finished.

   d) When a student is tagged a third time he loses the use of one of his legs. The student raises that leg and must hop in order to move. At this point he is regarded as being 'too unwell' to continue with the game. He needs to go to hospital to get well.

   e) Any tags to students beyond the third tag are not counted. Students only lose the use of three limbs maximum. After that, they are then expected to hop to hospital.

3. The hospital is a designated area of the room to which the student hops. On arriving at the hospital the student must perform exercises five times in order to get well. As the student performs each exercise he must say, 'I am well,' in order to recover. Options for exercises include:

   a) Five step-ups if enough step space is available.

   b) Five press-ups against the wall.

   c) For older groups the Instructor can have the students alternate between five press-ups on the floor and five sit-ups. The first time a student is sent to hospital they perform five press-ups, the second time five sit-ups, the third five press-ups and so on.

4. On completing the exercises in hospital, the student has regained the use of all of his limbs and can return to the game.
5. There is no Goose Guarding. Goose Guarding is when a student stands guard outside the hospital area with the intention of catching students out before they have a chance to get back into the game.
6. Tagging multiple times is allowed but only three tags count.
7. At times a student may feel that they are being picked on by a particular student or students. The Instructor needs to have his eyes on the class at all times. If a student is being targeted repeatedly by a student or students then the situation will need to be addressed. The students may have to be reminded that if they are not going to play a game properly then maybe the game cannot be played. If the targeting continues then the game will have to be stopped.
   a) If the game is stopped for this reason, everyone in the class should be told why the game was stopped and who was responsible. Peer pressure can be an effective tool in encouraging fair play and appropriate behaviour. Students don't like it when their game is stopped short.
   b) Students need to understand that their behaviour affects others.
8. Hospital Tag is played for a set amount of time. There doesn't need to be a particular outcome in order for the game to end.

4. Conditioning

The Instructor brings students back together to form a circle, standing up. Refer to session 1 (page 48) for the outline of setting up and managing the conditioning exercises. Remember, the students should only move as far as they feel comfortable. Avoid injuries. Encourage the students to relax and soften into each stretch.

Stretching 3rd form

Recommended time allocation: 8 minutes

Refer to session 3 (page 103) for the stretching 3rd form positions. Each member of the circle, from left to right or vice versa, is given a turn to say the breathing in and breathing out commands for the exercises (see session 2, page 84).

Brain exercises

Recommended time allocation: 3 minutes

Standing as part of the circle, the Instructor leads students through the brain exercises as described in sessions 1 (page 51) and 4 (page 127).

5. Constructive Response: self-protection

Group discussion: in what ways can people be mean?

Recommended time allocation: 15 minutes

Question 1

In what ways can people be mean?

Self-protection and keeping safe is a large topic. In session 2 we looked at keeping safe around physical contact with appropriate and inappropriate touching. We also explored keeping safe around angry adults.

When discussing emotions we explore keeping safe in relation to the management of our emotions. The exploration of keeping safe and self-protection in session 6 concerns direct threats that may cause harm to students.

In the martial arts, self-defence techniques are practised over and over again until they become automatic responses. While this certainly highlights the danger of reacting or striking without thinking, it is a training technique that can be used in a positive manner. If we consistently train our students to respond to confrontation in a calm, relaxed and responsive manner, they will be more likely to make choices that will serve their best interests. Therefore, as with all of the exercises and challenges in Warrior Kids, repetition is the key: regular and constant practice. The following Constructive Response training is re-visited frequently throughout Warrior Kids.

To begin, we are going to look at responding to physical threats. However, before getting physical it is important to prepare the students by holding a group discussion.

The Instructor and the students sit on the mats in a circle. Each student should be facing the centre of the circle and be clearly visible to the Instructor so that no one is in any way disassociated from the group, whether by their own positioning or by the positioning of another student. The self-protection discussion is generated by questions.

This question might generate a long list of behaviour that can be considered mean, including:

- name-calling,
- teasing,
- saying nasty things about your family,
- taking your things,
- saying mean things about you behind your back,
- not letting you play with them,
- breaking or ruining your stuff,
- trying to take your friends away,
- shoving/pushing,
- intimidating or being threatening,
- pulling hair,
- hitting/punching/kicking,
- shouting at you,
- hurting your friends, and
- hurting your family or pets.

Some students may share experiences at this point. As previously discussed, the Instructor needs to be conscious of disclosures. Refer to the outline for the Sharing Circle in session 1 (page 58), and

the outline of the Keeping Safe and safe touching discussion in session 2 (page 89).

I take this question further by asking, 'Can teachers and other adults be mean?' Adults don't always know the magnitude of a simple gesture, criticism or comment. Children can be emotionally devastated by a random or wayward remark, said intentionally or otherwise. A child may even take a comment the wrong way. Regardless, by asking this question we are allowing the students to process and make sense of this adult behaviour.

Question 2

How do you look after yourself when people are being mean to you?

When asking this question I point out to the students that, from time to time, they are likely to come across people who will be mean to them. Sadly, it is part of life and we need to know how to deal with this sort of behaviour in a way that looks after us. Even as adults we can still encounter meanness.

The answers given can be explored by the group to determine their effectiveness, appropriateness and safety. I query responses that are far-fetched, unsafe or simply not wise; other students in the group tend to set these right. Typical answers the students may give are:

- say, 'Stop it, I don't like it.',
- shout, 'No! Leave me alone!',
- stand up for yourself,
- protect yourself,
- run away or get away if need be. I always stress 'get away' as this encompasses all sorts of strategies, including trickery,
- use a big voice to attract others,
- tell somebody about what's happening,
- don't listen to mean words. Remember, there are people who love and believe in you. Remember the good things that loved ones have said. Remember the good things in your life,
- activate your Warrior Deflector Shield,
- get help.

Question 3

How can we support others when people are being mean to them?

This is an important question as it encourages social conscience and allows the students to think beyond themselves. In standing up for ourselves and for others we make our community a safer place. Some students may find it easier to think of keeping others safe rather than themselves. The answers to question 3 will tend to be a repeat of the answers to question 2, but with another person in mind.

Personal experiences or accounts of family members being treated in a mean way may arise. As previously mentioned, the Instructor needs to be conscious of disclosures and can refer to the outline given in the Sharing Circle in session 1 (page 58).

Constructive Response

Recommended time allocation: 25 minutes

Moving on from the discussion, the Instructor announces to the students that, 'Today we are going to look at self-protection and keeping ourselves safe.' The following are Constructive Response exercises.

Exercise 1

The Instructor explains to the class that a confident child, a child who stands tall with his head held high and who feels good about himself, is a lot less likely to get picked on. So, to start off the students are going to practise standing in the Warrior posture.

1. Remaining in a circle, the students stand up.
2. The students start by imagining their Warrior Deflector Shield is around them. Refer to session 3 (page 122).
3. Following the Instructor's example, the students practise standing tall in the Warrior posture, with their head held high. Breathe in, lengthening the spine and raising the head.
4. The Instructor tells the students to ask themselves, 'How does it feel to stand this way?'
5. The Instructor encourages the students to practise standing in the Warrior posture at home and at school, to practise feeling good about themselves, and to explore this way of being in their interactions with others.
6. Point out that any change takes time, so give it a while.

From this point we look at keeping ourselves physically safe. Each of the following exercises should be illustrated by the Instructor first; with the Instructor taking on the role of the *responder* and a suitable student taking on the role of the *aggressor*, in this case a bully.

When illustrating to the students the Instructor should be mindful of the assisting student and be gentle and considerate of his mental well-being. In other words, the Instructor should be soft and in no way fully direct his anger or intent at any student.

If the Instructor has the assistance of a co-instructor then he could use this person for the display.

As the bully approaches, the responder ...

Exercise 2

1. The students find a partner.
2. One partner will play the role of the *bully* while the other partner will be the *responder*.
3. The *responder* and the *bully* stand about five metres apart, facing one another.
4. The *responder* stands in the Warrior posture.
5. The *bully* walks up to the *responder*. The *responder* reacts by putting one foot back into the relaxed responsive posture. This posture enables the *responder* to create distance between him and the *bully*.
6. The partners swap roles and do the exercise again, with the *bully* approaching the *responder*.
7. Each pair should run through this exercise six times.
8. The Instructor walks around assisting pairs.

... steps back into the relaxed responsive posture.

Session 6

When the Instructor is demonstrating exercise 2 it is a good opportunity for him to acknowledge the signals of the bully's intent; to openly identify the build-up of an attack, that is, recognise the early warning signs. Questions can help lead the way, for example,

'How can you tell when someone is going to bully? What are the early warning signs? What happens to their body?'

When a person is about to bully, there are obvious body language signals that give them away. Some of the answers from the students may include the following:

- overtly angry or upset,
- low brow,
- stern glare,
- tight lips,
- locked jaw,
- distorted or scrunched-up face,
- an uneasy smile,
- puffing up to appear bigger,
- flexed muscles,
- clenched fists,
- concealing something that they may intend to use,
- verbally threatening,
- taunts, verbal or otherwise,
- put-downs,
- tone of voice, and
- showing off to peers.

These are warning signs; when identified they prepare the responder, allowing him to act to protect himself. By exploring and acknowledging these signs in class we are empowering the students and increasing their ability to exercise Constructive Response.

As the bully walks up to push, the responder …

Exercise 3

1. The students find a new partner.
2. One partner will play the role of the *bully* while the other partner will be the *responder*.
3. The *responder* stands in the Warrior posture.
4. The *bully* walks up to and attempts to place two hands on the upper body of the *responder* and push him. The *responder* responds by putting one foot back and raising his hands in the Responsive Posture. The movement is used to evade the force of the *bully's* push.
   a) If the *responder* makes contact with the *bully* in forming the Responsive Posture, it should be gentle.
5. The partners swap roles and do the exercise again.
6. Each pair should run through this exercise six times.

… steps back into the responsive posture, with hands raised and palms facing out.

At this point the Instructor should review the game of Hospital Tag played during the warm-up, in particular noting how evasion was a key part to that game. Evasion is also the key during this exercise.

No matter if the bully is trying to push, punch or kick, the responder should seek to evade the attack. The push in this exercise represents the various forms of attack.

I point out to the students that they aren't designed to get hit. I also remind them of how they had to evade my strikes with the foam sword (page 75). If the students are able to evade my strikes then they can certainly evade the strikes of another.

I stress to the students that they should get out of the way and not get hit. The ability to evade harm and danger is a natural survival instinct.

As mentioned in session 1, children who have been smacked have been conditioned to being hit. They are often told to stay still and to take their punishment. This conditioning can show up during the self-protection training.

I often clarify the difference between the two to these students. I don't condone smacking or hitting of any type, but it is important that students understand that in this instance I am expecting them to abide by their natural instincts and to get themselves out of harm's way. The reason it is important to make this clarification is that the student may go home and evade a smack from a parent, only to end up receiving a more severe punishment. Being hit is a reality for many children.

Exercise 4

The students find a new partner. This exercise is the same as exercise 2, but instead of stepping backwards the *responder* steps out in different directions to evade the *bully's* attack.

Hands should be kept up and ready to deflect the attacker's strike and to give protection. It is important that the hands are relaxed and open in the Responsive Posture as this denotes absence of aggression and won't provoke further aggression. It also means that the student is in a prepared state and is mentally, physically and emotionally ready to protect themselves.

With open hands the student is taking control and can guide and influence the situation. Open hands also encourage the student to keep an open mind. As soon as the hands are closed to make a fist, tension and friction extend up through the arm and into the body and the focus of the mind begins to narrow and close; the student is at risk of losing sight of the bigger perspective.

Exercise 5

Exercise 5 repeats exercise 2, but this time the emotional aspects of an encounter are addressed. Emotions are a part of everyday life; they are a given whether we like it or not. Our way of being with our emotions can either help us or hinder us.

We can choose to swallow our feelings and suppress them until they begin to eat at us from inside. Or we can choose to have our feelings rule our lives. Our anger can be a wild beast from which everyone needs to stay clear. Our fear can dictate our lives. Our hurt can be a constant companion, something to cling to, and our shame can be a shadow at our side. Or our emotions can be our allies, they can provide energy that we can harness and use.

It is natural for a person to feel fear when being confronted: they should. Fear is a survival instinct, it is an emotion designed to keep us safe. When we feel fear we become focused and alert. Our body

As the bully prepares to push, the responder …

… takes the left foot back and around to the side, making a responsive posture.

It is only through fear that we are brave.

and mind are ready for action. This is a perfect state to be in when threatened.

Fear is a friend that warns and prepares us when faced with danger, challenge or even change. It is something we can breathe in to, relax and pay heed to.

However, fear is not an emotion to show when someone is out to hurt or exert power over us. The demonstration of fear will only feed such an intent.

If a person was to cower to a bully and plead, 'Please don't hit me,' then the bully is more likely to hit that person as he can see an easy win. The majority of the time people only choose battles that they believe that they can win. This is saving face. That's why bullies tend to pick on those that they can overpower easily.

Impulsive, random acts of violence are rare. The majority of aggressive acts are calculated and planned. The early warning signs in the build-up to an encounter mentioned earlier demonstrate this. Aggressors choose their targets and their methods. Even in the schoolyard bullies look for an easy win. Such calculation is an exercise of choice. Those who hurt me as a child chose and took advantage of times and places very carefully. And even though my parents used their fists or any object that was close by, they chose to hit my body in places where marks wouldn't be visible to others.

Fear should not be presented in a confrontation. Rather, we should breathe and focus. Being able to do this at a time of challenge and confrontation isn't easy; it is achieved through practice and can take some time to acquire because it is ultimately entering a state of detachment. In the meantime, there is anger.

The wonderful thing about fear is that it is an initial emotion that is commonly followed by a secondary emotion: anger.

Anger can be used in a controlled manner as a self-affirming, constructive energy that keeps us safe and retains clear and firm boundaries in a positive and safe way. This is Controlled Anger and it is a powerful tool. Controlled Anger allows us to assert ourselves, which is essential at times when others are trying to overpower us or abuse and hurt us.

Controlled Anger is not about letting loose and beating the bully up or trashing the place. Nor is it about exerting power or one's will over others. These are abusive acts of anger and will only lead to trouble and hurt for the Responder as much as for the Bully. It is good to point out that it is not okay for the students 'themselves' to hurt or be mean towards others. Keeping safe works both ways; it is about making sure that we touch others in a safe way and that others touch us in a safe way.

Controlled Anger can be used to get someone to back off. In exercise 5 we asked the student to acknowledge their fear internally and then to allow their anger to come through.

'No one has the right to hurt you!' This is a statement that I repeat to the students, reminding them of their rights, reminding them that people are not allowed to hurt them. I prompt the students by saying, 'Show me fire, show me your Warrior Spirit.' The use of the word fire evokes the image and the energy of fire in the students, which gives them a good sense of what we want them to experience and helps them to retain the memory of the desired attitude through word association.

Some students will have difficulty in allowing themselves to feel anger, let alone express it. Even though this may be the case for some of the students, the Instructor should encourage everyone to have a go at exercise 5.

To practise being assertive in a positive way, students are asked to express their anger through their body language and voice.

Again, when demonstrating, the Instructor should be mindful of the assisting student and be gentle and considerate of his mental well-being. In no way should the Instructor fully direct his anger or intent at any student.

1. The students find a new partner.

2. One partner will play the role of the *bully*, the other partner will be the *responder*.

3. The *responder* stands in the Warrior posture.

4. The *bully* walks up and attempts to place two hands on the upper body of the *responder* to push them.

5. As the *bully* approaches, the *responder* stands tall with his head up, looking directly at the *bully* with a strong glare. When the *bully* is about to make contact the *responder* puts one foot back and raises his hands in the Responsive Posture, evading the force of the *bully's* push. At the same time the *responder* roars, 'Leave me alone!' in a loud, direct voice.

    a) 'Leave me alone!' is one option. Students could also roar, 'Back off!', 'Stop!' or 'No!' By being loud the *responder* will attract the attention of others who may be able to assist.

    b) There are many accounts in the martial arts world of people being defeated before they were able to attack, due to the manner of the responder. In some cases it was reported to be the eyes of the responder, the intent glare entering the *bully* through the eyes of the assailant and shattering his spirit. In other cases, it was the kiai or war cry from the responder that entered the assailant and shattered his willpower. There are accounts of the responder's posture being the mitigating factor. In other cases it was the demonstration of unwavering calmness that unnerved the attacker.

    c) It takes a lot of confidence and practice to be calm in the face of adversity, hence the use of anger and assertiveness in the beginning. However, for those students who pursue unwavering confidence, it is certainly something that they can attain.

6. The partners swap roles and do the exercise again.

7. Each pair should run through this exercise six times.

The Responsive Posture is not rigid. The arms should be relaxed. They should not be outstretched, nor should the posture be used as a strike.

By using this posture the *bully* will experience the *responder's* strength of spirit, which can then deter him from continuing with the attack, especially when the action is performed with a roar and a firm glare.

The hands should always be open in the Responsive Posture. If a teacher walks around the corner and sees the *responder* with fists up he will think that the *responder* is fighting. Open hands suggest a reluctance to fight and a desire to sort out issues amicably. Such a response will earn praise.

As a variation, instead of stepping backwards, the responder could ...

... step forwards into the responsive posture as the bully approaches and experience how powerful that feels.

A self-protection challenge

1. The Instructor assembles the students into a line, sitting down.

2. One by one, each student takes a turn to stand five metres in front of the Instructor, facing him in the Warrior posture.

3. It is now the Instructor who plays the role of the *bully*. Taking on the persona and mannerisms of a bully, the Instructor walks to the student with the intention of pushing him.

    a) The Instructor does not make physical contact with the responding student. It is simply the intent that the student is expected to experience and respond to.

4. As the *responder*, the student moves into the Responsive Posture and uses his eyes, voice and manner to deter the attack, as practised in exercise 5.

    a) Each student should be able to express anger using the confines given throughout the class. The Instructor should not be intimidated or fearful of the students. If the Instructor is fearful of witnessing or being faced with a student's expression of anger then the Instructor should find someone to assist with the exercises before the class.

    b) Encourage the students to stand strong and to be brave. They are expected to stand up to the bully, without the use of fists and other harming tactics.

5. Students who perform the challenge strongly pass. Those that do any of the following must repeat the exercise, with positive encouragement from the Instructor.

    a) Look away when the Instructor approaches.

    b) Laugh.

    c) Use a soft, indirect voice or soft, indirect language.

    d) Tremble or cower.

    e) Respond outside the challenge perimeters or behave inappropriately.

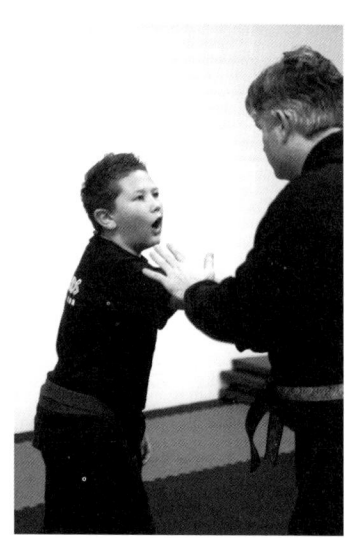

Session 6

Any student who continuously behaves inappropriately should be told that they are clearly not ready to do the challenge and be directed to sit down again in line with the other students.

6. If a student cries or collapses during the challenge they are clearly demonstrating that they are not in the right mental and/or emotional condition to face the challenge.

   a) The Instructor should take the student back to sit in the line with the other students. This is important as the student should not be isolated or singled out in any way, causing him to feel separate from the group.

   b) Have a fellow student or sibling (if there is one in the group) sit close beside the emotional student. If the parent or caregiver is in the room then they could support him. However, it is important to avoid rescuing. The supporting person shouldn't try to smother or stop the student from feeling the emotion. The idea is that the child gets to feel the emotion in a safely contained environment, and that the healthy expression of emotion is validated by the group. The supporting person need only sit close to the student, place a hand on his shoulder or even rub his back.

   c) If the child is very distraught then they could go and be with their parent in the room.

   d) If you are running a school programme, the teacher present could support the student.

   e) As an Instructor I may support the emotional student personally, hugging him to my side and reassuring him; telling him that he was brave for just coming to class, let alone standing up to have a go at the challenge.

   f) I would ensure that the emotional student doesn't feel bad in any way: the fact is, they did complete the challenge. The experience of each individual student will be unique to that student. It may have been more challenging for the emotional student to stand up in the first place than for another student to complete the whole challenge. There is no pass or fail. The experience itself, mentally, emotionally, physically and spiritually, and being with that experience, is the real challenge.

7. Each student who stood to face the challenge should be praised for their efforts.

2nd breathing exercise: activating the Warrior Deflector Shield

Recommended time allocation: 3 minutes

The Instructor and the students stand around the gym mats in a circle. Each student should be facing the centre of the circle and be clearly visible to the Instructor so that no one is in any way disassociated from the group, whether by their own positioning or by the positioning of another student.

The Instructor leads the students, demonstrating and talking them through the 2nd breathing exercise and the activation of the Warrior Deflector Shield. Refer to session 3 (page 121) for the outline of the 2nd breathing exercise.

Group discussion: recap

Recommended time allocation: 15 minutes

The class sits on the gym mats in a circle. The Instructor acknowledges the group's efforts during the self-protection aspect of the class. The Instructor talks to the students about the importance of creating distance and evading an attack. To help with this, the Instructor asks for two volunteers from the group to demonstrate one of the self-protection exercises.

1. The class moves back, increasing the size of the circle. The volunteers step into the middle to demonstrate one of the exercises.
2. The Instructor has the opportunity to praise or correct the volunteers' attempt.
3. On completing the exercise the volunteers rejoin their classmates in the circle.
4. The Instructor and students clap for the volunteers in appreciation of their efforts.

Following this, the Instructor asks for two more volunteers to demonstrate another of the self-protection exercises. Further volunteers can be requested beyond this so that all of the self-protection exercises are demonstrated once. The Instructor points out that the exercises practised are techniques that the students can use to keep themselves safe.

Once the self-protection exercises have been demonstrated the Instructor brings the students' attention back to the earlier group discussion by saying something like, 'To begin our self-protection training today we discussed the ways people can be mean. We also discussed how you can look after yourself when people are being mean to you. What are some of the ways that you could use to look after yourself when people are being mean?' This gives the students the opportunity to revisit the answers they gave earlier and to offer any new ones.

Following this, the Instructor should encourage the students to practise standing tall in the Warrior posture at home and at school and to practise feeling good about themselves and to explore this way of being in their interactions with others. Remind them that it takes practice to adopt this way of being.

The Instructor also reminds the students to be considerate in their dealings with others. Warrior Kids should practise being gentle with themselves, gentle with others and gentle with the world.

Finally, the Instructor presents the Koosh ball. Each member of the circle, from left to right or vice-versa, has a turn to hold the Koosh ball. When a student has the Koosh ball he says how the class was for him. The Instructor may encourage the students to say one thing they liked about the class and one they didn't like about the class.

This last exercise is a time of sharing. What students say cannot be discussed, only heard and acknowledged. The Instructor should speak last, out of respect to the students.

6. Closing words

Closing

Recommended time allocation: 1 minute

The Instructor directs students to assemble on the mats, standing in a circle as they did at the beginning of the class.

The Instructor asks for a volunteer from the group to say some words to end the class.

When the closing words have been said the Instructor acknowledges the speaker with appreciation and concludes with, 'Remember to take what you brought with you today, your shoes, socks, watches, water bottle, jersey and I'll see you next time.'

> Well done! You have completed session 6.
>
> As an Instructor you are a role model to your students, their families, to countless people in your community and beyond.
> Therefore, consider the following:
> Do you stand tall?; do you hold your head high?; do you feel good about yourself?
>
> The way that you feel about yourself is your responsibility.
> The way that you allow yourself to be treated is your responsibility.
> Only you can change it.
>
> Warrior Kids are expected to choose to have a good life through the making of constructive choices. Warrior Kids Instructors are expected to lead the way.
>
> Be gentle with yourself,
> gentle with others,
> and gentle with your world.

Session 7

> **EQUIPMENT**
>
> ▸ 8 x gym mats, size 1200 x 1800 mm
> ▸ Koosh balls (one for each student)
> ▸ chairs for parents and caregivers

Introduction

Session 7 starts off with what will become a popular warm-up game, Octopus. Students then revisit bodywork that featured earlier in the programme, namely rolling in four directions and handstands. The front break fall and cartwheels are introduced, taking the students' physical abilities further. The Run and Yell exercise allows the students to exert energy while expressing anger and frustration. Then it's on to emotional awareness using the Emotion Squares activity, where each student gets to share experiences. This is a session of depth and empowerment, enjoy.

The outcomes for session 7 are that the students will:

○ be more confident with basic body work,

○ be able to verbalise their feelings,

○ be more confident in identifying and appropriately expressing emotions.

Lesson overview

1. Opening words.
2. Round of introductions: a round of names and each student names a role model.
3. Warm-up game: Octopus.
4. Conditioning: Stretching 1st form; Brain exercises.
5. Body work: Rolling 4 directions; Front breakfall; Handstands and cartwheels.
6. Run and Yell.
7. 1st breathing exercise.
8. Emotion Squares.
9. Closing words.

1. Opening words

Recommended time allocation: 1 minute

The Instructor directs students to remove their shoes and socks and to sit on the mats in a circle. Once the group is settled the Instructor has the students stand up. The Instructor then asks for a volunteer to say some opening words to commence the class. Refer to session 1 (page 44).

2. Round of introductions

Recommended time allocation: 3 minutes

Each member of the circle, from left to right or vice-versa, takes their turn to say their name and to name a role model, someone that they look up to.

A role model is someone that a student admires, someone that inspires them and someone that they would like to be like. A role model could be someone that the student knows, a family member or a friend. A role model could be someone famous. It could be someone who is alive, someone from the past or even a fictional character such as a superhero (someone who saves and helps others). For some students it may be an animal or a pet that is a role model. It is the students' choice. Refer to session 1 (page 44) for the set-up of Introductions.

3. Warm-up game: Octopus

Recommended time allocation: 10 minutes

Refer to session 1 (page 45) for setting up and managing a warm-up game. The Instructor should remember to get the students to take note of their surroundings and clearly point out the boundary of the game to ensure safety and limit any chance of injury.

Octopus

Octopus is one of the most popular games in Warrior Kids. As with a number of the warm-up games, Octopus is commonly played in schools. Students may have played different versions of the game, however, the following version is the one I use.

The students stand in a line along one end of the room facing the Instructor, who is standing out in front. When the students are settled and ready to listen, the Instructor explains Octopus.

1. One student is chosen to stand in the middle of the room (or the predetermined game area if the room is large). The student in the middle is named the *octopus*. The remaining students are *fish*.

2. When the *octopus* is ready she calls out, 'Octopus!' When the *fish* hear 'Octopus!', they run to the other end of the room.

3. The *octopus* pursues and tags as many *fish* as possible before they reach the other end, where they are safe from the *octopus* and cannot be tagged.

4. *Fish* that are tagged become *seaweeds* and must stand on the spot where they were tagged. *Seaweeds* cannot move their feet. They must remain on the spot and aid the *octopus* by tagging any *fish* who come close.

    a) *Fish* who are tagged by *seaweeds* become *seaweeds*. They must stand on the spot where they were tagged and aid the *octopus* by tagging any *fish* who come close.

    b) The one time that *seaweeds* can move their feet is when all of the *fish* have reached one end. The *seaweeds* can then turn around to face them. However, they must be standing in the exact same spot where they were tagged.

    c) The role of the Instructor is to monitor the game and ensure that students are standing where they're supposed to be.

    d) Some students may try and move when the Instructor isn't looking. Any tag where a *seaweed* moves is dismissed.

5. *Fish* that run outside the predetermined game area instantly become *seaweeds*. The Instructor places such students somewhere in the game area where they must aid the *octopus*. Like the other *seaweeds*, they must remain standing on the spot where they are placed.

Fish that are tagged become *seaweeds*.

6. Disputes may rise from time to time about whether a student was tagged or not. Students will get tagged at one stage or another. This is something that they have to accept. If the Instructor is unsure and didn't see, she can hear from witnesses to help determine if a student was tagged or not. If the Instructor still isn't sure, she can inform the students that she will be watching next time.

7. If students do not run when 'Octopus!' is called, the *octopus* can count to five and any students remaining in the safe zone instantly become *seaweeds*. These students are placed somewhere in the game area where they must aid the *octopus*.

8. Tags must be safe and respectful.

9. Students need to watch out for one another and avoid knocking into others.

10. Students should demonstrate self-control throughout the game. An extra condition that I add to Octopus to help with self-control is that students are not allowed to touch the end walls. They must stop just before they reach the wall.

11. Once the *octopus* has tagged and turned each *fish* into a *seaweed*, the round is finished. Depending on time, the Instructor decides whether or not to play another round by choosing a different student to take on the role of the *octopus*.

12. Some students may find being the *octopus* a challenge, especially to tag the *fish*. It is important that the Instructor allows such a student to complete their role as the *octopus* and under no circumstances should the student be replaced or allowed to quit from the role. The Instructor can help the student by making changes to the game's boundaries or even by joining the game and allowing herself to be turned into a *seaweed*. However, the Instructor's overall attention should remain on the game and all of the students.

4. Conditioning

The Instructor brings students back together to form a circle standing up. Refer to session 1 (page 48) for an outline of setting up and managing the conditioning exercises. Remember the students should only move as far as they feel comfortable. Avoid injuries. Encourage the students to relax and soften into each stretch.

Stretching 1st form

Recommended time allocation: 8 minutes

Refer to session 1 for the stretching 1st form positions (page 49). Each member of the circle, from left to right or vice-versa, is given a turn to say the breathing in and breathing out commands (see session 2, page 84).

Brain exercises

Recommended time allocation: 3 minutes

Standing as part of the circle, the Instructor leads students through the brain exercises, as described in session 1 (page 51) and session 4 (page 127).

5. Body work
Recommended time allocation: 10 minutes

Refer to session 1 (page 52) for the outline of setting up and managing the tumbling exercises.

Remaining in the circle, the Instructor looks around the group and chooses two students who have modelled appropriate and constructive behaviour and acknowledges their behaviour aloud to the class. The Instructor then leads both students to the front of the mats and has them sit down, with ample space between them. The Instructor tells the remaining students that at the command 'Go' they are to line up behind one of the two leaders, make two lines and sit down. The Instructor should ensure that no one moves until she says go.

Once all the students are lined up and the lines are as even as possible, the Instructor introduces the next activity and goes on to explain and demonstrate the first exercise.

Rolling 4 directions

In session 7 the students are given the opportunity to practise rolling 4 directions from the Crouching Frog posture. The 4 directions are:

1. rolling sideways to the left,
2. rolling sideways to the right,
3. rolling forwards, and
4. rolling backwards.

The students practised these rolls for the first time during sessions 1 and 2 of Warrior Kids.

Side rolls
Revisit and run through the side roll techniques explored in session 1 (page 53). Each line should run through twice, one time rolling from the left and the second time rolling from the right.

Forward roll
After the side roll revisit the forward roll techniques explored in session 1 (page 53). Each line should run through twice.

Back roll
Revisit and run through the back roll techniques explored in session 2 (page 88). Each line should run through twice.

I like to alternate the lines so that one student rolls at a time. Doing this means an instructor can observe each student's progress.

Front breakfall

A breakfall is a technique for breaking one's fall. It is a way of falling and landing to minimise the risk of injury. Breakfalls are a good skill for students to practise and adopt as they help them to be mindful in the care and protection of their bodies.

The first breakfall technique that students learn in Warrior Kids is the front breakfall, used to prevent injury when falling forwards.

The student at the front of each line steps out on to the centre of the mats. This is important as it creates distance from the line of students directly behind her, which means no one will get kicked.

Start seated in the 1st knee posture (see photo, below left). Fall forwards, putting hands and forearms in a triangular shape in front of the body. The arms from the elbow through to the fingertips are laid flat on the floor. Prior to impact, turn the face sideways, protecting it from the ground. When colliding with the floor, raise the right leg out to the rear to help lessen the impact of the landing.

Each student should have two attempts at the front breakfall then move to the back of the line so as the next student can have their turn.

The first knee posture.

With smaller groups, there is no need for lines when practising techniques such as the front breakfall.

Turning the face to the side means students will avoid banging their nose on the floor when they collide.

Handstands

Revisit and run through the handstand techniques explored in session 2 (page 97). Each line should run through twice.

Cartwheels

As with the rolls and handstands, I give the students two ways of performing a cartwheel. They can give both ways a go or just choose one.

The students stand up in their lines. The student at the front of each line steps out on to the centre of the mats, creating distance from the line of students directly behind her.

Each student should have two attempts at a cartwheel then move to the back of the line.

Assisting students with cartwheels

Some students will never have performed a cartwheel. However, the Instructor would be best to avoid trying to physically assist them. Instead of becoming reliant on the Instructor, students should be encouraged to utilise their skill and ability in finding their own cartwheels.

1st cartwheel

The 1st cartwheel is an essential start for students who haven't done cartwheels before or who may have not done one for some time. It slowly and safely leads into cartwheels without pressure and the technique builds confidence.

Stand with one leg forward, hands above the head, facing sideways. The leg in front should be the leg that feels most comfortable. (Typically with cartwheels a student will favour one side, either the left or the right. Students should focus on getting confident performing a cartwheel on their favoured side before attempting it on the other side.)

If starting with the left leg in front, the body will be facing right. Bending down, place the left hand on the floor, followed by the right hand, which is placed ahead of the left. Lift the right leg sideways and out to the right, then lift the left leg and vault forwards, keeping the hands on the floor. It can help if the student is set up to vault their legs over a line on the floor or a join in the mats.

The students are not expected to raise their legs high when attempting the 1st cartwheel. In fact, it is best if they keep their legs low for the first few times. For some children, just giving it a go will be an achievement.

After practising the 1st cartwheel, students can be encouraged to lift their legs higher and maybe to straighten the legs, pointing the toes at the ceiling. This takes the students closer to the 2nd cartwheel.

The 1st cartwheel is a safe start for students who are inexperienced at doing cartwheels. By having the students take their legs out to the side that they are facing, we are limiting the risk of injury. If a student moved their legs in the opposite direction to the one that they are facing, there is a risk that they will damage a wrist, arm or shoulder.

The 1st cartwheel …

… is a safe way …

… of starting …

… to learn …

… the basic mechanics of cartwheeling.

2nd cartwheel – *cartwheel with the left leg in front*

Some students will already be confident performing cartwheels. This method will allow them to practise their form.

Stand with the left leg forward and the right leg back. Face the right with hands above the head. Turn the body sideways in a wheel-like fashion, raising the right leg and lowering the torso to place the left hand on the floor, followed by the right hand. At this point the left foot also leaves the floor. Wheeling over, the right foot is placed on the floor ahead of the right hand, the left hand is lifted off the floor followed by the right hand, as the left foot lands after the right foot. The

cartwheel finishes with the student standing upright.

Students practising the 2nd cartwheel can be encouraged to slow their movement and count each time they touch the floor. Their left hand would be 'one', the right hand 'two', the right foot 'three' and the left foot 'four'. The Instructor can even challenge the students to see how slowly they can go.

The Instructor acknowledges and praises each honest attempt from the students and points out any areas of their cartwheels that they could work on to improve.

Students can take the first cartwheel further by raising their legs higher.

Further challenge

For those students who are well practised at performing the second cartwheel and demonstrate a high level of competency and skill, challenge them to give their other side a go. Students will favour one side of their body for doing cartwheels and those that have a lot of experience have often worked on strengthening one side while neglecting the other. By practising on both sides students will develop greater co-ordination and skill.

Students practising their other side may be back to square one, just like a beginner, which is a humbling experience for some. The Instructor should encourage such students to give it a go. Remind them that they can already do cartwheels on one side, so they'll certainly be able to do it on the other.

Tell the students to mentally visualise themselves performing a cartwheel on their other side, to see each movement. Encourage the students to think of the mechanics of the movement. Which hand will touch the floor first? Which part of the body will be second, third and so on? The student can even start with the first cartwheel.

Run the lines through the cartwheel practice two or three times.

Further challenges are explored as the students progress through the grades.

6. Run and Yell

Recommended time allocation: 10 minutes

The Instructor has the students line up along one end of the room. The Instructor stands in front. Each student should be facing the Instructor and be clearly visible so that no one is in any way disassociated from the group, whether by their own positioning or by the positioning of another student. When each student is settled and listening the Instructor prepares them for the next challenge.

The Run and Yell exercise is a fun challenge that allows the students to let go and burn off excess energy. The Run and Yell is used in later sessions to prepare and to help students get in touch with their anger. It is also a good exercise for refocusing and changing the energy in a class.

Run and Yell: part 1

1. When the Instructor calls 'Go!' the students run to the other end of the room.

2. The Instructor points out that she is looking to see which students have good self-control. On reaching the other end, students must stop running at a designated point, such as on a line or before a wall, without touching it. An assistant could stand at a point and be the visual reference that the students are not allowed to run past.

3. Students must be aware of those around them. No one is allowed to be knocked over or pushed.

4. The Instructor moves to the side, out of the path of the students.

5. When each student is settled and behind the starting point, the Instructor calls 'Go!' and monitors the students as they race to the other end.

6. The Instructor points out students who demonstrated great self-control and points out those who could be doing better.

7. Repeat four times.

Run and Yell: part 2

1. When the Instructor calls 'Go!' the students run. This time, however, the students must demonstrate their Warrior Spirit and yell as loudly as they can, all the way to the other end.

    a) I point out to the students that I am an adult, standing in front of them, asking them to be as loud as they possibly can. That normally doesn't happen, so make the most of it!

    b) It is important to stress that students are expected to yell, not scream. Screaming uses the voice box in a completely different way from yelling, and as yelling is a part of the Constructive Response training, we really want the students to practise and get used to using their voice in this way. Screaming is also a lot harder on the ears!

    c) Students must not yell out words. They yell as they would if they were giving a war cry.

2. Again, the Instructor points out that she is looking to see which students have good self-control. On reaching the other end, students must stop running and yelling.

3. Students must be aware of those around them. No one is allowed to be knocked over or pushed.

4. The Instructor moves to the side, out of the path of the students.

5. When each student is settled and behind the starting point, the Instructor calls 'Go!' and monitors the students as they race to the other end.

6. The Instructor points out students who performed the challenge well and points out those who could be doing better.

7. Repeat four times.

7. Breathing exercise

Recommended time allocation: 2 minutes

The Instructor has the students form a standing circle around the outside of the mats. The Instructor leads the students, demonstrating and talking them through the 1st breathing exercise. Refer to session 1 (page 57) for the outline of the 1st breathing exercise.

8. Emotion Squares

Recommended time allocation: 40 minutes

The students sit in a line in front of the mats. When everyone is settled and ready to listen, the Instructor explains the Emotion Squares activity. This activity is another opportunity for students to share. Emotion Squares works with specific emotions, allowing the students to identify, express and manage emotions and emotional triggers.

Emotion Squares allows the students to focus on one particular emotion that relates to an experience they have had.

Refer to the Sharing Circle (page 58) and the 'Issues that may arise in Warrior Kids sharing activities' in session 1 (page 59) for the outline and guidelines for running sharing activities.

Emotion Squares utilises eight gym mats. The Instructor steps out on to the mats and points out that there are eight mats in total, however, for the Emotion Squares activity, two mats are counted as one so that four squares are created.

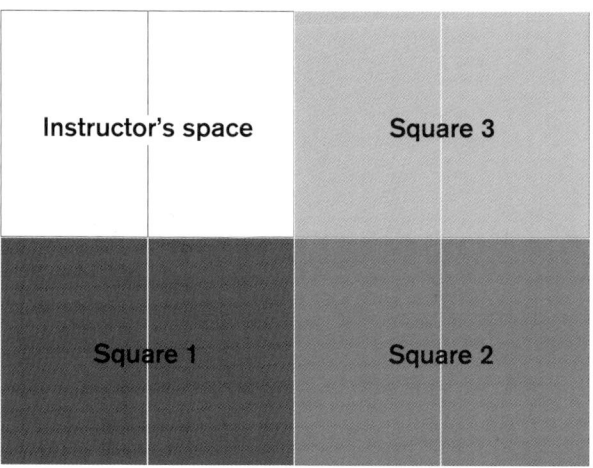

Emotion Squares: part 1

The Instructor moves on to the two mats identified as Square 1 and says to the students, 'If in the last week you can think of a time when you felt *annoyed*, a little bit angry, then when I say "Go" you will come and sit in square number one.'

The Instructor moves on to the two mats identified as Square 2 and says, 'If in the last week you can think of a time when you felt *angry* about something, then when I say "Go" you will come and sit on square number two.'

The Instructor moves on to the two mats identified as square 3 and says, 'If in the last week you can think of a time when you felt *furious*, really angry about something, then when I say "Go" you will come and sit on square number three.'

The Instructor moves back on to Square 1 and says, 'You have a choice, you can choose to share an experience when you felt a little bit angry or,' the Instructor moves on to the Square 2, 'you can choose to share an experience when you felt angry or,' the Instructor moves on to Square 3, 'you can choose to share an experience when you felt furious, really angry. So, we have little, middle and big.'

Session 7

The use of Koosh balls

If there are enough Koosh balls, the Instructor could give one to each student. This will help stimulate the students' thought processing, allowing them to prepare what it is that they have to say. Koosh balls will also help the students to focus on the task at hand. Refer to the One 2 One activity in session 5 (page 151) for guidelines.

'Now, there are 24 hours in a day, 7 days in a week. Lots of things happen in our lives every day and we go through a whole range of emotions. There is nothing wrong with feeling angry. Anger is natural. I can tell you right now that I have felt annoyed this week, I have felt angry and I have felt furious, and that's normal and healthy.'

Hearing that the Instructor feels anger in her life will normalise the natural experience for each of the students. This is not about the behaviour derived of the feeling, it is the experience of the emotion itself.

The two mats identified as the Instructor's space are for the Instructor only. Students must choose one of the three allocated squares to sit on. Students that are not sure or for any reason find the activity difficult, should start by sitting on Square 1. The Instructor may have to come back to these students, allowing them more time to think of an experience to share.

Every student is expected to share. However, by giving a choice of three squares we are allowing the students to choose a level of sharing that they feel comfortable with, relieving them of any pressure to share embarrassing, shameful or regretted moments. The students have to feel safe with their sharing.

When the Instructor says 'Go' the students sit on their chosen squares.

The Instructor sits on the mats identified as the Instructor's space. Each student should be facing the Instructor and be clearly visible to her. The Instructor says to the students, 'Each person is going to have the opportunity to share why they felt angry, so make sure that you are sitting up, that you are comfortable and that you are ready to listen.' Some students may try and lie down. The Instructor will need to ensure that the students sit upright throughout the activity. Some students may move about excessively. The Instructor will need to contain such interruptions.

The Instructor looks to Square 1 and asks a student who is ready to share why they felt annoyed. The Instructor listens and reflects back to the student what he heard the student say, allowing the student to clarify her experience.

Most experiences will simply require the Instructor to thank the student and move on to the next student. However, certain experiences shared may require further exploration by the Instructor to ensure that the student responded in a safe and appropriate manner. For example, if a student speaks of being annoyed or angry due to being bullied at school, what did they do about it? If a student was angry with a sibling or Mum, how did they respond? Was it appropriate and constructive, deserving of praise, or did the student choose to behave in a way that brought about negative consequences? Did they yell, break things or lash out?

Regardless of how the student responded, we want to highlight and identify constructive responses that will keep the student safe and free from punishment or retribution; behaviour that brings the student the best possible outcome.

The Instructor needs to avoid telling off or shaming a student for non-constructive behaviour. The Instructor must remain neutral and detached, while also maintaining care and consideration for the student's overall well-being. If the students know that Instructors are there to support them, they will trust us. I would convey my feelings of sadness, frustration or

Unlike the Sharing Circle, the Instructor does not share during Emotion Squares. The Instructor's role is to facilitate and oversee the process.

Emotion Squares: part 2

disappointment about non-constructive behaviour, however, I would not tell a student off. Asking the student, 'What would you do differently next time?' is a way of getting her to consider alternative responses and behaviour.

When the students seated on Square 1 have shared (apart from any that may not be ready yet), the Instructor turns her attention to Square 2, where students are willing to share an experience when they felt angry. The Instructor elicits accounts from these students.

When the students in Square 2 have completed sharing, the Instructor can check back with Square 1 for any students that weren't ready to share earlier. Following this, the Instructor can then move to Square 3 and allow those students to share an experience when they felt furious.

At the completion of sharing anger experiences, the Instructor acknowledges the students' efforts and thanks the students for their sharing, then moves on to part 2.

Now it is time to change the emotion. The emotion that the Instructor chooses depends on the amount of class time remaining. If the activity is flowing well and time allows for two or three more rounds of Emotion Squares, the Instructor could choose to have the students share an experience of when they felt sad.

To do this the Instructor moves on to Square 1 and announces to the students, 'If in the last week you can think of a time when you felt a *little sad* or disappointed, then when I say "Go" you will come and sit on square number one.'

The Instructor moves on to the two mats identified as Square 2 and says, 'If in the last week you can think of a time when you felt *sad* about something, then when I say "Go" you will come and sit on square number two.'

The Instructor moves on to the two mats identified as Square 3 and says, 'If in the last week you can think of a time when you felt *really sad* about something, then when I say "Go" you will come and sit on square number three.'

The Instructor says 'Go!' and the students sit on their chosen squares. Again, every student is expected to share. However, by giving the students the choice of the three squares we allow them to determine their level of sharing.

Alternatively, the Instructor could choose to have the students share an experience of when they felt scared. Square number one would be a *little scared*, maybe nervous, square number two would be *scared* and square number three would be *frightened*.

The Instructor may choose to have the students share an experience of when they felt ashamed. Shame is an important emotion to explore and in Emotion Squares I focus on shame in terms of conscience, guilt and regret, rather than embarrassment, for example, of falling over or being teased. I would ask the students to think of a time when they did something that wasn't good, something that they regretted doing. Maybe they hurt someone, maybe they lied or maybe they got into trouble.

In processing shame the students are learning the value of the emotion and how such a feeling can encourage us to make better choices in our treatment of others. By declaring shame the students are then free of it and can move on and take responsibility for their

Session 7

actions. Square 1 would be a *little ashamed*, Square 2 would be *ashamed* and Square 3 would be *really ashamed*.

When the students have shared one or two of the emotions mentioned above, the Instructor can then move the students to part 3 of Emotion Squares.

Emotion Squares: part 3

To finish Emotion Squares the students get to share an experience when they felt happy. Finishing with happiness is extremely important as it ensures that the students leave the class on a high note. I want students to leave class feeling good about themselves and to have a balanced view of life.

Square 1 would be a *little happy*, Square 2 would be *happy* and Square 3 would be *excited*.

On completion of Emotion Squares the Instructor acknowledges the students' efforts and thanks them for their sharing.

9. Closing words

The Instructor directs students to assemble on the mats in a standing circle.

Closing

Recommended time allocation: 1 minute

The Instructor asks for a volunteer from the group to say some words to end the class.

When the closing words have been said the Instructor acknowledges the speaker with appreciation and concludes with 'Remember to take what you brought with you today, your shoes, socks, watches, water bottle, jersey and I'll see you next time.'

> Session 7 is done!
>
> All aspects of Warrior Kids will help to keep you healthy.
> By practising the body work and the conditioning exercises, and by practising the sharing of your own experiences and feelings, along with the appropriate management of emotions and stress, you will be able to maintain a healthy existence, physically, mentally, emotionally and spiritually.
>
> Make time to do your own training and practice. Train in the body work and conditioning aspects of Warrior Kids.
> Take time to share with another your experiences of life, the good times and the not-so-good times.
> Talk about your feelings. Manage your emotions and your stress.
> Practise what you teach.
> Be true to your authentic self and plan to succeed.

Session 8

EQUIPMENT

- 8 x gym mats, size 1200 x 1800 mm
- Koosh balls (one for each student)
- chairs for parents and caregivers

Introduction

Session 8 begins with two warm-up games: Instructor Says, where the students get to go over the Warrior Kids postures, and then it's Posture Tag, where the postures are used to evade a Koosh ball. Later, the students are introduced to two evasive forms, the core components of Constructive Response and self protection in Warrior Kids. The students get to use the movement practised in the 1st evasive form as a release to a wrist grab. Following this, the students partner up for the One 2 One activity and share what they like about their classmates. The session concludes with the Sharing Circle.

The outcomes for session 8 are that the students will:

- be more confident in using the Warrior Kids postures as self protection,
- have a basic understanding of the first two evasive forms,
- be able to perform a release from a wrist grab,
- be able to identify and deliver compliments affirming others.

Lesson overview

1. Opening words.
2. Round of introductions: a round of names and a job that each student would like to do when they are older.
3. Warm-up games: Instructor Says; Posture Tag.
4. Conditioning: Stretching 2nd form; Brain exercises.
5. Constructive Response: self protection.
   a) Evasive forms.
   b) Release from a wrist grab.
6. 2nd breathing exercise and the Activation of the Warrior Deflector Shield.
7. One 2 One: what do you like about your partner?
8. Sharing Circle: a low and high point.
9. Closing words.

1. Opening words

Recommended time allocation: 1 minute

The Instructor directs students to remove their shoes and socks and to sit on the mats in a circle. Once the group is settled the Instructor asks the students to stand. The Instructor then asks for a volunteer to say some opening words to commence the class. Refer to session 1 (page 44).

2. Round of introductions

Recommended time allocation: 3 minutes

Each member of the circle, from left to right or vice-versa, takes their turn to say their name and a job that they would like to do when older.

When presenting this introduction I tell the students that they are young and that they can change their mind as many times as they want in regard to a job or career that they would like to do, but for right now, at this very moment, what job do they think they would like to do when they get older?

Refer to session 1 for the set-up of introductions (page 44).

3. Warm-up games

Overall recommended time allocation: 15 minutes

Refer to session 1 (page 45) for the outline of setting up and managing a warm-up game. The Instructor should remember to get the students to take note of their surroundings and clearly point out the boundary of the game to ensure safety and limit any chance of injury.

In session 8 there are two warm-up games. The game called Instructor Says prepares the students for the second warm-up game called Posture Tag.

Instructor Says

Recommended time allocation: 5 minutes

The Instructor has the students step back to make their initial circle larger. He then takes the students through a few rounds of Instructor Says. Refer to session 1 for the outline and set-up of Instructor Says (page 69).

Posture Tag

Recommended time allocation: 10 minutes

Now that the students have revisited the postures of Warrior Kids, it is time to move on to the second game, Posture Tag. Posture Tag allows the students to practise the postures further and encourages them to enhance their evasive skills. This game requires one Koosh ball. When the students are settled and ready to listen, the Instructor explains Posture Tag.

1. The Instructor starts Posture Tag as the *tagger*.

2. The *tagger* tosses the Koosh ball into the air, allowing it to fall on the floor a few metres from him. As soon as the Koosh ball leaves the *tagger's* hands, the students can move away from him.

3. When the *tagger* picks up the Koosh ball the students must stand still, forming any one of the Warrior Kids postures. The students must try to form a different Warrior Kids posture each time.

4. Throwing the Koosh ball from where it landed, the *tagger* tries to hit one of the students.

   a) The Koosh ball is thrown lightly so as not to hurt the student.

   b) The Koosh ball cannot be thrown at the head or face. Such tags are not counted.

   c) The Koosh ball cannot be thrown recklessly. The *tagger* should be aware of lights and other hazards in the room. I've had the odd Koosh ball get stuck up in a roof, so it is best to encourage the *tagger* to keep the ball low.

   d) Any student who goes outside the perimeters of the game will require a warning. A further breach could result in the student having to sit out the remainder of the game. As with all Warrior Kids activities, safety is essential.

5. To evade the Koosh ball the students can take one step into another Warrior Kids' posture. For example, a student standing in the central posture can evade the Koosh ball by taking a step backwards and forming the responsive posture.

6. If a student is hit by the Koosh ball, he becomes the *tagger*. As soon as he picks up the Koosh ball the students must stand still in a Warrior Kids posture.

7. If the *tagger* misses in his attempt to tag someone, the students are able to move away. As soon as the *tagger* has picked up the Koosh ball the students must stand still in a Warrior Kids Posture.

   a) If the Koosh ball goes out of the designated game area the students do not have to stop in a posture until the *tagger* has stepped back on to the game area holding the Koosh ball.

   b) The *tagger* throws the Koosh ball from where he re-enters the game area.

8. Students wanting a turn at being the *tagger* may try to crowd around the student with the koosh ball, hoping to get tagged. The Instructor should advise the *tagger* to ignore these students and to go for those who are playing the game properly. However, there are times when moving closer to the *tagger* is appropriate. Some older students may take the initiative and stand close to let a younger *tagger* get an easy shot.

9. To help *taggers* who are finding the role difficult, the Instructor can stop the game and call 'Change Tagger'. The Instructor nominates a new *tagger* and the game continues. To ensure that the game continues to flow, the Instructor can tell the newly nominated *tagger* that he cannot tag the last person who was in.

10. Posture Tag is played for a set amount of time. There doesn't need to be a particular outcome in order for the game to end.

4. Conditioning

The Instructor brings students back together to form a standing circle. Refer to session 1 (page 48) for an outline of setting up and managing the conditioning exercises. Remember, the students should only move as far as they feel comfortable. Avoid injuries. Encourage the students to relax and soften into each stretch.

Stretching 2nd form

Recommended time allocation: 8 minutes

Refer to session 2 for the stretching 2nd form positions (page 84). Each member of the circle, from left to right or vice versa, is given a turn to say the breathing in and breathing out commands (see session 2, page 84).

Stretches can be taken further.

Brain exercises

Recommended time allocation: 3 minutes

Standing as part of the circle, the Instructor leads students through the brain exercises as described in session 1 (page 51) and session 4 (page 127).

5. Constructive Response

Recommended time allocation: 15 minutes

The five evasive forms

In session 8 we further the students' Constructive Response skills. To achieve this they follow the Instructor and perform the 1st and 2nd evasive forms. 'Forms' are a collection of postures.

The evasive forms are the core components of Constructive Response. The evasive forms are set arrangements of movement used to evade physical threats. These can be performed in a number of ways.

The movements are relaxed and flowing, which indicate control and confidence. Throughout the forms the hands are open, with palms facing forwards. The hands are kept up to shield and are used to deflect. The evasive forms employ eight directions of movement.

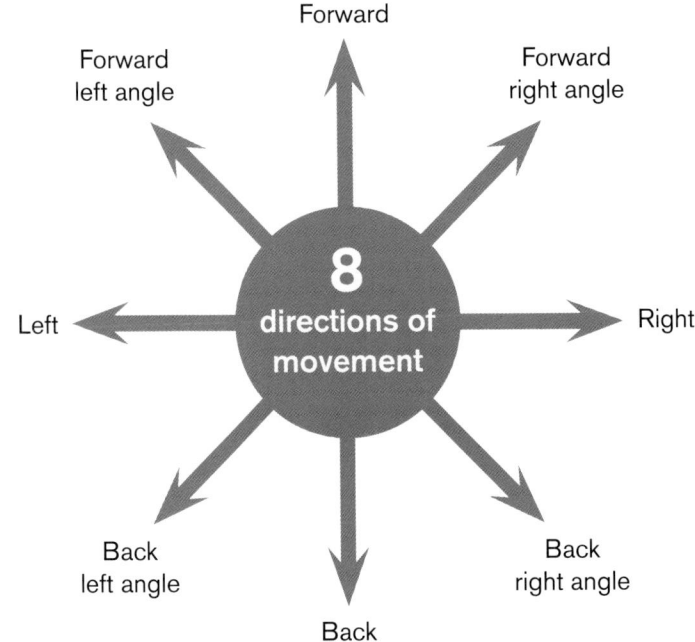

This diagram will aid in the understanding and teaching of the evasive forms. Refer to session 1 for the description of postures (pages 49 and 50) and to session 6 for the outline and set-up for teaching Constructive Response (page 159).

The Instructor has the students form a line across the room. The Instructor stands in front so that he is clearly visible to all of the students. The class faces forwards.

1st evasive form

The 1st evasive form consists of two parts. The first part is a step back into the Responsive Posture, evading a physical threat. The step back into the Responsive Posture was first practised in session 6 (page 162).

The second part of the 1st evasive form is the step forward into another Responsive Posture. This movement is to encourage students to be brave and upright when faced with aggression. By moving forwards with hands open and up, the student will be able to hold and prevent any further attack in a non-aggressive manner. The second part will help students to understand that they are not expected to back down, but rather to be brave and to face their attacker confidently.

1. Begin by standing in the Warrior posture.
2. Step back with the right foot into a left Responsive Posture. Hands are up in a relaxed fashion, with palms open to act as a shield. With the left foot in front, the left hand will be in front with the right hand back.
3. Step forwards with the right foot into a right Responsive Posture.
4. Finish by returning to the Warrior posture.
5. Run through five times on the left side. Then run through five times on the right side, with the left foot stepping back into a right Responsive Posture.

Start in the Warrior posture.   Step back to evade.   Step forwards to prevent further attack.

2nd evasive form

The 2nd evasive form also consists of two parts. The first part is a 45° step to the rear side to evade. Then it is a step forward into a Responsive Posture to prevent further advances.

While the step back was the key point of evasion in the 1st evasive form, the angled step is the key evasive aspect in the 2nd evasive form.

1. Begin by standing in the Warrior posture.
2. Step 45° with the right foot into the back right angle position, forming a left Responsive Posture.
3. Step forwards with the right foot into a right Responsive Posture.
4. Finish by returning to the Warrior posture.
5. Run through five times on the left side. Then run through five times on the right side with the left foot stepping back into a right Responsive Posture.

The Warrior posture.   Step back on a 45° angle to evade.   Step forwards to prevent further attack.

3rd evasive form

The 3rd evasive form is a little more complicated than the first two evasive forms and it may take students a little while to be able to perform. However, once they do they will find it easy to remember.

In the 2nd evasive form we took a 45° step to the rear. For the 3rd evasive form we take a 45° step to the front. The movement is used to sidestep away from an advance and a circular arm action is used to deflect the advance.

1. Start by standing in the Warrior posture.
2. Step 45° with the left foot into the forward left angle position, as shown in the second photo below.
3. At the same time, circle the right arm low across the body to the left, then up and over, backwards to the right. The left arm follows the right arm as the right foot is taken back and to the left to align with the left foot in a left Responsive Posture.
4. Finish by returning to the Warrior posture.
5. Run through five times on one side. Then run through five times on the other side with the right foot stepping into the forward right angle position.

The evasive form always starts in the Warrior posture. | Take a 45° step to the front while bringing the right hand across to the left, … | … up and around … | … to deflect a strike. The right foot aligns behind the left to form … | … a responsive posture.

4th evasive form

The 4th evasive form uses the cross-step posture. The body shifts in the direction of the cross-step, allowing the person to evade an advance. The cross-step posture can be used as a first step when walking away.

Stepping across to evade.

1. Begin by standing in the Warrior posture.
2. Shift the body to the left, taking the right leg across the front of the left leg to form a right cross-step posture, with the right hand out in front and the left hand back, as in the Responsive Posture.
3. Finish by returning to the Warrior posture.
4. Run through five times on one side. Then run through five times on the other side with the body shifting to the left and the right leg crossing in front of the left to form a right cross-step posture.

5th evasive form

Using the hips to evade … … and the hands to deflect.

In the 5th evasive form the feet are fixed in the Warrior posture. The feet do not move. This method of evasion relies on the shifting of the centre through the movement of the hips, and suits advances where movement is restricted. The 5th evasive form is about absorbing the threat.

Where the previous evasive forms are practised on one side at a time, the 5th evasive form is practised on both sides by swinging the hips from left to right, and vice versa.

The students follow the Instructor as he demonstrates the 3rd evasive form.

1. Begin by standing in the Warrior posture.
2. Keeping the back straight, turn the left hip forwards, aligning the navel with the front right angle position. At the same time the left knee is shifted slightly forwards and the right knee is pulled slightly back. The arms swing with the movement, with the left hand rising out and in front and the right hand rising behind it, as in the Responsive Posture. Hands are used to deflect an advance.
3. Keeping the back straight, turn the right hip forwards, aligning the navel with the front left angle position. At the same time the right knee is shifted slightly forwards and the left knee is pulled slightly back. The arms swing with the movement, with the right hand rising out and to the front and the left hand rising behind it as in the Responsive Posture. Again, hands are used to deflect an advance.
4. Finish by returning to the Warrior posture.
5. The turn to the right followed by the turn to the left should be counted as one form. Run through the form 10 times.

Release from a wrist grab

This is how to release yourself from a wrist grab using the movement of the 1st evasive form.

The Instructor has the students sit down in a line and watch as he demonstrates the release. The Instructor chooses a student who has modelled appropriate and constructive behaviour and acknowledges his behaviour aloud to the class. This student then helps to demonstrate the release from a wrist grab.

1. The Instructor stands in the Warrior posture.
2. The student walks up to the Instructor and grabs his left wrist with his right hand.
3. The Instructor responds by stepping back with the left foot into a right Starlight posture (page 71). While moving into the posture, the Instructor uses the momentum to raise his left wrist upwards and outwards, twisting it free via the student's thumb.
    a) The step back is relaxed, utilising the weight of the body, rather than muscle. Natural relaxed movement will help to de-escalate an altercation; muscle tension will serve to escalate an altercation.
    b) Point out that easing through four digits will be more challenging than easing through one thumb. So, students should be encouraged to ease through the thumb. Again,

The student uses ...

... body weight and ...

... the gap between the thumb and the fingers ...

... to get free.

Using distraction

it is not about musclebound pulling, but rather gently twisting and easing, utilising the natural body-weight movement so that the aggressor has little clue of what the releaser is doing until it is too late.

c) The movement of the arm during the release is upwards and outwards while moving back into the Starlight posture, as opposed to trying to pull the arm through the aggressor's grasp or pulling downwards.

d) The more relaxed and subtle the technique, the greater chance of it working.

4. If the student is grabbed by the right wrist they respond by stepping back with the right leg into a left Starlight posture. Stepping back on the same side that they are held creates greater distance and allows the natural body movement to create the opportunity for release.

   a) If the student is grabbed on the left wrist the student steps back with the left foot into a right Starlight posture.

   b) If the student is grabbed on the right wrist the student steps back with the right foot into a left Starlight posture.

5. A variation is that while the Instructor is easing his wrist from the aggressor's grasp, he can use his free arm to apply weight on the student's arm, thereby leveraging free.

The Instructor has the students run through the wrist release in pairs. Students should get to practise the release 10 times each. The Instructor can move around assisting pairs and testing each student by holding their wrist and getting them to perform the release.

Students should be assisting one another to learn the release. No one is going to be an expert the first few times they practise. Encourage the students to take their time and to move slowly while they are learning. Anyone who chooses to be difficult for their partner will need to be reminded of this and may even need to be partnered up with someone else.

Distraction is a tactic to disrupt the aggressor's intention, causing him to soften his hold and allowing the student to escape more easily. A student might disrupt the aggressor's intention by waving out to somebody with his free hand or even by talking to the aggressor and asking him questions. There are many ways a student can disrupt an aggressor and the students may have some ideas of their own. What is important is that we want to de-escalate altercations, not to make them worse. Students should be mindful of this when using distraction techniques. Distraction also helps when the size of an aggressor is an issue. Students should be reminded that they are clever and cleverness is the greatest asset for staying safe.

The Instructor concludes the Constructive Response practise by acknowledging every students' efforts, pointing out well-performed techniques and correcting any errors.

6. 2nd breathing exercise

Recommended time allocation: 2 minutes

The Instructor has the students form a circle standing around the outside of the mats. The Instructor leads the students, demonstrating and talking them through the 2nd breathing exercise and the Activation of the Warrior Deflector Shield. Refer to session 3 for the outline of the 2nd breathing exercise (page 122).

7. One 2 One: what do you like about your partner?

Recommended time allocation: 25 minutes

Koosh balls

If there are enough Koosh balls on hand, one could be given to each student to assist them in staying focused. Refer to session 5 for the outline of using the Koosh balls in the One 2 One activity (page 151).

The Instructor informs the students that at the word 'Go' they are expected to find a partner and to find a space in the training area of the room and sit down. It is important that the pairs have plenty of space around them as this allows privacy for their sharing.

When each pair is quiet, settled and ready to listen, the Instructor explains the One 2 One activity. Refer to session 5 for the outline and set-up of the One 2 One activity (page 151).

1. One person in each pair is chosen to speak first. One way to do this is to ask for a person in each pair to put up their hand. The Instructor can then choose the student with their hand up or choose the student with their hand down to speak first.

2. In session 5 the students had to express what they liked about themselves. In session 8 students have three minutes to tell their partner what they like about them, for example, 'What I like about you is …'

    a) Some students may know each other from school, some may come from the same neighbourhood or some may have got to know each other during the course of the programme. Students need to think and express what they like about their partner.

    b) It could be that a student likes his partner's smile, hair, eyes or dress sense. It could be that a student likes his partner's friendliness, kindness, patience or respectfulness. Maybe the partner is brave, confident or considerate. Perhaps the partner is really skilled at something such as rolling, wrestling or one of the other activities in Warrior Kids. It could be anything.

    c) Encourage the students to personalise their feedback. 'I like it when you're nice to me,', 'I like it when you play with me,' or 'You make me laugh.'

3. The student sharing must say five or more qualities that they like about their partner. The partner is expected to listen.
   a) The partner counts with his fingers for each compliment he receives.
   b) If a student says something that is not nice to their partner then they are expected to say an additional five complimentary remarks to make up. The exercise is supposed to be a positive experience for all involved and students should understand that they are expected to give positive feedback.

4. To assist the students in understanding One 2 One, the Instructor should model the activity. To do this the Instructor chooses a student to receive his feedback.
   a) The Instructor and the student sit so they are visible to the rest of the class. The Instructor tells the student five things that he likes about him.
   b) The receiving student counts each positive affirmation that he receives.
   c) This is great for the students to witness and also for the parents and other family members at the side to witness.

5. During the activity, the Instructor should be on hand to assist students who have trouble sharing. Some students may have trouble understanding what they are supposed to do while others may find it a challenge to vocalise feelings. When assisting a student the Instructor could openly acknowledge one or two things that he likes about the partner, to spur the student on. However, the Instructor should avoid doing the student's job.

6. When three minutes have passed the roles are swapped. The student who shared first now listens as his partner says what he likes about him.

7. If students finish parts of the activity early, they must wait for the remainder of the class before moving on to the next part. In this instance the Instructor also has the opportunity to increase the expectations of these students: instead of sharing five things that they like about their partner, they could share 10.

8. It is important to stress that it is not about the quantity of what is said but about the quality. Once students get the hang of the activity some may race off and say 30 or more things that they like about their partner. However, five thoughtful affirmations will have far greater impact than 30 random ones.

9. When time is up and both students have had a chance to share what they like about their partner, they thank one another. This signifies the end of the first round of the activity.

10. The Instructor moves one student from each pair and places them with a new partner.

11. A new cycle of the One 2 One activity begins with a designated student in each pair telling their partner what they like about them.

a) In the second round the students will be more confident in complimenting their partner so the pace of the activity will increase.

b) There may be one or two students who still find the activity a challenge and require the Instructor's support.

12. Before beginning the second round of One 2 One, the students should be given a moment to take a good look at their new partner. The students need to understand that this is a new partner so they shouldn't be giving the same compliments they gave to their first partner. Students need to respect their new partner by paying them new compliments.

13. When time is up and both students have had a chance to share what they like about their partner, they thank one another. This signifies the end of the second round of the activity. If there is enough time the Instructor could take the students through a third and maybe even a fourth round.

14. When the One 2 One activity is completed the Instructor nominates two students to collect the Koosh balls.

15. The Instructor acknowledges everyone for their efforts in the One 2 One activity.

8. Sharing Circle

Recommended time allocation: 15 minutes

The Instructor and the students sit in a circle on the mats. Each student should be facing the centre of the circle and be clearly visible to the Instructor so that no one is in any way disassociated from the group, whether by their own positioning or by the positioning of another student.

The Instructor presents a Koosh ball and announces that it is time for the Sharing Circle, where each student will have a turn to share a low point and a high point from their week. Refer to session 1 for the outline of the Sharing Circle (page 58).

9. Closing words

The Instructor directs students to assemble on the mats, standing in a circle as they had done at the beginning of the class.

Homework

To lead up to the homework task the Instructor asks the class the following questions:

1. Earlier on you partnered up with someone and had the opportunity to tell them some nice things. What was it like to compliment someone?

   The Instructor elicits three or four answers from the group then goes on to the next question.

2. What was it like to have someone say nice things about you?

   The Instructor elicits three or four answers from the group.

Session 8

> ### *The homework task*
>
> The homework for session 8 is for the students to tell their Mum, Dad or caregiver five things that they like about them. This could be done in the car on the way home from Warrior Kids. The sooner the better really, as it will still be fresh in the student's mind.
>
> By openly announcing the homework task to the class I am indirectly enlisting the participation of the parents watching from the side. As Instructor, you will know that the parents have heard you when they smile or look to one another. The task is simply a way of students sharing the activity with their parents. It allows the parents to be a part of their child's Warrior Kids experience.

Closing
Recommended time allocation: 1 minute

The Instructor asks for a volunteer from the group to say some words to end the class.

When the closing words have been said the Instructor thanks the speaker. Following this the Instructor acknowledges to the class that there are only two more classes of the Warrior Kids programme remaining. Now is the time when he will be considering what grade each student has achieved. The Instructor points out that he will be getting feedback from parents and teachers and hopes that everyone has been doing their best in order to achieve a Red or Orange belt in Warrior Kids.

Newsletters

This is the time to hand out newsletters or notices regarding future Warrior Kids programmes or community classes, and to tell the group about the shared lunch to celebrate the completion of the programme (if you are choosing to have one).

The Instructor concludes with 'Remember to take what you brought with you today, your shoes, socks, watches, water bottle, jersey and I'll see you next time.'

> This concludes session 8.
>
> Students will express sadness and disappointment in learning that the programme will soon be over. Parents may also be disappointed.
> You, the Instructor, will miss the students.
> That is the way it should be.
>
> By being a successful Instructor, you and the students will have connected and bonded over the 10 weeks.
> Friendships will have formed and for many students you will have become a significant person in their lives.
> You are a support, a rock, someone that they can look up to and to whom they can turn for help.
>
> Moving on at the end is what happens and only with ongoing classes are students able to continually attend.
> However, you know that when you start your next programme it will be with new students who need and want just as much.
> You will become a significant person in their lives, a support, that rock, someone that the children can look to and to whom they can turn and many will want to share a connection with you.
>
> You will be a light and you will inspire.
> This is you being a leader in your community.

Session 9

EQUIPMENT

- 8 x gym mats, size 1200 x 1800 mm
- foam stick
- chairs for parents and caregivers

Introduction

The second to last session of the Warrior Kids in-school programme starts with the check-in activity, which first featured in session 2 (page 78) and gives each student the opportunity to share something troublesome from their week, and to share an achievement. The warm-up activity for session 9 is leaping, where students are challenged to leap over a foam stick held at various heights. Later, safe play is revisited with Warrior Kids Wrestling, but this time students are confronted with matches consisting of three students at a time. Hospital Tag follows if there is extra time. Great fun! Great learning!

The outcomes for session 9 are that the students will:

○ gain an understanding of the value of leaping,

○ gain further skills and awareness during Warrior Kids Wrestling, and

○ further their understanding and ability to play safe and to look after and care for others.

Lesson overview

1. Opening words.
2. Round of introductions: a round of names and a favourite place.
3. Check-in.
4. Warm-up challenge: Leaping.
5. Conditioning: Stretching 3rd form; Brain exercises.
6. Wrestling: 2 on 1 challenge.
7. Extra time activity: Hospital Tag.
8. Closing words.

1. Opening words
Recommended time allocation: 1 minute

The Instructor directs students to remove their shoes and socks and to sit on the mats in a circle. Once the group is settled the Instructor has the students stand up. The Instructor then asks for a volunteer to say some opening words to commence the class. Refer to session 1 (page 44).

2. Round of introductions
Recommended time allocation: 3 minutes

Each member of the circle, from left to right or vice-versa, takes their turn to say their name and a favorite place. A favourite place can be anywhere that a student has been. It might be a place that the student knows and to which they have some personal connection. It might be a place that has meaning, a sanctuary, or a place of which they have fond memories. It could be their bedroom at home, a tree in their yard, a restaurant, school, a holiday park, a beach or a theme park on the other side of the world.

Refer to session 1 for the set up of Introductions (page 44).

3. Check-in
Recommended time allocation: 20 minutes

The Instructor and the students sit on the mats in a circle. Each student has a turn to share something troublesome from their week and an achievement from their week.

Refer to session 2 for the outline and set up of the check-in activity (page 78).

4. Warm-up challenge: leaping
Recommended time allocation: 15 minutes

For session 9 there is a warm-up challenge as opposed to a game. The outline for setting up and managing a warm-up challenge will be the same as the outline given for games in session 1 (page 45).

Leaping is a basic skill practised in Warrior Kids. Leaping works and strengthens the body, enhancing motor skills and co-ordination. It can also be an effective tool in Constructive Response, especially when it comes to evasion. Also, leaping is fun to practise.

> One family reported that their five-year-old son, one of my students, had stepped out on to a road crossing. At that moment a reckless driver sped around the corner in a car, oblivious to the child directly in his path. My student, who had been practising leaping the week before in class, responded by leaping back off the road, out of harm's way, saving his life. I often share this account with students as it highlights the need to be safe around roads and demonstrates the value of leaping.

The Instructor chooses a student who has modelled appropriate and constructive behaviour and acknowledges their behaviour aloud to the class. The Instructor then leads this student to the gym mats and has her sit down in front of them. The Instructor tells the remaining students that at the command 'Go' they are to line up along one side of the appointed leader, around the outside of the gym mats. This will enable each student to see the leaping demonstration.

The Instructor produces the foam stick. As with session 1, some of the students will respond to the sight of the stick and may think that they are about to get hit. When this happens, I will pause, look directly at any concerned students and ask, 'Have I ever hurt you?' When they reply, 'No,' I then tell the class that I would never hurt

Any student who rushes for a place in the line should be sent to the back of the line. Students should be encouraged to relax and to be considerate of others.

When presenting leaping to the class I talk about it being similar to work in the classroom at school. For this challenge the students need to focus on what is in front of them and to get it done. Further, students should be reminded that they are expected to respect others. No one is to laugh at or ridicule a student's attempt at leaping. Students can verbally support one another. The Instructor should monitor the level of noise.

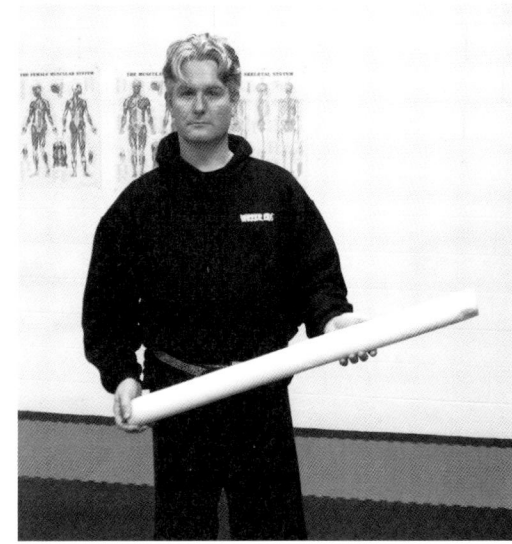

The foam stick. This one has been cut from a flotation noodle.

them. This is valuable as it establishes further trust between the Instructor and the students.

Demonstrating leaping

The Instructor can demonstrate the following method of leaping to the students. This can be done before or after the students perform leaping part 1.

1. Stand in the Warrior posture, feet shoulder-width apart.
2. Bend the legs slightly, then spring upwards, lifting both feet inwards towards the groin, while pointing the knees out to the sides (much like a frog does when swimming).
3. Return to the floor in the Warrior posture.

The Instructor sits down on the gym mats and rests her arms on her legs, holding the foam stick horizontally over the mats. The Instructor then asks the leading student to stand in front of the stick, facing it side on.

Leaping: part 1

1. The student leaps forwards with both feet over the foam stick, landing softly on the other side.
   a) It is important that the student leaps with both feet as it prepares and warms her up for the upcoming challenge.
   b) Both feet should land at the same time.
   c) If the leap is not performed correctly, the student has to return to the front of the line and do it again.
   d) If a student fails the leap on purpose, she forfeits her turn and goes to the back of the line.
2. One by one, the line of students follows their leader and leaps over the obstacle. Following the leap, each student goes to the back of the line.
3. Only one student should be on the mats at a time. This will mean that the remaining students are at a safe distance.
4. The Instructor verbally acknowledges each attempt.

Leaping: part 2

1. When the lead student returns to the front of the line the Instructor lifts the foam stick higher so that it is in line with her navel.
2. The leader leaps with both feet over the foam stick and lands softly on the other side.
3. The remaining students file through, each having their turn to leap over the obstacle.

Leaping: part 3

1. When the lead student returns to the front of the line for a third time, the Instructor lifts the foam stick higher so that it is in line with his solar plexus.
2. The leader leaps with both feet over the foam stick.
3. The remaining students file through.
    a) Some students may find this height a challenge, especially younger ones. If you feel the foam stick is too high for a particular student, you can lower it. However, the activity is about being challenged, therefore it should be getting progressively more difficult.
    b) Students who find it difficult will need encouragement.
        i) If it is obvious to the Instructor that the student would get over with some effort then she should tell the student that she believes that she can do it.
        ii) Some students will mentally give way to the challenge, telling themselves that they can't do it. Encourage these students to change their mindset from 'can't' to 'can and will'.
        iii) The students who give up mentally will be obvious as they will not bend their knees and raise their legs when leaping. They will have psychologically failed the leap even before they stand facing the stick.
        iv) If it is clear at any point that a student is unable to make it over the obstacle, the Instructor can lower the foam stick. However, be sure not to shame or embarrass the student.
        v) Some students get self-conscious and get lost in the attention of the other students. Remind the student to focus on the task.
        vi) Some students may get themselves into a rhythm of continually failing the leap, even if the foam stick is low. In this case the student needs a 'disruption' to her thought processing. To do this I ask the student to stop in front of the obstacle and face me. I may clap, which can disrupt her cognitive state. I will ask the student to breathe in and out. I may even have her close her eyes and picture herself successfully leaping over the foam stick. 'This is easy for you,' I will say. 'I already know that you can do it, so let's just get it done.'
        vii) If further unsuccessful attempts follow then I will ask the student to move to the back of the line, prompting her to take a break and allowing her to refocus and prepare for another try.

Session 9

viii) If a student isn't successful on the day then they're sure to get it the next time. Each student has their own way of learning, their own way of processing what is going on. Give them time.

ix) All Warrior Kids should be wearing suitable clothes for physical activity. Now and then a student may turn up to class dressed inappropriately. For example, a girl wearing a short skirt may have issues when leaping a certain height.

Leaping: part 4

1. When the lead student returns to the front of the line for the fourth time the Instructor has the remaining students sit down in their line.

2. The Instructor announces that this time each student will choose a height to leap over. When the leader has her turn she moves the foam stick to the height that she wants to attempt to leap over. The Instructor encourages the students to challenge themselves.

    a) It is important that the students do not compare or compete with others. Their leap is their individual leap. It's not about what the other students are doing. I always point out that I am not comparing but that 'I just want to see you challenge yourself.'

    b) Some students will be able to spring high, some will not. This does not matter. All that matters is that all students challenge themselves in choosing their own height and give it an honest attempt.

    c) I want every student to succeed, so some may need to change their height. Sometimes I will adjust a height slightly and have the student leap over that. If she makes it over easily I will have the student do it again, however, this time I will sneak the foam stick back up to the original height that she chose, without telling her. I will tell the student, 'You've already done it once so you can certainly do it again.' When she makes it over, I tell the student of my actions and tell her that she made it over her original height.

    d) Alternatively, when a student chooses a height and makes it over easily, I make a point of showing him how high he was above the obstacle, indicating that he can leap higher than his chosen height.

    e) Some students who have a fear of failing may try to always choose a safe height. Encourage them to challenge themselves. Allow them to fail and allow them to know that they are still okay. Great achievement comes with the risk of failure. We must be prepared to fail in order to succeed.

    f) Students should also know that the foam stick cannot be set at a height that is too low; some students may choose to opt out of the challenge by moving the foam stick to a height just off the ground.

3. Each student takes a turn to choose a height to leap over.

Leaping: part 5

1. The Instructor returns to resting her arms on her legs, holding the foam stick horizontally over the mats as she did in part 1.
2. This time the students take three leaps. First they leap forwards with both feet over the foam stick, landing softly on the other side. Then they reverse, leaping backwards with both feet over the foam stick. Lastly the student leaps forwards one more time.
   a) Leaping backwards presents a psychological challenge for some students. However, if they can leap a certain height forwards then they can leap the same height backwards.
   b) The Instructor can count for each leap: 1 for forwards, 2 for backwards and 3 for forwards.
3. One by one, the line of students take their turn to leap over the obstacle.

The leaping activity can end at this point. However, if there is enough time, the Instructor can take the students through leaping parts 6 and/or 7.

Leaping: part 6

1. When the lead student returns to the front of the line the Instructor lifts the foam stick higher so that it is in line with her navel.
2. The students take three leaps. First they leap forwards, then backwards and lastly forwards again.
   a) Some students may find the height challenging. The Instructor should encourage each student to make it over the obstacle.

Leaping: part 7

1. When the lead student returns to the front, the Instructor has the remaining students sit down in their line.
2. The Instructor announces that this time each student will choose a height to leap over. When a student has her turn on the mats, she moves the foam stick to the height that she wants to leap over. However, the height for the leap forwards will be the same height for the leap backwards.
3. The Instructor encourages the students to challenge themselves.

5. Conditioning

The Instructor brings students back together to form a standing circle. Refer to session 1 (page 48) for the outline for setting up and managing the conditioning exercises. Remember, the students should only move as far as they feel comfortable. Avoid injuries. Encourage the students to relax and soften into each stretch.

Stretching 3rd form

Recommended time allocation: 8 minutes

Refer to session 3 for the stretching 3rd form positions (page 103). Each member of the circle, from left to right or vice versa, is given a turn to say the breathing in and breathing out commands, as explained in session 2 (page 84).

Session 9

Brain exercises

Recommended time allocation: 3 minutes

Standing as part of the circle, the Instructor leads students through the brain exercises, as described in session 1 (page 51) and session 4 (page 127).

6. Wrestling: 2 on 1 challenge

Recommended time allocation: 25 minutes

Warrior Kids Wrestling (WKW) is an exploration of safe play. Students work together to look after and care for others, while at the same time being challenged physically and having fun.

The students should be encouraged to relax and give it a go. Stress that no one is allowed to get hurt. Refer to session 3 for the set up, outline for running and rules of WKW (page 114). The set-up process is designed to get the students feeling confident about participating in WKW. It is the Instructor's responsibility to ensure that a high level of safety and respect is maintained throughout the challenge.

The Instructor has the students sit down in a circle around the outside of the gym mats.

1. A WKW match in session 9 consists of three 1- or 2-minute rounds.
2. In session 9 three students will be on the gym mats for each match.
   a) The three students will remain on their knees throughout the match.
   b) It is best to pick older, more responsible students in the class to wrestle first, as they will set the tone for the following WKW matches.
3. Two of the three students will start at different corners of the gym mats. The third will begin in the centre of the mats. Choose the most able or the largest of the three students to be in the centre first.
4. When the Instructor calls 'Go' the first round begins. The students in the corners of the mats work together to try to pin down the student in the centre so that she cannot get up.
5. The job for the student in the centre is to pin down both of the students working against her at the same time.

Session 9

> In one of my early programmes I had a young girl who roared the whole time she was on the mat, which resulted in the other students, who were boys, backing down. It was a very valuable lesson for everyone in the class, especially the girls. The roaring girl never hurt the boys, but her attitude put them off. As you can imagine, this girl has grown into a strong, confident woman. No one is going to mess with her and she certainly won't put up with any nonsense.

   a) This is quite a challenge for the student in the centre; however, pinning two students down at once has been done plenty of times in Warrior Kids. The challenge calls for the student in the centre to be clever and to have the right attitude.

6. The Instructor could support the student in the centre by giving her some pointers prior to the round commencing.

   a) The student should be encouraged to relax her body, to avoid tensing up. This will preserve energy and allow her to remain calm and sensitive to the intentions and actions of the two students opposing her.

   b) The student can use body weight to escape and evade wrist grabs by exiting through the thumbs (see session 8, page 191).

   c) The student could use one of the two students opposing her as a shield. She does this by keeping one of the opposition between herself and the second opponent.

   d) The use of voice can aid in the challenge. A well-timed roar can put the opposition off guard, allowing the student to get the upper hand.

   e) By being soft and fluid, the student will be able to read the actions and body language of the opposition. With little resistance, it is common for the opposition to become overconfident. They will trap themselves by overexerting and creating a vulnerability. The student in the centre then has the opportunity to take advantage of her opponent's vulnerability.

      i) The student in the centre should expend energy only to keep herself from being pinned or when it is clear that she can gain the upper hand. Even so, the student should be encouraged to utilise her weight rather than her strength.

      ii) Two-on-one wrestling are valuable self-protection training as attacks from multiple aggressors are (sadly) a common occurrence.

7. The main rule for WKW is to have fun. WKW is not about hurting others or getting hurt. If students want to win at WKW then they should relax, have fun and finish their turn with no one hurt and smiles on their faces. This mean all three students 'win'.

8. When time ends for the first round the Instructor calls 'Stop' and the three students return to their starting positions (two in corners of the gym mats and one in the centre). The Instructor then has the student in the centre swap places with one of the students in the corners. The new student in the centre will be the second-most able or second largest of the three.

9. The second round begins when the Instructor calls 'Go'. The student in the centre has a turn to try and pin two students as they work together to pin her.

10. When round two is complete, the last student of the three takes her turn in the centre of the mats.

Session 9

Brain exercises

Recommended time allocation: 3 minutes

Standing as part of the circle, the Instructor leads students through the brain exercises, as described in session 1 (page 51) and session 4 (page 127).

6. Wrestling: 2 on 1 challenge

Recommended time allocation: 25 minutes

Warrior Kids Wrestling (WKW) is an exploration of safe play. Students work together to look after and care for others, while at the same time being challenged physically and having fun.

The students should be encouraged to relax and give it a go. Stress that no one is allowed to get hurt. Refer to session 3 for the set up, outline for running and rules of WKW (page 114). The set-up process is designed to get the students feeling confident about participating in WKW. It is the Instructor's responsibility to ensure that a high level of safety and respect is maintained throughout the challenge.

The Instructor has the students sit down in a circle around the outside of the gym mats.

1. A WKW match in session 9 consists of three 1- or 2-minute rounds.

2. In session 9 three students will be on the gym mats for each match.

    a) The three students will remain on their knees throughout the match.

    b) It is best to pick older, more responsible students in the class to wrestle first, as they will set the tone for the following WKW matches.

3. Two of the three students will start at different corners of the gym mats. The third will begin in the centre of the mats. Choose the most able or the largest of the three students to be in the centre first.

4. When the Instructor calls 'Go' the first round begins. The students in the corners of the mats work together to try to pin down the student in the centre so that she cannot get up.

5. The job for the student in the centre is to pin down both of the students working against her at the same time.

Session 9

> In one of my early programmes I had a young girl who roared the whole time she was on the mat, which resulted in the other students, who were boys, backing down. It was a very valuable lesson for everyone in the class, especially the girls. The roaring girl never hurt the boys, but her attitude put them off. As you can imagine, this girl has grown into a strong, confident woman. No one is going to mess with her and she certainly won't put up with any nonsense.

a) This is quite a challenge for the student in the centre; however, pinning two students down at once has been done plenty of times in Warrior Kids. The challenge calls for the student in the centre to be clever and to have the right attitude.

6. The Instructor could support the student in the centre by giving her some pointers prior to the round commencing.

   a) The student should be encouraged to relax her body, to avoid tensing up. This will preserve energy and allow her to remain calm and sensitive to the intentions and actions of the two students opposing her.

   b) The student can use body weight to escape and evade wrist grabs by exiting through the thumbs (see session 8, page 191).

   c) The student could use one of the two students opposing her as a shield. She does this by keeping one of the opposition between herself and the second opponent.

   d) The use of voice can aid in the challenge. A well-timed roar can put the opposition off guard, allowing the student to get the upper hand.

   e) By being soft and fluid, the student will be able to read the actions and body language of the opposition. With little resistance, it is common for the opposition to become overconfident. They will trap themselves by overexerting and creating a vulnerability. The student in the centre then has the opportunity to take advantage of her opponent's vulnerability.

      i) The student in the centre should expend energy only to keep herself from being pinned or when it is clear that she can gain the upper hand. Even so, the student should be encouraged to utilise her weight rather than her strength.

      ii) Two-on-one wrestling are valuable self-protection training as attacks from multiple aggressors are (sadly) a common occurrence.

7. The main rule for WKW is to have fun. WKW is not about hurting others or getting hurt. If students want to win at WKW then they should relax, have fun and finish their turn with no one hurt and smiles on their faces. This mean all three students 'win'.

8. When time ends for the first round the Instructor calls 'Stop' and the three students return to their starting positions (two in corners of the gym mats and one in the centre). The Instructor then has the student in the centre swap places with one of the students in the corners. The new student in the centre will be the second-most able or second largest of the three.

9. The second round begins when the Instructor calls 'Go'. The student in the centre has a turn to try and pin two students as they work together to pin her.

10. When round two is complete, the last student of the three takes her turn in the centre of the mats.

The points on this page arise from a Constructive Response perspective. From an emotional awareness perspective, there's nothing better than to see students exerting their frustration, anger and emotional hurt in a safe and controlled way. Sometimes it's better to allow them to forget techniques and strategies and simply let them go for it and become an entanglement of tension, where they can have resistance to push and pull against. This is a great physical outlet, especially for those who don't have someone to wrestle against at home.

For some children, the Constructive Response angle will be more resonant, allowing them to experience a new way of being and tapping into their internal Warrior and deeper confidence. For others, the emotional awareness that arises from the activity will be of greater benefit; they find the opportunity to 'let go' invigorating.

There may be students who need more exposure to being careful in their treatment of others, so a stronger emphasis on relaxing and being considerate and aware of others is required.

7. Extra time activity: Hospital Tag

Recommended time allocation: 5 minutes

11. At the end of three rounds, when the three students have had a turn in the centre of the mats, the match is finished.

12. When the match has ended, the Instructor has the three students stand up and face her. She asks each student how the challenge was and how they are feeling at that moment. Are they hurt anywhere?

    a) If the foundations for safe WKW are clearly laid out in the beginning of the activity there shouldn't be any injuries. If there has been an injury, the rules need to be re-emphasised.

    b) Accidents are a lot less likely to occur if the students are following the rules, taking care of one another and making sure that the activity is a fun experience for everyone.

       i) If a wrestling match is looking too rough the Instructor should stop it immediately and re-emphasise the rules.

       ii) If the Instructor has to keep intervening then the students in question lose their opportunity to wrestle and should be replaced.

       iii) The Instructor can observe a wrestling match from the side. However, if there are concerns over a match or the Instructor cannot see the match clearly, then the Instructor should stand on the mats, moving around the wrestling students, closely supervising the match.

       iv) The whole class should be encouraged to assist in the management of WKW. A student's safety is the responsibility of every student. In doing this, many eyes and voices are helping to keep safe boundaries in place.

    c) If the three students in the centre had a good experience, with no injuries, the Instructor should verbally acknowledge their efforts to the class and thank them for being great role models. The Instructor should then say that everybody is expected to do the same.

    d) When each group of students has completed their three-round match, I usually have them go and get a drink if water is available in the same or an adjacent room. It wouldn't be wise to allow students to go further than this.

13. When a WKW match finishes three new students are then chosen to go on to the mats and wrestle.

14. WKW finishes when everyone has had a turn in the centre of the mats.

If there is extra time following Warrior Kids Wrestling, the Instructor could take the class through a short game of Hospital Tag. Refer to session 6 for the outline of Hospital Tag (page 156).

8. Closing words

Check-out
Recommended time allocation: 1 minute

Closing words
Recommended time allocation: 1 minute

The Instructor directs students to assemble on the mats, standing in a circle as they had done at the beginning of the class.

Each member of the circle, from left to right or vice-versa, takes their turn to say one word that describes their experience of the class. The Instructor says, 'Say one word to describe how the class was for you today.'

The Instructor asks for a volunteer from the group to say some words to end the class.

When the closing words have been said the Instructor thanks the speaker. Following this she acknowledges to the students that there is only one class left in the programme.

The Instructor concludes with 'Remember to take what you brought with you today, your shoes, socks, watches, water bottle, jersey and I'll see you next time.'

Session 9 is complete.

As the programme draws to a close and you consider what grade to award each student, consider your own performance while running the programme.

Consider your manner and the way you are and have been with the students and their families.
Do the families feel welcome to attend each session? Are the students enjoying their Warrior Kids experience? How specific is your feedback to the students?

Consider your group management skills.
How well are the students interacting as a group? How well are the students supporting one another? How well are the students focused in class? How is your time management?

Consider your ability to communicate.
How clear are your instructions? How well do the students follow instructions? Are you having to raise your voice? If so, how often?

Consider your openness to personal development and change.
In terms of your ability as an Instructor, what worked for you? What would you do differently next time?

Consider your openness to the effectiveness of Warrior Kids. Remember Warrior Kids is proven to work. It simply relies on the Instructor to make it work. Can you make it work? Have you made it work?

Practice makes perfect.
Keep going.

Session 10

EQUIPMENT

- 8 x gym mats, size 1200 x 1800 mm
- padded sword
- affirmation cards
- pens and paper (enough for each student)
- certificates if they are to be awarded at the end of the session
- chairs for parents and caregivers

Introduction

Session 10 brings the Warrior Kids in-school programme to an end. The warm-up game for the session is the Warrior Kids Medley, a mix of the basic skills taught and practised throughout the programme. Shared stretching adds difference to the conditioning aspect of the class and allows students to choose a stretching position to demonstrate. Constructive Response is revisited through the 1st evasive form and this leads up to the final challenge, which is a test that involves the use of intuition. A cognitive conditioning exercise features towards the end of the session, which introduces students to affirmations and visualisations and their use to clarify and achieve goals.

As session 10 marks the conclusion of the programme, spot questions are given to the students to help revise topics discussed in the class. These questions are asked 'on the spot', at different points of the session. There are five spot questions, however not all five need to be used. Depending on time, the Instructor may choose two spot questions to use. Any of the five questions can be chosen. If there is plenty of time, three or four questions might be used.

The outcomes for session 10 are that the students will:

- further their knowledge and ability with the basic skills of Warrior Kids,
- have an understanding of intuition,
- understand the value of affirmations and visualisations and how they can help to achieve goals.

Lesson overview

1. Opening words.
2. Round of introductions: a round of names and each student's favourite subject in the classroom.
3. Warm-up game: The Warrior Kids Medley.
4. Conditioning: Shared stretching; Brain exercises.
5. Spot question 1: 'What should you do when someone is trying to touch you in a way that is not safe?'
6. Constructive Response, part 1: 1st evasive form
7. Spot question 2: 'How do we look after ourselves when people are being mean to us?'
8. Constructive Response, part 2: sidestep
9. Spot question 3: 'How can you look after yourself when you feel angry?'

Session 10

10. Test time.
11. 1st breathing exercise.
12. Spot question 4: 'Tell me one thing that you like about being you.'
13. Cognitive conditioning: constructive affirmation and visualisation.
14. Spot question 5: 'Do you feel that you deserve to pass Warrior Kids?'
15. Closing words.

1. Opening words

Recommended time allocation: 1 minute

The Instructor directs students to remove their shoes and socks and to sit on the mats in a circle. Once the group is settled the Instructor has the students stand up. The Instructor then asks for a volunteer to say some opening words to commence the class. Refer to session 1 (page 44).

2. Round of introductions

Recommended time allocation: 3 minutes

Each member of the circle, from left to right or vice versa, takes their turn to say their name and their favorite subject in the classroom at school.

A favourite subject is a working subject within the classroom such as maths, writing, art, spelling, science and so on. The subject cannot be something outside of the classroom, for example PE, fitness or sport. Refer to session 1 for the set up of Introductions (page 44).

3. Warm-up game: The Warrior Kids Medley

Overall recommended time allocation: 10 minutes

Refer to session 1 for the outline of setting up and managing a warm-up game. The Instructor should remember to get the students to take note of their surroundings and clearly point out the boundary of the game to ensure safety and limit any chance of injury.

The Warrior Kids Medley

The Warrior Kids Medley is an ideal game to finish the programme with as it gives the students the opportunity to revise and practise key body work techniques explored throughout the programme, but at the same time we add some variation.

The students remain standing in a circle, as they were at the beginning of class. When the students are settled and ready to listen, the Instructor explains the Warrior Kids Medley.

1. The Instructor stands to one side of the predetermined game area, where he can observe the game.
2. The Instructor runs through the lists of commands that he will randomly call out at a steady pace and explains what the students are expected to do when each command is called. The students have to perform the commands to the best of their ability, as quickly as they can. The commands are:

- ○ 'Run to the end!' The Instructor points to an end of the game area and the students run there.
- ○ 'Run backwards!' The Instructor points to an end of the game area and the students run there backwards, looking over their shoulders to see where they are going.
- ○ 'Run sideways!' The Instructor points to an end of the game area and the students run there sideways.
- ○ 'Show me a posture!' Students demonstrate a posture that they have practised in class.
- ○ 'Show me another posture!' Students demonstrate a different posture that they have practised in class.
- ○ 'Leap forwards!' Students leap forwards.
- ○ 'Leap backwards!' Students leap backwards.
- ○ 'Leap sideways!' or 'Leap to the left!' Students leap sideways or to whichever direction the Instructor calls.
- ○ 'Leap to the other side!' or 'Leap to the right!'
- ○ 'Leap up!' Students leap as high as they can.
- ○ 'Drop down!' Students drop to the floor.
- ○ 'Roll forwards!' Students perform a forward roll.
- ○ 'Roll sideways!' or 'Roll to the left!' Students perform a sideways roll to the side the Instructor calls.
- ○ 'Roll to the other side!' or 'Roll to the right!' Students perform a sideways roll to the side.
- ○ 'Roll backwards!' Students perform a backward roll.
- ○ 'Handstand!' Students perform a handstand.
- ○ 'Cartwheel!' Students perform a cartwheel.
- ○ 'Front break fall!' Students demonstrate the front break fall they practised in session 8.
- ○ 'Chicken dance!' Students perform the chicken dance from the game Mice, Tigers and Elephants in session 2. The students put both feet together and bend their knees slightly. With the left hand they make a tail out the back and with the right hand a cockerel crown on top of the head. The students dance around in a circle, performing a chicken dance and making the sound of a chicken.

3. Commands can be repeated.

4. The Instructor openly acknowledges students who respond promptly to each command and who are quick to be ready for the next one. The Instructor encourages the students to keep going and to give their best attempt at fulfilling each command.

5. Later in the game the Instructor might choose a student to call out the commands. In this case the student stands in the same position as the Instructor, at the side of the mats, and gives the commands, which the other students perform.

6. Depending on time, more than one student could be given a turn at calling out the commands.

7. The Warrior Kids Medley is played for a set amount of time then simply stopped. There doesn't need to be a particular outcome for the game to end.

4. Conditioning

The Instructor brings students back together to form a circle standing up. Refer to session 1 (page 48) for the outline of setting up and managing the conditioning exercises. Remember, the students should only move as far as they feel comfortable. Avoid injuries. Encourage the students to relax and soften into each stretch.

Shared stretching

Recommended time allocation: 10 minutes

For the shared stretching in session 10, each member of the circle, from left to right or vice versa, is given a turn to take the class through a stretching technique that they can remember from the stretching forms practised over the 10 sessions.

When it is a student's turn to share, he simply leads the class through his chosen stretch, then through the breathing in and breathing out commands as explained in session 2 (page 84).

The stretching techniques must be from the Warrior Kids stretching forms: 1st, 2nd or 3rd, as outlined in sessions 1, 2 and 3 (pages 49, 84 and 103 respectively).

If there are 10 or fewer students in the class, run through shared stretching two times and allow each student to demonstrate a second stretch. If the number of students is well below 10 a third round of shared stretching is possible.

If a student demonstrates a stretch on one side of the body, allow them to perform the same stretch on the other side before moving on to the next student's turn.

Everyone is given a turn to share a stretch.

Brain exercises

Recommended time allocation: 3 minutes

Standing as part of the circle, the Instructor nominates a student to lead the class through the brain exercises as described in session 1 (page 51) and session 4 (page 127). The student chosen should be someone who is confident about knowing the brain exercises and, more importantly, someone who has demonstrated commendable behaviour and conduct throughout the 10 sessions.

5. Spot question 1

Recommended time allocation: 3 minutes

The class pauses for a spot question. This exercise should be performed quickly and is not a group discussion. It involves a simple question from a previous session and requires simple answers. The first question is about keeping safe and is from session 2 (page 89). The Instructor can refer to this session to be familiar with the surrounding questions and the outline and set-up of the Keeping Safe discussion.

Question 1

In session 2 we talked about keeping safe and safe touching. We discussed people trying to hurt you or trying to touch your private parts or trying to get you to touch theirs, or touching you in a way that's uncomfortable, or touching you in an adult way, is not okay and is not safe. So, what should you do when someone is trying to touch you in a way that is not safe?

The students put up their hand to answer the question and the Instructor elicits five appropriate answers from the group. Each appropriate answer given should be repeated for the class by the Instructor so that everyone understands.

6. Constructive Response, part 1: 1st evasive form

Recommended time allocation: 8 minutes

> It would be wise to have the student practise the downward strike under the Instructor's guidance first, before proceeding with the evasion demonstration. This will allow the Instructor to correct the student and to ensure that he will perform the strike in a safe and trustworthy manner.
>
> This practice strike can be performed in front of the class. This will enable the other students the opportunity to learn aspects of the strike through observation, which may prove useful in future classes when particular students are absent.

The Instructor gets the students to form a line across the room and says, 'Because it is session 10 and the conclusion of the programme, each student will be presented with a test. But I'm going to be nice to you. I'm going to get you prepared for the test. In order to prepare yourselves you are going to practise your first evasive form.'

The Instructor leads the students through the 1st evasive form as described in session 8 (page 188). The form is practised five times on the right side and then five times on the left side.

On completion of the form the students remain in the line and sit down. Once everyone is seated and is settled and ready to listen, the Instructor asks the class, 'Put up your hand if you're confident that you know the first form.' When the students have answered, the Instructor says, 'Right, let's see,' and brings out the padded sword.

The Instructor demonstrates the move first. An assistant strikes down at him with the padded sword. If an assistant is not available, then the Instructor could nominate a trustworthy student to strike down at him.

1. Each student has a turn to stand in the Warrior posture in front of the Instructor.

2. The Instructor steps back, raising the padded sword, then takes a step forwards, bringing the padded sword slowly down, towards the student. No student should ever be struck with the padded sword.

3. The student evades the strike by stepping back into the Responsive Posture, just as they did in the 1st evasive form. The shift back doesn't have to be exactly as it is in the 1st evasive form. The important aspect of the 1st evasive form is the evading backward movement. The Instructor should avoid getting locked in the form. Students step back in a way that is most comfortable for them, a way that ensures they are beyond the reach of the strike.

4. Once each student has taken a turn to evade the vertical strike, they return to sitting in a line with the other students.

7. Spot question 2

Recommended time allocation: 3 minutes

The class pauses for a spot question. The second spot question is from session 6, part 5 (page 160).

Question 2

In session 6 we discussed the ways that people can be mean. So, the second spot question is, how do we look after ourselves when people are being mean to us?

The students put up their hand to answer and the Instructor elicits eight appropriate answers from the group.

8. Constructive Response, part 2: sidestep

Recommended time allocation: 5 minutes

The students remain seated in their line as the Instructor explains part 2 of the Constructive Response exercise. For part 2 the students get to practise the sidestep evasive manoeuvre. The sidestep features in the 2nd, 3rd and 4th evasive forms, however, now the students have the opportunity to amplify the movement. As this is the last part of the preparation for the test, students will want to get it right.

Unlike the 1st part of the Constructive Response practised in session 10, the students do not run through an evasive form before attempting the sidestep in front of the Instructor. The students respond to a vertical strike using a sidestep. As with the 1st evasive form, the Instructor demonstrates the move first by having an assistant strike at him with the padded sword.

1. Each student has a turn to stand in the Warrior posture in front of the Instructor.

2. The Instructor takes a step back, raising the padded sword. He then steps forwards, bringing the padded sword slowly down towards the student.

3. The student evades the strike by stepping with both feet out wide to the side, into a Responsive Posture. The movement can be to any side. What is important is that the student has removed himself from the path of the downward strike and the range of the padded sword.

4. Once each student has taken a turn to evade the vertical strike they return to sitting in a line with the other students.

When evading ...

... to the side ...

... the student needs to ensure that ...

... they are beyond the reach of the sword.

9. Spot question 3

Recommended time allocation: 3 minutes

The class pauses for a spot question. The third spot question refers to learning from session 4, part 7 (page 136).

Question 3

In session 4 we looked at anger and did the wrap-up challenge. We also discussed ways to look after ourselves when we feel angry. So, let's revisit that question. How can you look after yourself when you feel angry?

The students put up their hand to answer and the Instructor elicits five appropriate answers from the group.

10. Test time

Recommended time allocation: 15 minutes

Note It is advised and would be wise for the Instructor to practise performing the test before actioning it with the students in the class.

To conclude the Constructive Response practised in session 10, the students are required to perform a test. The test is about the students trusting themselves and having confidence in their intuition.

The students remain seated in their line as the Instructor explains the test.

In the Constructive Response practised in session 1 and 6 we explored intuition and natural survival instincts. In the *New Zealand Oxford Dictionary* (2005), intuition is described as:

1. immediate apprehension by the mind without reasoning,
2. immediate apprehension by a sense, and
3. immediate insight.

When explaining intuition within the framework of keeping safe, the Instructor can refer to prey animals, such as a gazelle, being stalked by a lion, or a bird being stalked by a cat. Often these animals cohabit and it is only when the hunter turns its attention and focuses on capturing the prey that the prey becomes nervous and flighty. The prey senses the danger.

When beginning the test, the Instructor's attention should not be on the student. I usually think of eating an ice-cream!

The Instructor turns on the intention, focusing on the back of the student's head.

Students will be used to sensing this level of intensity. They know when their parents are not happy, even without seeing or hearing them.

Another example of intuition that can help prepare the students for the test is the experience of feeling someone is watching them from across the room, or a parent knowing that their baby is awake and crying in another part of the house, even though they can't hear them. There is also the example of walking into a room and knowing that the people in the room are uneasy, such as when a student enters

Session 10

> The strike in the test should never be performed fast or in a true attack fashion. At no point should a student be at risk of being hit. The students are learning to register consciously and avoid another person's intent to hit them.

home and has a feeling that Mum and Dad are unhappy before seeing them. The Instructor may have other examples that he could share.

With the other Constructive Response activities practised in session 10 it was advised that the Instructor demonstrate the evasive moves in front of the class. However, the Instructor should not demonstrate the test. The test should be solely for the students to perform. Instructors who would like to practise the test themselves would be best to do it in their own time with another Instructor, outside of class and away from the students.

Further, students are not trained to perform the test, which requires intent and focus.

1. Each student has a turn to stand in the Warrior posture in front of the Instructor, but this time they do not face the Instructor, they face away from the Instructor so that the vertical strike is coming at them from behind.

2. The Instructor takes a step back, raises the padded sword and announces to the student that he 'will be striking any time now'. At this point the Instructor should remain still, look off to the side and think of eating an ice-cream or about taking a nice walk along some beach so that no attention is given to the student in front.

3. This test is about the student learning to trust his intuition, to trust himself. The student must relax so that he is open to sensing danger, open to sensing the intent of the strike (which is much like a student 'feeling' when Mum or Dad is angry with him). On sensing the intent, without looking or relying on hearing, the student is expected to evade the strike by taking a large step forwards and away from the Instructor, then turn back into a responsive posture to face him.

4. With the student standing relaxed in front of him, the Instructor chooses a moment to 'turn on' the intent of bringing the padded sword slowly down at him. Without stepping, he looks directly at the student in front of him, focusing his full attention on the back of his head.

    a) Now the test is on. The aim for the student is to intuitively pick up the intent of the Instructor, and most importantly, respond to the Instructor's intent by stepping beyond the strike range.

    b) The student might be nervous and try to guess when the Instructor is going to strike. If the student moves before

The more relaxed the student can be, the more likely the student will be able to pick up the intent.

Sensing danger or a threat is a survival instinct.

This test is exciting for the students.

Session 10

At no point should the student be under threat of being hit.

The sword is brought down slowly and stops above the student's head. The student is evading the intention.

Further evasive challenges are explored in Warrior Kids beyond the 10-week programme.

the intent of the strike is given, then the student returns to standing in the Warrior posture facing away from the Instructor and performs the test again.

c) The Instructor should encourage each student to let go, relax, and trust themselves.

d) If the student senses the intent and moves before the Instructor steps forwards to strike, it is a pass. The student is expected to pick up the intent and this can happen before the strike is in play. The strike from the Instructor may not even be required, only the intent.

e) Some students who may not feel confident will not move, yet it may be evident that they feel the intent of the Instructor. This will be shown with a slight movement in the student's body, such as a tremor in the leg or a twitch of the shoulder.

  i) This is where the Instructor will say, 'There it is, that's it, you felt it. Well done, now next time trust yourself, take the step and get out of harm's way.'

  ii) The student repeats the test again.

5. If a student doesn't respond to the initial intent then the Instructor slowly steps forwards. The Instructor must avoid making any noise while striking. As the Instructor moves forwards, he brings the padded sword slowly downwards.

a) If a student fails to move, the padded sword should be stopped just above the student's head.

b) If a student moves before the padded sword stops, the student has passed the test.

c) A pass is a pass regardless of when a student senses the intent and evades, and regardless of whether the strike happens or not. There is no lesser pass.

6. Some students may not pass the test. There is nothing wrong with that. It is usually just a matter of time and, if the student has the opportunity to perform the test again, they will eventually pass. The concept of intuition is something that some students may take time to understand.

a) A student who does not pass the test after two or three tries should be acknowledged for their efforts and asked to sit down. Whether they passed or not doesn't have to be announced.

b) If other students ask whether or not another student passed, tell them just to worry about themselves passing. The test is a personal experience and comparisons should not be made.

c) If required, the Instructor can relieve a failing student of any ill-feeling by saying, 'Don't worry about it, it takes time. I have complete confidence that you'll get it next time. The biggest thing is giving it a go, well done.'

7. Each student should be openly acknowledged for their efforts.

11. 1st breathing exercise

Recommended time allocation: 2 minutes

The Instructor has the students form a standing circle around the outside of the mats. The Instructor nominates a student to lead the class through the 1st breathing exercise. Refer to session 1 for the outline of the 1st breathing exercise (page 57).

12. Spot question 4

Recommended time allocation: 4 minutes

The Instructor and the students sit on the mats in a circle in preparation for the fourth spot question. Each student should be facing the centre of the circle and be clearly visible to the Instructor so that no one is in any way disassociated from the group, whether by their own positioning or by the positioning of another student.

The fourth spot question is from the learning in session 5, part 7. Instructors should refer to this session to be familiar with the outline and set up of the One 2 One challenge (page 151).

Question 4

In session 5 you partnered up with someone and told them what you like about yourself. Today I want you to tell me one thing that you like about yourself.

Each member of the circle, from left to right or vice-versa, takes their turn to say one thing that they like about themselves.

13. Cognitive conditioning: constructive affirmation and visualisation

Recommended time allocation: 15 minutes

The students remain seated in a circle on the gym mats for the cognitive conditioning exercise. The students can move back to increase the size of the circle if more space is required.

Session 10 includes two cognitive conditioning exercises that promote constructive thinking through the use of affirmation and visualisation. Affirmations and goal-orientated visualisations are used by leading athletes and a great number of successful people to condition themselves for success on a mental and emotional level.

By conditioning their minds, the students are preparing themselves for achieving and developing a belief and the confidence that they can achieve, thereby opening them to endless possibilities. Affirmations and visualisations will encourage the students to clarify their goals, enable them to be more focused, creative and diligent in achieving their goals. They will become more receptive when identifying opportunities that bring them closer to their goals, and developing the gumption to take advantage of those opportunities. Affirmations also develop a 'can do' attitude when faced with problem-solving.

Developing an achieving attitude has become a science used by many, including sports psychologists and professional people who seek the assistance of life coaches and motivators.

> The subconscious can be reprogrammed. The only reason we behave the way we do is because of neural pathways in our brain. These are formed over our lifetime and we come to see them as who we are. But the brain is

'plastic'; it is constantly changing. In the time it has taken you to read this paragraph, millions of new nerve connections have formed within your brain.

— Keith McGregor, Director of Personnel Psychology NZ Ltd, *The New Zealand Herald*, 28 October 2009

Many students will have self-esteem issues. They will battle with negative conditioning about who they are and what they can and cannot do. They may have been on the receiving end of negative treatment, opinions and remarks. They may be holding on to statements that they believe to be reality, statements such as 'I'm naughty,' 'I can't do it,' or 'I can't do maths.' These statements are nothing more than what I call Negative Thought Patterns (NTP).

Affirmations and visualisations are actions that open possibilities; the possibility of achieving, of feeling good about who we are and shifting beyond limitations (whether they be our own or external limitations). Affirmations and visualisations have the power to change and influence behaviours. By repeating an affirmation and visualisation, our brain begins to weaken existing neural connections and form new pathways. Negative Thought Patterns are replaced with Constructive Thought Patterns (CTP).

The affirmation and visualisation exercises presented here have proven to be positive for students and there have been numerous accounts of successes as a result. Students have become better at reading, improved in maths, achieved in sports and made new friends. The practice of constructive affirmation and visualisation has even impacted on families when parents and siblings have adopted the practice. What is important is that the affirmations and visualisations are real, down-to-earth and achievable.

For the affirmation exercise the Instructor will require A4 cards, with an affirmation printed on each card. You will also need paper and a pen for each student.

Page 218 lists common affirmations I have used for this exercise. Feel free to use them, or you may have others that you would like to offer to your students. There are many books and websites promoting the use of affirmations.

Notice that the affirmations are short and to the point. They are not over-complicated or too wordy and therefore are easy to retain and easy to recite. Also, there is no 'I will' or 'I want' in the affirmations. Instead, they give the sense that the goal has already been achieved. Affirmations of 'I will' or 'I want' will only leave the student 'willing' and 'wanting' the goal. 'I want' and 'I will' focus on tomorrow and tomorrow never comes. Such affirmations remain future orientated.

> Changing neural wiring requires work. Athletes train hard for events because they have to change the structure of their body. They know it requires repetition and persistence. They don't have to believe that their body will change — they know it just does.
>
> If I want to change my pathways around being organised or remembering names, I have to do the work. This means diligently repeating to myself, 'I am organised and efficient,' 'How come I remember names so easily?', 'I am thrilled how well my speech went.' Notice that these are all stated in the

Affirmations

I am strong and confident.
Great for dealing with anxiety and preparing for confronting situations such as public speaking.

I am fit, well and happy.
Creating an image of health and well-being and spurring one on to achieve that condition.

I attract good things.
Sometimes people adopt the belief that they attract negative things. This belief will cause them to only see the negative aspects of their lives and possibly even to seek negative experiences. 'I attract good things' is establishing a CTP.

I am blessed.
Similar to the above in the sense that it is creating the belief that good things happen to you. This also helps in the elimination of worries. Worrying thoughts are not facts, yet they create and maintain stress, anxiety and fear; and as worries do not solve problems they are unconstructive. If we have a problem we address it; the act of worrying doesn't address problems. Worrying tends to make a mountain out of a molehill.

I have lots of friends.
A lack of friends and isolation is a common issue that students have when they arrive at Warrior Kids. By having the students visualise that they have friends, and to experience what that feels like, they can then be open to the possibility of friendship and behave as such, becoming more approachable to others.

I can do anything I set my mind to.
Sometimes a challenge just requires a bit more focus and commitment in order to see it through. Such openness and willingness to achieve will pay off.

I believe in myself, I believe in me.
Promoting confidence and self-belief.

I am healthy and strong.
An image of health and well-being.

My body is my best friend.
It is easy to think at times that our body is working against us, letting us down. Yet by not being at war with our body we are more able to work with it in order to change.

I am a Master.
Great for the students who want to be a martial arts master or want to be a master at anything that they do. Encourages them to focus and to relax and simply do rather than to try too hard.

I'm really good at …
The student fills in the blank with whatever he would like to be good at. 'I'm really good at skateboarding.' 'I'm really good at spelling.'

Good things happen to me.
The same as 'I attract good things.' However, the way an affirmation is worded can have more resonance for a student. The more personal the affirmation, the more power it will have.

I can be whatever I want to be.
Encouraging one to rise above limitations.

People feel happy when they see me.
Allows one to be open to friendship and a sense of community. Also encourages a constructive outlook.

I am kind and considerate.
Encourages empathy and allows one to be more considerate in their treatment of others. It also allows one to feel good about themselves and their contribution.

I will achieve, I will succeed.
Spurring one on with the confidence to achieve their goals.

I'm a good …
Again, fill in the blanks. 'I'm a good friend.' 'I'm a good tennis player.' 'I'm a good Warrior Kids Instructor.'

I am magnificent and beautiful.
Encouraging one to feel good about themselves.

I am lucky.
Establishing a positive outlook and being open to opportunities and challenges.

I'm good at being me.
Very encouraging to be good at something and one can only rise upwards from there.

I am confident, I can do it!
Great for achieving one's goals.

I feel happy.
Creating a positive outlook and allows negative feelings to shift.

I always make good choices
This is a very valuable affirmation. We are faced with choices daily, from what we eat and how we treat others to how we deal with situations. Students will be faced with these same choices, and tough choices around drugs and alcohol, violence and abuse, sex and being less than who they are; at a young age they are very vulnerable. By helping them to adopt the belief that they can make good choices, we help them to attain a truly wholesome life.

I am clever.
Imagine if every child arrived at school every day believing that they were clever. Think of that attitude and what it could achieve.

I have a great mind.
Same as above and open to learning.

I do my best all the time.
Creating an achiever.

I am a good person.
Encouraging good choices and a positive outlook.

I am a great friend.
Helping to establish good friendships.

I am a good leader.
Opens possibilities and allows a person to really fulfil the leadership role, mentally and emotionally.

Cognitive conditioning, part 1: affirmations

Affirmations are not a magic wand. However, they do challenge negative thoughts and beliefs and they open up possibilities for the students.

past or present tense — the subconscious, like all computers, doesn't cope with the word 'will'.

— Keith McGregor, Director of Personnel Psychology NZ Ltd, *The New Zealand Herald*, 28 October 2009.

Students should focus their affirmations on what they want to achieve as opposed to what they don't want. For example, 'I am not bad at maths' is very different to 'I am good at maths.' The use of not and bad used with the word maths would rule out the possibility of improving at maths. The same could be said for 'I am not a bad person' or 'I am not fat.' The subconscious will give attention to the negative words when what the student really wants is to focus on achieving the goal and feeling better about themselves.

1. The Instructor explains affirmations, making sure to mention that sportspeople, celebrities and superstars use affirmations to help them achieve and win their goals.

2. The Instructor presents the affirmation cards. The cards are passed around the circle and the students choose an affirmation that stands out for them. The cards may even spur a student to come up with his own personal affirmation to help him achieve a chosen goal.
   a) When the students are creating their own affirmations it is important that the affirmations are short (fewer than 10 words) and to the point, with a clear goal in mind.
   b) When a student chooses an affirmation that they would like to use from the cards, they should still pass the card on, as the same affirmation may work for another student.

3. The affirmation cards are passed around the circle until they return to the Instructor. Then they are placed in the middle of the circle where all of the students have access to them.

4. The Instructor passes paper and a pen to each student.

5. Students write their name at the top of the paper, then write down the affirmation that they have chosen to focus on.
   a) The students should understand that what they write is confidential. They may have to share it quietly with the Instructor, but they do not have to share it with the other students.
   b) It is wise if the students understand that they may have to share their affirmation with the Instructor, as he may need to give some guidance.
   c) Younger students who create their own affirmation may require assistance with the spelling and writing of that affirmation. Older, more capable students who finish their affirmations quickly may be able to help younger ones. Or a parent from the side may like to help. Otherwise the Instructor will have to give assistance.

6. Once each student has finished writing their affirmation, the affirmation cards and pens are collected and removed. This ends part 1 of the cognitive conditioning exercise.

Session 10

Cognitive conditioning, part 2: visualisation

The conscious mind is a verbal processor, which means that we communicate and think in words. The subconscious is different: it is an image processor. Therefore, it is not enough to simply say an affirmation. The affirmation needs to be linked to an image; a visualisation. The students need to run a 'mental video' of themselves achieving their goal or having already achieved it. They need to see themselves achieving, and to see themselves having achieved.

1. The Instructor has the students say their affirmation in their mind, and to repeat it.

2. The students are asked to close their eyes and to picture themselves achieving or having achieved their affirmation as they say it. If their affirmation is to feel good about themselves, they could see themselves feeling great about who they are. If their affirmation is to do well at giving a speech, then they could see themselves delivering the speech masterfully or being applauded and praised for having given such a terrific speech.

3. The Instructor asks the students to keep their eyes closed, to keep repeating their affirmation and to keep seeing themselves achieving it.

   a) The Instructor asks the students to feel that achievement. What does it feel like?

   b) What smells are associated with that achievement. What does it smell like?

   c) What tastes are associated with the achievement. What does it taste like?

4. The Instructor keeps the students repeating their affirmation and visualising it for 60 to 90 seconds. The Instructor tells the students to open their eyes.

5. The cognitive conditioning exercise concludes with the giving of the homework task.

Moving on from negative behaviours and changing destructive cycles requires tenacity, which in itself requires self-belief.

Homework

Homework tasks have been given to students in some previous sessions. As the students are about to finish the programme after completing session 10, it is good to send them away with something they can practise to keep their Warrior Kids experience alive and to keep them focused on achieving what they want. As with the previous homework tasks, there is no pass or fail.

The homework task for session 10 is for the students to take their affirmation with them and to practise saying and visualising it every day for two minutes until they have achieved their goal. The affirmation and visualisation could be practised on the way to school, or on the way home. The students could say their affirmations and visualise in the morning when they are getting dressed. They could say the affirmation in their head when in the presence of others or, as I prefer, aloud in a private space, such as a bedroom. Remind them to see themselves achieving in their minds, to play the mental video. Others in their family may be keen on giving an affirmation a go too.

If at any time a student feels that their affirmation isn't working for them, they can change it to a new one that is more in line with the goal they want to achieve. It can take time to figure out exactly what it is that we want; often it can be a windy path to discovering our true goals, with various subsidiary goals along the way.

14. Spot question 5

Recommended time allocation: 3 minutes

The Instructor directs students to assemble, standing in a circle as at the beginning of the class, in preparation for the closing words. Before concluding the last session, the Instructor asks the final spot question.

Question 5

Considering your behaviour and the choices that you have made over the period of the programme, do you feel that you deserve to pass Warrior Kids?

Each member of the circle, from left to right or vice-versa, takes their turn to say whether they feel that they deserve to pass Warrior Kids. During the answering the Instructor may like to ask three or four students why they gave the answer that they did, regardless of whether the answer is a yes or a no: 'Why do you deserve to pass?' or 'Why don't you deserve to pass?' The students' answers should be kept short to stay on schedule.

15. Closing words

At this point the Instructor may choose to go into the Warrior Kids Grading and the presenting of ranks and certificates. The Warrior Kids Grading is explained in the next chapter (page 223).

Otherwise, the Instructor acknowledges to the students that they have reached the end of the Warrior Kids programme. From here some of the students may continue their training by repeating the programme or by taking part in an ongoing community-based Warrior Kids class. Others will be moving on.

Now is the time for the Instructor to say any last words. I usually say something like, 'It has been a real honour to spend this time with you. I have really enjoyed getting to know you all. I'm going to miss you. If you ever get the chance to do Warrior Kids again, I would be very happy to have you in my class. You are welcome to stay in contact with me and let me know how you are getting on. Otherwise, be a Warrior Kid every day, be brave, be safe and have a great life.'

The Instructor asks for a volunteer from the group to say some words to end the programme.

When the closing words have been said the Instructor thanks the speaker, then concludes with, 'Remember to take what you brought with you, your shoes, socks, watches, water bottle and jersey.'

This brings the Warrior Kids programme to an end.

Take a deep breath.
You did it! Congratulations!
You took a group of students through the Warrior Kids 10-week programme.

As the students go back to their lives, consider what you have given them.
There may be something that you have said or done during the course of the programme that will change a life forever.
Sometime, somewhere in the future, these students will look back on their experience with you and find strength to get through a challenging part of their lives.
You gave them that.

When a programme is at completion …   … bring the students and their families together and …   … celebrate!

> You and your contribution are like a pebble dropped in a pond. The ripples will spread out, reaching the edges of your community. Even though you may not see it, you are causing change. Change in the students, change in families, change in your community.
> You are a hero in the truest sense.
> The more you fulfil your role as a Warrior Kids Instructor, the greater impact you will have. The more ripples you will create.
>
> Don't stop now.
> Keep going.
> Be the Warrior.

Grading

Progress in Warrior Kids is acknowledged through belt grades. In order to pass each grade, students must demonstrate the appropriate manner and conduct; the higher the grade the higher the expectations. The belt grades in Warrior Kids are: Red, Orange, Yellow, Green, Blue, 1st Purple, 2nd Purple, Black Belt 1st Dan and beyond, demonstrating that mastering the art of living is ongoing.

At the end of the 10 week in-school programme, students are eligible to be graded for their first rank. There are three possible outcomes for each student.

1. **Orange Belt** The highest rank given in an in-school programme. Awarded to students who have demonstrated a level of excellence while behaving in a consistently outstanding manner and conduct in and out of class.

2. **Red Belt** Awarded to students whose overall manner and conduct throughout the programme is satisfactory, or to students who have made significant changes and effort in their manner and conduct.

3. **White Belt** The lowest rank signifies the completion of the Warrior Kids in-school programme and is awarded to students whose manner and conduct has been less than appropriate through the programme.

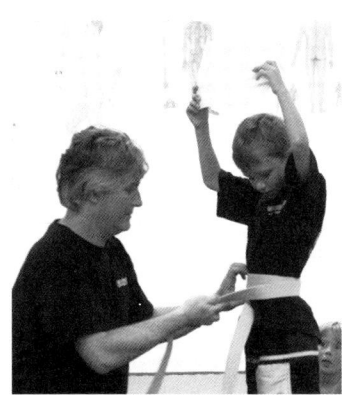

In order to achieve a Red or Orange belt, students must not only demonstrate knowledge of the Warrior Kids syllabus, but also the appropriate skills, manner and conduct in their classroom at school, in the playground and at home. In other words, they must be conducting themselves in a manner that serves them. If they are getting into trouble, hurting others or in any way making life harder for themselves, then they are not making good choices and will earn a White Belt.

To help the Instructor determine the grades, the questionnaire on the next page is given to parents and teachers in week 8 of the programme. This questionnaire will give the Instructor an insight in to how the teacher, school and parents see the child. The Instructor needs to remain autonomous when it comes to deciding grades; teachers, principals and parents may try to influence or even determine a child's grade. A teacher may pressure an Instructor to award a student a White Belt as she finds the student difficult to deal with in class. However, this may be more about the teacher's ability to relate to the student and manage the class rather than the actual behaviour of the student.

WARRIOR KIDS™

Grading questionnaire

To the Parents and Caregivers of Warrior Kids

It is now time to consider which grade each student has achieved in Warrior Kids. In order to pass each grade, children must not only demonstrate knowledge and skill of the Warrior Kids syllabus, but also the appropriate manner and conduct in the programme, in the classroom, around the school and at home. Hence, feedback is sought from these areas. There are three possible outcomes for the students. These are as follows.

1. **Orange Belt** The highest rank given in an in-school programme is awarded to students for excellence in demonstrating an outstanding manner and conduct in and out of class.

2. **Red Belt** Awarded to students whose overall manner and conduct throughout the programme is satisfactory, or to students who have made significant changes and effort in their manner and conduct.

3. **White Belt** The lowest rank signifies the completion of the Warrior Kids in-school programme and is awarded to students whose manner and conduct has been less than appropriate through the programme.

The Instructor considers all feedback when making his/her decision.

Considering your child's manner and behaviour at home and school, please take a moment to answer the following questions and return this form to your child's school. Feel free to use the back of this page if you need more room.

What would you like your child to work on or improve?

What is your child doing well?

SIGNED: .... DATE: ....

Thank you.

Parents can also try to sway the Instructor's decision. While some may try to have their child awarded the highest grade possible, others may try to punish by requesting that their child receive a White Belt.

What has to be remembered is that the parents have had a huge impact on a child's behaviour. While many inappropriate behaviours are simply a child learning and developing, there are behaviours that are a direct result and reflection of trouble at home, and a child shouldn't be punished for someone else's mistakes; especially their parents'.

That is not to say that I am judging parents. My role, and the Instructor's role, is simply to ascertain where the child is and in what way we can best serve them. It is not the parents or teachers going through the challenges and tasks of Warrior Kids. I have passed many students when parents have asked me not to. The reason I passed the student was the student deserved to pass.

Parents and schools don't always get it right. They make mistakes. Parents can be very good at 'do as I say, not as I do.' As Instructors we need to be able to see through this behaviour in a compassionate manner yet acknowledge the true child and not the perceived little monster or the perceived angel as the case may be.

Students are not expected to be perfect. Perfection is a never-ending pursuit. Students are not being rated on the grades that they get at school. They simply have to be striving to do their best and to be choosing constructive outcomes in the different areas of their lives. We're all entitled to make mistakes.

The grading is a powerful experience for the students, one they won't forget. The Instructor can have a life-long impact on a child's life at that very moment, and that comes with a lot of responsibility. Therefore, care is required.

Grading: an outline

Recommended time allocation: 30 minutes

The grading can be performed at the end of the programme, or at another pre-arranged time.

1. Students sit on the mats in a circle. Each student should be facing the centre of the circle and be clearly visible to the Instructor so that no one is in any way disassociated from the group, whether by their own positioning or by the positioning of another student.

2. Standing as part of the circle, the Instructor nominates the student to his left or right to stand in the centre of the circle and face him.

3. One by one, each student will take their turn to stand in the middle of the circle and face the Instructor.
    a) The reason each student stands in the circle, surrounded and observed by their peers and everyone else present, is to remind them that their manner and conduct affect those around them, and that each student is accountable and responsible to their family and their community. It is also about being seen for who they really are and facing and standing up to that. The Instructor explains this to the class.
    b) The student needs to be standing respectfully, without slouching or having their hands in their pockets.

c) The students seated in the circle need to be respectful of the person in the middle and refrain from talking, moving or lying down. Koosh balls can help to keep students focused.

4. The Instructor addresses the student in the centre, saying something like, 'It was an honour to have you in the programme and an honour to have the opportunity to get to know you a little.' The Instructor should ensure that when addressing the students his words are, as much as possible, different for each individual. Otherwise, the students and others present will question the Instructor's sincerity and the validity of his words.

5. Keeping it short and clear, the Instructor goes on to present his feedback in the following order.

    a) **Positive affirmation**.   Acknowledge two areas where the student has done well, in or out of the programme. Maybe he was good at tumbling, rolling, handstands or cartwheels. Maybe he was good at the games. Perhaps it is aspects of his manner and conduct that you would like to acknowledge, such as his willingness to listen and follow instructions. Was he friendly and warm with others? Was he considerate and thoughtful? Respectful? Was he great at sharing? It might even be his manner and conduct in his classroom or at home with his family that deserves acknowledgement. This is also the time to acknowledge any memorable highlights from the student's Warrior Kids experience.

    b) **Constructive feedback**.   Acknowledge two areas that the student could work on, in or out of the programme. A student may require uplifting remarks such as, 'Be brave, you're a clever boy so give things a go,' or 'I like listening to you and what you have to say. I would have liked to hear more from you. Please speak up, you have so much to offer,' or 'You deserve to feel really good about yourself, you're a wonderful person. Remember this moment, remember what I'm saying to you.'

    Some students may require prompting for appropriate behaviour. For example, 'It's really sad that you're still choosing to hurt others, Michael. You're better than that. Your behaviour in Warrior Kids has been outstanding, but I'm really sad to hear that you've been making different choices in the playground,' or 'I like it when you listen, Jamie. I like it when you focus on what you're supposed to be doing. Please focus more,' or 'It's time you were helping out at home. From now on I want you to make your bed every morning, and I want you to get yourself ready for school before turning the television on,' or 'Lately you have been making choices that have been getting you into trouble, Tom. I want you to make constructive choices, Tom. Choices that bring you good things.'

    Students who have demonstrated excellent manners and conduct throughout the programme may not require much in the way of constructive feedback.

6. Finally, the Instructor declares the belt grade that the student has achieved and why. He then presents the student with his certificate and belt. Some schools may like the presentation of certificates and belts to be done in an assembly, where the greater school community can witness the achievement. This is great for integrating Warrior Kids and the Warrior Kids messages into the wider community.

7. When the student has learnt his grade the Instructor has the class clap for him. Then he returns to sitting as part of the circle and the next student along takes his turn in the center of the circle for his feedback.

8. On completion of the grading, the students stand up. Turning sideways, the Instructor and the students step closer to the centre, making the circle smaller to the point that they can reach across the circle to touch one another. The Instructor and the students bend and place a hand down low into the centre of the circle. The students' hands go on top of the Instructor's hand. The Instructor and the students then start to hum softly. As the hum gets louder the Instructor and the students raise their hands, and end by throwing their hands up in to the air with a loud, celebratory cry.

Beyond the programme

Tim presents training and seminars. For more information visit the official Warrior Kids website: www.warriorkids.org

Tim's picture books and novels for teenagers are available and can be used in conjunction with the Warrior Kids programme.

Notes

Notes

Notes

Notes